C000077708

The *A. E. Waite Reader:*
A Selection of Occult Essays

By Arthur Edward Waite

Copyright © 2021 Lamp of Trismegistus. All rights reserved. No part of this publication may be reproduced or transmitted in any form or by any means, electronic or mechanical, including photocopying, recording, or by any information storage and retrieval system, without permission in writing from Lamp of Trismegistus. Reviewers may quote brief passages.

ISBN: 978-1-63118-515-1

Esoteric Classics

Other Books in this Series and Related Titles

The Devil in Love by Jacques Cazotte (978–1–63118–499–4)

Confessions of an English Opium–Eater by T De Quincey (978–1–63118–485–7)

On the Cave of the Nymphs in the Odyssey by Thomas Taylor (978-1-63118-505-2)

Aurora of the Philosophers by Paracelsus (978-1-63118-507-6)

Rosicrucian Rules, Secret Signs, Codes and Symbols by various (978–1–63118–488–8)

The Poem of Hashish by A Crowley & C Baudelaire (978-1-63118-484-0)

Fortune–Telling with Dice by Astra Cielo (978–1–63118–466–6)

The Janeites, The Man Who Would Be King and Other Stories of Freemasonry
by Rudyard Kipling (978–1–63118–480–2)

Crystal Vision Through Crystal Gazing by Frater Achad (978–1–63118–455–0)

Rosa Alchemica, The Tables of Law & The Adoration of the Magi
by William Butler Yeats (978–1–63118–421–5)

The Star and the Garter by Aleister Crowley (978-1-63118-406-2)

Thirty–One Hymns to the Star Goddess by Frater Achad (978–1–63118–422–2)

Ghosts in Solid Form by Gambier Bolton (978–1–63118–469–7)

A Collection of Magical Writings, Fiction, Poetry & Essays
By Aleister Crowley (978–63118–424–6)

The Sword of Welleran and Other Stories by Lord Dunsany (978-1-63118-501-4)

Arcane Formulas or Mental Alchemy by W W Atkinson (978–1–63118–459–8)

The Machinery of the Mind by Dion Fortune (978–1–63118–451–2)

*A Collection of Fiction and Essays by Occult Writers on Supernatural
and Metaphysical Subjects* by various (978–1–63118–510–6)

The Leadbeater Reader: A Selection of Occult Essays (978–1–63118–483–3)

Audio versions are also available on Audible, Amazon and Apple

Other Books in this Series and Related Titles

Paracelsus, the Four Elements and Their Spirits by M P Hall (978-1-63118-400-0)

The Magician's Heavenly Chaos by Thomas Vaughan (978-1-63118-500-7)

Masonic and Rosicrucian History by M P Hall & H Voorhis (978-1-63118-486-4)

Tao Te Ching & Commentary by Lao Tzu & C Johnston (978-1-63118-495-6)

The Influence of Pythagoras on Freemasonry and Other Essays (978-1-63118-404-8)

The Golden Verses of Pythagoras: Five Translations (978-1-63118-479-6)

On the Philadelphian Gold by Philochrysus & Philadelphus (978-1-63118-511-3)

History, Analysis and Secret Tradition of the Tarot by Hall &c (978-1-63118-445-1)

The Kabbalah of Masonry & Related Writings by E Levi &c (978-1-63118-453-6)

A Collection of Early Writings on Astral Travel (978-1-63118-477-2)

The Ceremony of Initiation: Analysis & Commentary (978-1-63118-473-4)

The Old Past Master by Carl H Claudy (978-1-63118-464-2)

The Path of Light: A Manual of Maha-Yana Buddhism (978-1-63118-471-0)

The Hymns of Hermes by G. R. S. Mead (978-1-63118-405-5)

Clairvoyance and Psychic Abilities by Leadbeater & Besant (978-1-63118-403-1)

Catholicism, Yoga and Hinduism by Hartmann &c (978-1-63118-478-9)

American Indian Freemasonry by A C Parker (978-1-63118-460-4)

Ancient Mysteries and Secret Societies by M P Hall (978-1-63118-410-9)

*A Collection of Writings Related to Occult, Esoteric, Rosicrucian and Hermetic Literature,
Including Freemasonry, the Kabbalah, the Tarot, Alchemy and Theosophy*
various authors *Volumes 1-4*
(978-1-63118-713-1) (978-1-63118-714-8)
(978-1-63118-715-5) (978-1-63118-716-2)

Audio Versions are also available on Audible, Amazon and Apple

Table of Contents

INTRODUCTION

The word "esoteric" can be difficult to define. Esotericism in general can be seen less as a system of beliefs and more as a category, which encompasses numerous, different systems of beliefs. It's a bit of juxtaposition, since the word "esoteric" indicates something that few people know about, while the term itself broadly covers numerous philosophies, practices, areas of study and belief systems.

In a greater sense, Esotericism acts as a storehouse for secret knowledge, which is often considered ancient (by *tradition, if not by fact),* passed down from generation to generation, in private. At various times in history, simply possessing the knowledge of some of these subjects, was considered illegal and a jailable offence, if discovered. This usually included such general topics as Alchemy, Qabalah, Hermeticism, Occultism, Ceremonial Magic, Astrology, Divination, Rosicrucianism and so on. Collectively, these areas of study were often referred to as the esoteric sciences.

Sometimes, the outer garment of a subject isn't esoteric, while what is hidden beneath it, is. As an example, Freemasonry isn't necessarily esoteric by nature (at *least not anymore),* but certain signs, passwords and handshakes given to the candidate during their initiation, are in fact, esoteric, in the sense that they are hidden from the general public.

Today, in the twenty-first century, such topics are readily available at bookstores across the country, and numerous mainsteam publishers offer beginners guides and coffee-table volumes on many of these subjects, intended for mass appeal. Books like *"The Secret"* have turned previously arcane topics into household knowledge. All that being the case, however, it isn't to say that there still aren't buried secrets to uncover, ancient wisdom being ignored and forgotten mysteries to be explored. In fact, it is often that we are only able to further our own studies by standing on the shoulders of these disappearing giants.

Lamp of Trismegistus is doing its part to help preserve humanity's esoteric history by making some of these classics available to those students who are seeking to unearth the knowledge of these ancient colossi.

So, be sure to check other titles from our *Esoteric Classics* series, as well as our *Occult Fiction, Theosophical Classics, Foundations of Freemasonry Series, Studies in Alchemy, Supernatural Fiction, Eastern Studies, Paranormal Research Series, Studies in Buddhism* and our *Christian Apocrypha Series*. You can also download the audio versions of most of these titles from Audible, Amazon and Apple, for learning on the go.

THE HERMETIC AND ROSICRUCIAN MYSTERY

We are only beginning, and that by very slow stages, to enter into our inheritance from the past; and still perhaps in respect of its larger part we are seeking far and wide for the treasures of the mystic Basra. But these treasures are of more than one species and more than a single order; for that measure to which we are approximating and for that part which we hold, we shall be well advised to realize that there are some things which belong to the essences while some are of the accidents only. I do not think that among all the wise of the ages, in whatsoever regions of the world, there has been ever any difference of opinion about the true object of research; the modes and form of the quest have varied, and that widely, but to one point have all the roads con-verged. Therein is no change or shadow of vicissitude. We may hear of shorter roads, and one would say at first sight that such a suggestion may be true indubitably, but in one sense it is rather a convention of language and in another it is a commonplace which tends to confuse the issues. It is a convention of language because the great quests are not pursued in time or place, and it would be just as true to say that in a journey from the circumference to the centre all roads are the same length, supposing that they are straight roads. It is a commonplace because if anyone should enter the byways or return on his path and restart, it is obvious that he must look to be delayed. Further-more, it may be true that all paths lead ultimately to the centre, and that if we descend into hell there may be still a way back to the light, as if one ascended to heaven; but in any house of right reason the issues are too clear to consider such extrinsic possibilities. Before I utilize these random and, I think, too obvious considerations to present the root-thesis of this paper, I must recur for one moment to the question of the essence and the accident, because on the assumption from which the considerations originate- namely, that there is a secret tradition in Christian times, the place of which is in the West- or rather that there are several traditions- it seems desirable to realize what part matters vitally among them. I will take my illustration from alchemy, and it should be known that on the surface it claims to put forward the mystery of a material operation, behind which we discern- though not, it should be understood, invariably-another subject and another intention. Now, supposing that we were incorrect in our discernment, the secret tradition would remain, this notwithstanding, and it would remain also if the material operation were a dream not realized. But I think that a tradition of the physical kind would have no part in us, who are concerned with another conversion than that of metals, and who know that there is a mystic stone which is unseen by mortal eyes? The evidences of the secret tradition are very strong in alchemy, but it must be accepted that, either therein or otherwise, I am not offering the proofs that the tradition exists. There are several schools of occult literature from which it follows that something was perpetuated belonging to their own order, as, for example, the schools of magic; concerning these latter I must say what to some persons may seem a rule of excessive severity- that they embody nothing which is essential to our purpose It is time that we should set apart in our minds the domain of phenomenal occultism as something which, almost automatically, has been transferred to the proper care of science. In so doing it is our simple hope that it may continue to extend a particular class of researches into the nature of man and his environment which the unaccredited investigations of the past have demonstrated already as productive to those who can he called open to conviction. The grounds of this conviction were manifested generations or centuries ago, and along both lines the research exhibits to us from time to time that we -or some of us- who know after another manner, have been justified very surely when, as if from a more remote region, we have returned to testify that the great mysteries are within.

I have no need to affirm that the secret tradition, either in the East or the West, has been always an open secret in respect of the root-principles concerning the Way, the Truth and the Life. It is easy, therefore, to show what it is not, and to make the distinction which I have attempted between the classes of the concealed knowledge. It is not so easy to define the most precious treasures of the King- in respect of that knowledge-according to the estimate concerning them which I have assumed tacitly to be com-mon between persons confessing to mystic predispositions at this day. The issues are confused throughout, all our high predilections notwithstanding, by the traditional or historical notion concerning the adept, which is that of a man whose power is raised to the transcendent degree by the communication or attainment, after some manner, of a particular and even terrible knowledge of the hidden forces of nature. I have heard technical and imputed adepts of occult associations state that those who possess, in the actual and plenary sense, the gifts which are ascribed to themselves by the simplicity of an artificial title, are able so to disintegrate the constituted man that they can separate not only the body from its psychic part but the spirit also from the soul, when they have a sufficient cause in their illumination against a particular victim. If things of this kind were possible, they would belong to the science of the abyss-when the abyss has been exalted above all that is termed God; but there is no need to attribute an over-great seriousness to chatter and traffic of this kind, which has been all too prevalent in a few current schools of inexactitude. The tendency contributes, as I have said, to confuse the issues and, though it may seem a perilous suggestion, one is tempted to say that, in all its higher aspects, the name itself of adept might be abandoned definitely in favour of that of the mystic- though on account of the great loose thinking it is only too likely- and there are signs sufficient already- that it would share a similar fate of misconstruction.

There was a time perhaps when we could have listened, and did even, to descriptions of this kind, because we had only just begun to hear of adepts and sages, so that things were magnefied in the half-light. The scales have fallen now, and though the light into which we have entered is very far from the high light of all, it is serviceable sufficiently to dispel many shadows and to dissipate many distractions. The difficulty which is here specified is increased by the fact that there are certainly powers of the height, and that the spirit of man does not in its upward path take all the heavens of aspiration without, after some manner, being set over the kingdoms which are below it. For ourselves, at least, we can lay down one irrevocable law- that he who has resolved, setting all things else aside, to enter the path of adeptship must look for his progress in proportion as he pursues holiness for its own sake and not for the miracles of sanctity. It will be seen that I am disposed to call things by their old names, which have many consecrations, and I hope to command sympathy- but something more even- when I say further that he who dreams of adeptship and does not say sanctity in his heart till his lips are cleansed and then does not say it with his lips, is not so much far from the goal as with-out having conceived regarding it. One of the lesser masters, who has now scarcely a pupil amongst us, said once, quoting from somewhere Vel sanctum invenit, vel sanctvm facit; but I know that it must be long resident in our desires before it can he declared in our lives.

I have searched the whole West and only in two directions have I found anything which will compare with pure monastic mysticism; one of these is the mystic side of alchemy, while the other is that body of tradition which answers most fully to the name of Rosicrucianism. There are other places in which we find the same thing, or the substance of the same thing, and I believe that I have given faithful testimony already on this point;

even in the lesser schools I am sure that it was always at the roots, but except in so far as a personal sympathy may direct us, or the accidents of an historical study, I do not know that there is a direct gain- or that there is not rather a hindrance- by going any distance afield for what is so close to our hands, and into side issues for what is in the straight road- whether this be broad or narrow. There is no doubt that from one point of view Christian mysticism has been on the external side bewrayed rather seriously by its environment, because of the inhibitions of the official churches in saying this, I hope that the time has come to all of us when the cheap conventions of hostility towards these churches, and especially towards the Latin Rite, have ceased to obtain in our minds and that we can appreciate, in however detached a manner, the high annals of their sanctity. If so, we shall be able to appreciate also, at the proper value, an external and historical side on which the Latin Church approached too often that picture in the story of the Holy Graal of a certain King of Castle Mortal, who sold God for money. The difficulty which the Rite has created and the inhibitions into which it has passed arise more especially not alone on the external side but from the fact that it has taken the great things of symbolism too generally for material facts. In this way, with all the sincerity which can be attached to its formal documents, produced for the most part by the process of growth, the Church Catholic of Latin Christianity has told the wrong story, though the elements which were placed in its hands are the right and true elements. I believe that the growth of sanctity within the Latin Church has been- under its deepest consideration- substantially hindered by the over-encrustation of the spirit with the literal aspect, though this at the same time is indispensable to expression. I believe that in the minds of the mystics this hindrance has operated; of all men on earth they have recognized assuredly the working of the spirit; but they sought to attain it through the veils of doctrine and they did not utterly and wholly part the curtains thereof. The result was that these trailed after them and were an impediment as they entered the sanctuary. The process itself was, in one sense, the wrong process, though on account of their environment it was almost impossible that they should adopt another. We have agreed long ago that to work up from Nature to Grace is not really the method of the wise, because that which is below is the branches and that which is above is the roots, and the tree of life is really in this sense, and because of our distance from the centre, as it were, upside down. So also the true way of experience in the mystic life is to work outward from within. It is natural, of course, and this is of necessity also, that we should receive our first intimations through the letter, but when it has exhibited to us some reflections of the light which is behind we must not suffer our course to be hindered by the office of the letter, but should set it aside rather, to abide in the root-meaning which is behind the symbols. There is a later stage in which we shall revert to the external and to the meaning that is without, bringing back with us the inward light to interpenetrate and trans-form it. Perhaps an illustration will explain better the order of procedure than a formal statement merely, though I do not think that there is even a surface difficulty concerning it. We have been taught in the infancy of the mind the great story which is the root and heart of external Christianity. That is not the letter which kills but the cortex of a vessel behind which are the eternal fountains of life. I need not say that many of us do not get be-yond this cortex and, fortunately, it is not a dead husk, but a living body through which Grace flows to us after the measure of our capacity. But it may come to pass that the inward sensorium is opened- by the mediation, as it may well be, of the great books of the Church, or in what manner soever- and we then see that the great story, the old story, the story which is of all things true, is that of our own soul. I mean this not in the sense of the soul's geniture, but in the sense of its progress, as it is here and now environed. We are then looking towards the real road of our redemption, and it is at this stage that the letter should be set aside for a period because everything has to be enacted anew. The virgin must conceive and bear her son; in the grand rough outline of Saint Martin the son must be born in the Bethlehem of our human life; he must be presented in the temple which stands in the Jerusalem within; he must confound the doctors of the intellect; he must lead the hidden life of Nazareth; he must be manifested and must teach us within, in which way we shall return to the world of doctrine and shall find that all things are made new. It is not that there are new doctrines, but there is another quality of life; thereby the old symbolism has been so interpenetrated that the things which are without have become the things which are within, till each seems either in the power of the grace and in the torrent of the life. It is then that we cease to go out through the door by which we went in, because other doors are open, and the call of many voices, bidding us no longer depart hence, says rather: Let us enter the sanctuary, even the inmost shrine.

I desire, therefore, to make it plain that the Secret Church Mystic which exists and has always existed within the Church Militant of Christendom does not differ in anything from the essential teaching of doctrine- I mean Quod semper, quod ubique, quod ab omnibus; that it can say with its heart what it says also with its lips; that again there is no change or shadow of vicissitude; but in some very high sense the ground of the essentials has been removed. The symbolum remains ; it has not taken on another meaning; hut it has unfolded itself like the flower from within. Christian Theosophy in the West can recite its Credo in unum Deum by clause and by clause, including in unam sanctum catholicam et apostolicam ecclesiam, and if there is an arriere pensee it is not of heresy or Jesuitry. Above all, and I say this the more expressly because there are still among us- that is to say, in those circles generally- certain grave misconceptions, and it is necessary to affirm that the path of the mystic does not pass through the heresies.

And now with respect to the secret schools which have handed down to us at this day some part or aspects of the secret tradition belonging to Christian times, I must leave out of consideration, because there are limits to papers of this kind, the great witness of Kabalism which although it is a product of the Christian period is scarcely of it, and although therein the quest and its term do not assuredly differ from that of the truth which is in Christ, there are perhaps other reasons than those of brevity for setting it apart here. Alchemy may not have originated much further East than Alexandria, or, alternatively, it may have travelled from China when the port of Byzantium was opened to the commerce of the world. In either case, its first development, in the forms with which we are acquainted, is connected with the name of Byzantium, and the earliest alchemists of whom we have any remains in literature constitute a class by themselves under the name of Byzantine alchemists. The records of their processes went into Syria and Arabia, where they assumed a new mode, which bore, however, all necessary evidence of its origin. In this form it does not appear to have had a specific influence upon the corpus doctrinale. The records were also taken West, like many other mysteries of varying importance, and when they began to assume a place in western history this was chiefly in France, Germany and England. In other words, there arose the cycle of Latin alchemy, passing at a later date, by the way of translation, into the vernaculars of the respective countries, until finally, but much later, we have original documents in English, French and German. It follows, but has not so far been noticed, that the entire literature is a pro-duct of Christian times and has Christianity as its motive, whether subconsciously or otherwise. This statement applies to the Latin Geber and the tracts which are ascribed to Morien and Rhasis. The exception which proves the rule is the Kabalistic Aesh Mezareph, which we know only by fragments included in the great collection of Rosenroth. I suppose that there is no labyrinth which it is quite so difficult to thread as that of the Theatrum Chemicum. It is beset on every side with pitfalls, and its clues, though not destroyed actually, have been buried beneath the ground. Expositors of the subject have gone astray over the general purpose of the art, because some have believed it to be: (a) the transmutation of metals, and that only, while others have interpreted it as (b) a veiled method of delineating the secrets of the soul on its way through the world within, and besides this nothing. Many text-books of physical alchemy would seem to have been re-edited in this exotic interest. The true philosophers of each school are believed to have taught the same thing, with due allowance for the generic difference of their term, and seeing that they use the same language it would seem that, given a criterion of distinction in respect of the term, this should make the body of cryptogram comparatively easy to disentangle. But as one of the chief difficulties is said also to reside in the fact that many of them do not begin at the same point of the process, the advantage of uniformity is cancelled largely.

There are affirmed to be experimental schools still existing in Europe which have carried the physical work much further than it is ever likely to be taken by any isolated student; but this must be accepted under several reserves, or I can say, at least, that, having better occasions than most people of knowing the schools and their development, I have so far found no evidence. But there are testified otherwise to be- and I speak here with the certainty of first-hand knowledge-other schools, also experimental, also existing in Europe, which claim to possess the master-key of the mystical work. How far they have been successful at present in using that key I am not in a position to say, nor can I indicate its nature for reasons that, I think, must be obvious. It so happens, however, that the mystery of the processes is one thing and that which lies on the surface, or more immediately beneath the externals of the concealed language, is, fortunately, another thing. And, as often happens also, the enlightening correspondences are offering their marks and seals- if not at our very doors- at least in the official churches. Among all those places that are holy there is no holy place in which they do not abide a mane usque ad vespertinum, and the name of the correspondence-in-chief is the Holy Eucharist.

I propose now to tabulate certain palmary points of terminology which are common to all the adepts, including both schools indifferently, though we are dealing here- and this is understood- with the process of one school only. By the significance of these points or terms we shall see to what extent the symbolism of the higher alchemy is in conformity with mystic symbolism and with the repose of the life of the Church in God. It should be realized, however, that there is nothing so hard and so thankless as to elucidate one symbolism by the terms of another- and this notwithstanding an occasional identity which may manifest in the terms of each.

It must be understood further and accepted that all alchemists, outside the distinctions of their schools, were actuated by an express determination to veil their mystery and that they had recourse for this purpose to every kind of subterfuge. At the same time they tell us that the whole art is contained, manifested and set forth by means of a single vessel, which, amidst all manner of minor variations, is described with essential uniformity throughout the great multitude of texts. This statement constitutes a certain lesser key to the art; but as on the one hand the alchemists veil their hallow-in-chief by reference, in spite of their assurance, as above noted, to many pretended vessels, so has the key itself a certain aspect of subterfuge, since the alleged unity is in respect only of the term final of the process in the unity of the recipient. This unity is the last reduction of a triad, because, according to these aspects of Hermetic philosophy, man in the course of his attainment is at first three- that is, when he sets out upon the great quest; he is two at a certain stage; but he is, in fine, one, which is the end of his evolution. The black state of the matter on which the process of the art is engaged is the body of this death, from which the adepts have asked to be detached. It is more especially our natural life. The white state of the stone, the confection of which is desired, is the vesture of immortality with which the epopts are clothed upon. The salt of the philosophers is that savour of life without which the material earth can neither be salted nor cleansed. The sulphur of the philosophers is the inward substance by which some souls are saved, yet so as by fire. The mercury of the sages is that which must be fixed and volatilized- naturally it is fluidic and wandering- but except under this name, or by some analogous substitute, it must not be described literally outside the particular circles of secret knowledge. It is nearer than hands and feet.

16

Now the perfect correspondence of these things in the symbolism of official Christianity, and the great mystery of perfect sanctification, is set forth in the great churches under the sacramentalism of the Holy Eucharist. This is my point, and I desire to make it clear: the same exalted mystery which lies behind the symbols of bread and wine, behind the undeclared priesthood which is according to the order of Melchisedeck, was expressed by the alchemists under the guise of transmutation; but I refer here to the secret school of adeptship which had taken over in another and transcendent interest the terminology and processes of occult metallurgy.

The vessel is therefore one, but the matter thereto adapted is not designated especially, or at least after an uniform manner it is said to be clay by those who speak at times more openly in order that they may be understood the less, as if they also were singing in their strange chorus:-

Let us be open as the day,

That we may deeper hide ourselves.

It is most commonly described as metallic, because on the surface of the literature there is the declared mystery of all metals, and the concealed purpose is to show that in the roots and essence of these things there is a certain similarity or analogy. The reason is that the epopt, who has been translated, again finds his body after many days, but under a great transmutation, as if in another sense the panis quotidianis had been changed into the panis virus et vita/is, but without mutation of the accidents. The reason is also that in normal states the body is here and now not without the soul, nor can we separate readily, by any intellectual process. the soul from the spirit which broods thereover, to fertilize it in a due season. It is, however, one vessel, and this makes for simplicity; hut it is not by such simplicity that the art is testified to be a lusus puerorum. The contradistinction hereto is that it is hard to he a Christian, which is the comment of the man born blind upon the light that he cannot see. There is also the triumphant affirmation of the mystical counter-position, that to sin is hard indeed for the man who knows truly. The formula of this is that man is born for the heights rather than the deeps, and its verbal paradox is facilis ascensus superno. The process of the art is without haste or violence by the mediation of a graduated fire, and the seat of this fire is in the soul. It is a mystery of the soul's love, and for this reason she is called "undaunted daughter of desire." The sense of the gradation is that love is set free from the impetuosity and violence of passion and has become a constant and incorruptible flame. The formula of this is that the place of unity is a centre wherein there is no exaggeration. That which the fire consumes is certain materials or elements, which are called recrementa, the grosser parts, the superfluities; and it should he observed that there are two purgations, of which the first is the gross and the second the subtle. The first is the com-mon process of conversion, by which there is such a separation of seemingly external components that what remains is as a new creature, and may be said to be reborn. The second is the exalted conversion, by which that which has been purified is so raised that it enters into a new region, or a certain heaven comes down and abides therein. It is not my design in the present place to exhaust all the sources of interpretation, because such a scheme would be impossible in a single paper, and I can allude, therefore, but scantily to the many forms of the parables which are concerned with the process up to this point. The ostensible object, which was materialized in the alternative school, is the confection of a certain stone or powder, which is that of projection, and the symbolical theorem is that this powder, when added to a base metal, performs the wonder of transmutation into pure silver or gold, better than those of the mines. Otherwise, it prolongs life and renews youth in the adept- philosopher and lover of learning. In the second case, it is spoken of usually as an elixir, but the transmuting powder and the renewing draught are really one thing with the spiritual alchemists. It must be also affirmed that in virtue of a very high mysticism there is an unity in the trinity of the powder, the metal and the vase. The vase is also the alchemist on his outer side, for none of the instruments, the materials, the fires, the producer, and the thing produced are external to the one subject. At the same time the inward man is distinguished from the out-ward man; we may say that the one is the alchemist and the other the vessel. It is in this sense that the art is both physical and spiritual. But the symbolism is many times enfolded, and the gross metal which is placed within the vessel is the untransmuted life of reason, motive, concupiscence, self-interest and all that which constitutes the intelligent creature on the normal plane of manifestation. Hereof is the natural man enclosed in an animal body, as the metal is placed in the vessel, and from this point of view the alchemist is he who is sometimes termed arrogantly the super-man. But because there is only one vessel it must be understood that herein the stone is confected and the base metal is converted. The alchemist is himself finally the stone, and because many zealous aspirants to the art have not understood this they have failed in the great work on the spiritual side. The schedule which now follows may elucidate this hard subject somewhat more fully and plainly.

There are (a) the natural, external man, whose equivalent is the one vessel; (b) the body of desire, which answers to the gross matter; (c) the aspiration, the consciousness, the will of the supernatural life; (d) the process of the will working on the body of desire within the outward vessel; (e) the psychic and transcendental conversion thus effected; (f) the reaction of the purified body of desire on the essential will, so that the one sup-ports the other, while the latter is borne upward, and from such raising there follows this further change, that the spirit of a man puts on itself a new quality of life, becoming an instrument which is at once feeding and is itself fed; (g) herein is the symbol of the stone and the great elixir; (h) the spirit is nourished from above by the analogies of Eucharistic ministry; (i) the spirit nourishes the soul, as by bread and wine; (j) the soul effects the higher conversion in the body of desire; (k) it thus comes about that the essence which dissolves everything and changes everything is still contained in a vessel, or- alternatively- that God abides in man.

This process, thus exhaustively delineated in the parables of alchemy, is put with almost naked simplicity by Eucharistic doctrine, which says that material lips receive the supersubstantial bread and wine, that the soul is nourished and that Christ enters the soul. It seems, therefore, within all reason and all truth to testify that the panis vivus et vitalis is even as the trans-muting stone and that the chalice of the new and eternal testament is as the renewing elixir; but I say this under certain reasonable reserves because, in accordance with my formal indication, the closer the analogies between distinct systems of symbolism the more urgent is that prudence which counsels us not to confuse them by an interchangeable use.

All Christian mysticism came forth out of the Mass Book, and it returns therein. But the Mass Book in the first instance came out of the heart mystic which had unfolded in Christendom. The nucleus of truth in the missal is Dominus prope est. The Mass shows that the great work is in the first sense a work of the hands of man, because it is he officiating as a priest in his own temple who offers the sacrifice which he has purified. But the elements of that sacrifice are taken over by an intervention from another order, and that which follows is transfusion.

Re-expressing all this now in a closer summary, the apparatus of mystical alchemy is indeed, comparatively speaking, simple.

The first matter is myrionimous and is yet one, corresponding to the unity of the natural will and the unlimited complexity of its motives, dispositions, desires, passions and distractions, on all of which the work of wisdom must operate. The vessd is also one, for this is the normal man complete in his own degree. The process has the seal of Nature's directness; it is the graduation and increasing maintenance of a particular fire. The initial work is a change in the substance of will, aspiration and desire, which is the first conversion or transmutation in the elementary sense.

But it is identical even to the end with the term proposed by the Eucharist, which is the modification of the noumenal man by the communication of Divine Substance. Here is the lapis qui non lapis, lapis tingens, lapis angularis, lapis qui multiplicetur, lapis per quem justus aedificabit domum Domini, et jam valde aedificatur et terram possidebit, per omnia, etc. When it is said that the stone is multiplied, even to a thousandfold, we know that this is true of all seed which is sown upon good soil.

So, therefore, the stone transmutes and the Eucharist trans-mutes also; the philosophical elements on the physical side go to the making of the stone which is also physical; and the sacramental elements to the generation of a new life in the soul. He who says Lapis Philosophorum, says also: My beloved to me and I to him: Christ is therefore the stone, and the stone in adept humanity is the union realized, while the great secret is that Christ must be manifested within.

Now it seems to me that it has not served less than an useful purpose to establish after a new manner the intimate resemblance between the higher understanding of one part of the secret tradition and the better interpretation of one sacrament of the church. It must be observed that we are not dealing in either case with the question of attainment. The analogy would remain if spiritual alchemy and Christian sacramentalism abode in the intellectual order as theorems only, or as part of the psychic dream which had never been carried into experience. It would be more easy (if there were here any opportunity) to offer the results of the experience as recorded in the lives of the saints than to discuss the traditional attainments which are held to have passed into actuality among the secret schools; but the veiled literatures must be left to speak for themselves, which- for those who can read- they do, like the annals of sanctity as to these- those who will take the pains may seek verification for themselves. My task in respect of spiritual alchemy ends by exhibiting that this also was a mystery of sanctity concerned ex hypothesi with the communication of Divine Substance, and that this is the term of the Eucharist. It is this which the doctrine of sanctity offered, to those who entered the pathway of sanctity, as the foretaste in this life of the union which is consummated in eternity, or of that end be-yond which there is nothing whatever which is conceivable. We know from the old books that it has not entered into the heart of man, but the heart which has put away the things of sense conceives it by representations and types. This is the great tradition of that which the early alchemists term truth in the art; the end is representation after its own kind rather than felicity, but the representation is of that order which begins in ecstacy and ends in absorption. Let no man say, therefore, that he loses himself in experience of this order, for, perchance, it is then only that he finds himself, even in that way which suggests that after many paths of activity he is at length coming into his own.

It might seem that I have reached here a desirable point for my conclusion, but I am pledged, alike by my title and one antecedent reference, to say something concerning Rosicrucianism, which is another witness in the world on the part of the secret tradition. There is one respect in which it is simpler in its apparatus than the literature of the purely Hermetic tradition, for it lies within a smaller compass and has assumed a different mode. It is complicated by the fact that very few of the texts which are available among the things of the outside world have a title to rank in its tradition. This, I suppose, is equivalent to an intimation that the witness is still in the world after another and more active manner, which is true in more than a single way. I am not the ambassador, and much less the plenipotentiary, of the secret societies in the West, and independently of this statement I feel sure that I shall not be accused of endeavouring to assume the role or to create the impression. I know only that the societies exist, and that they are at the present time one means of perpetuating that tradition. I do not suggest that there are no other means, because I have indicated even from the beginning that the door looking towards heaven and the sanctuary which is its ante-chamber was opened long centuries ago by the official churches. But the tradition itself has been rather behind the churches and some part of the things for which we are all seek-ing is to he found therein- all which is without detriment to the light of the East, because this is also the light of the West under another veil. Even in the esoteric assemblies which are now and here among us, the tradition is, in a sense, veiled, and, of course, in speaking publicly one has always to cloud the sanctuaries rather than to say: Lift up your eyes, for it is in this or that corner of London, Paris or Prague.

If there is one thing more regrettable than the confusion in forms of symbolism, it is the identification of separate entities under a general term which has only a particular meaning so far as history is concerned. The name Rosicrucian, has suffered from abuse of this kind, being used almost interchangeably with that of Alchemist by popular writers. I must ask to be dis-associated from this error when I say that the external history of the Rosy Cross, in so far as it can be said to exist, has only one point of correspondence with Rosicrucian traditions perpetuated by secret societies in a few centres of Europe. The point of correspondence is the legend-in-chief of the Order, detached from the pseudo-historical aspect which it bore in the early documents, and associated with a highly advanced form of symbolism. It is in this form only that it enters into the sequence of the mysteries, and exhibits how the priest-king does issue from Salem, carrying bread and wine. We have, therefore, the Eucharistic side in the higher Rosicrucian tradition, but if I may describe that which is greater in the terms of that which is lesser- because of the essential difficulty with which I am confronted- it has undergone a great change, not by a diminution of the sacraments but because they are found everywhere. The alchemical maxim which might be inscribed over the gate of any Rosicrucian temple is-

Est in Mercurio quicquid quaerunt sapientes.

The Eucharistic maxim which might be written over the laboratory of the alchemist, in addition to Laborare est orare would be-

Et antiquum documentum Novo cedat ritui:

Praestet fides supplementum Sensuum defectui.

The maxim which might be written over the temples of the official churches is Corporis Mysterium, that the mystery of the body might lead

them more fully into the higher mystery of the soul. And, in fine, that maxim which might, and will be, inscribed over the one temple of the truly catholic religion when the faiths of this western world have come into their own- that which is simplest of all, and of all most pregnant, would be mysterium fidei, the mystery which endures forever and forever passes into experience.

In conclusion as to this part, Rosicrucianism is the mystery of that which dies in manifestation that the life of the manifest may be ensured. I have found nothing in symbolism which accounts like Rose-Cross symbolism for that formula which on one side is the summary expression of mysticism: "And I look for the resurrection of the dead and the life of the world to come."

And now in conclusion generally:-

I have spoken of three things only, and of one of them with great brevity, because the published literatures have to be set aside, and of that which remains it does not appear in the open face of day. The initiations are many and so are the schools of thought, but those which are true schools and those which are high orders issue from one root. Est una sola res, and those whose heart of contemplation is fixed upon this one thing may differ widely but can never be far apart. Personally, I do not believe- and this has the ring of a commonplace- that if they came to understand one another they would be found to differ widely. I know not what systems of the eons may intervene between that which is imperishable within us and the union wherein the universe will, in fine, repose at the centre. But I know that the great systems ay, even the great processes- of the times that are gone, as of those which now encompass us- do not pass away, because that which was from the beginning, is now and ever shall be- is one motive, one aspiration, one term of thought remaining, as if in the stillness of an everlasting present. We really understand one another, and our collective aspirations are united, world without end.

MYSTICAL REALIZATION

The testimony to mystical experience has been borne in the modem world, in the main on the faith of the records, and under the Christian aegis - through all the Christian centuries-it has been borne at first hand by those who have attained therein some part at least of that which awaits the souls of men in the fruition of Divine Union. The annals of old sanctity and the commentaries of expert theology constitute together an exceedingly large literature, over and above which there is a yet larger testimony going back into remote ages and concerned with the same experience under the denominations of other religions in the sacred world of the East. Yet it seems to me that in what has been called the "general and popular world" of thoughtful and literate people there is still only a very slight and imperfect understanding of the whole subject. There is, I think, none on which statements, are looser and fundamental misconceptions, more frequent. The terms Mysticism and Mystical are still used to characterize the dealings of "occult science" and as synonyms for the scheme of things, which are usually connoted by the title of "new thought." They are labels in common, used indifferently by friends and enemies of both. Those who affirm that there are no occult sciences, though there are many grades of self-induced hallucination, are apt to term them mystical as a by-word of reproach. Those in whose view the literary ventures which carry the mark of new thought are goods that are labeled falsely, regard it as the last word of condemnation to describe them as mystical. On the other hand, both literatures belong, in the opinion of many defenders, to the realm of mysticism, which they understand to mean higher thought. The point of union between the two parties resides in the fact that they are indifferently misusing words.

It happens that mysticism is the world-old science of the soul's return to God and that those who apply it to (1) any form of conventional metaphysics, (2) any branch of mental philosophy, (3) any reveries high or low, are no less mistaken than those who use it as a term of scorn. I care nothing in this connection for the etymological significance of the word, as denoting what is secret and withdrawn. It has come in the course of the years to have one meaning only in the accurate use thereof, and we must abide by this and no other-for the sake of ordered thought-unless and until the keepers of mystical science shall agree between themselves on another and more definite term as an expression of the whole subject.

I have been speaking of the outer circles, from whom it seems idle at present to expect accuracy; but there is a more extraordinary want of understanding on the part of some whom we should expect to be capable at least of thinking rightly within the elementary measures of mysticism. Here it is no longer a question concerning the mere word, or the use of denominations in the sense of the mystical path when they belong more properly to the end, after all the travellings are over. I refer especially at the moment to misapprehensions respecting the place of the science in the life of modern man and woman, and this involves a consideration of the now recurring question whether that science can be acquired by practice in the daily life of the world. There can be no expectation of presenting in a brief space any views that will differ materially from those which I have expressed already in much longer studies; but it may be possible to offer something simply, for understanding on the part of those who cannot examine the subject in ordered and lengthy books. The question is, therefore, whether those excellent people are right who seem to think that the principles of mystical science may be so put forward that they can be taken into the heart, not indeed of the men in the street - though no one wishes to exclude them-but of men and women everywhere who have turned already to God, or are disposed in that direction. Alternatively, is it-shall I say ?-a science which is reserved to experts only? We know that it is not possible to become acquainted readily and easily with the higher mathematics, with chemistry or biology. There are certain natural qualifications in virtue of which the poet is born, as well as made subsequently; there is also the scientific mind, which presupposes gift and faculty, as well as opportunity and application. In the science of the mystics, in their peculiar art of life, are there certain essential qualifications to be postulated in every case, and is there a long apprenticeship? Before attempting to answer, let us see what is being said and how far it exhibits any adequate acquaintance with the problems belonging to the debate.

It has been suggested recently that religion is at work revising institutions and theology, that reconstruction is in the air everywhere and that mysticism needs reconstruction as much as anything else. In the face of this statement a certain caution is necessary lest we begin to talk foolishly. It appears, however, that the remark applies rather to notions, theories and systems, to "the spell of medieval mysticism" and to the reconstruction of these. Yet the tendency is to regard mysticism as a mode of thought, an attitude -if you like- towards the universal, so that we can have done with archaic forms and devise others which are modern. It is, however, as I have said, a science, the end of which is attained in the following of certain methods. One does not change sciences -as, for example, mathematics- but we can reconstruct and, it may be, improve our way of acquiring them. Medieval mysticism is the same as modern mysticism, but there may be other ways of reaching it, in respect of the externals, than were known and practiced in convents. Fundamentally speaking, however, the ways are one-whether in the East or West, for those who follow *Vedanta* and those to whom the *Imitation* is a source. The only change that we can make is by taking out of the way that which is unnecessary thereto. As I tried to show some four or five years since, in *The Way Of Divine Union,* there is no question that the end of mysticism was reached by the ascetic path during many past centuries of Christendom, but it belonged to the accidents of the quest; and other ways are possible, which I tried also to indicate. The alleged reconstruction of religion is taking place only in a subsidiary sense, within narrow measures, or here and there in the corners. The great Latin Church is revising nothing, while the Greek -I suppose- is stewing in the waters of its own incapacity. But if they were both at the work of remaking and at one in their activity with the sects and the Anglican Church, the case of the mystics would still differ, because pure mysticism has no institutions to revise and no conventional or official theology to expand, reduce, or vary. It is a path of advancement towards a certain end, and the path is one: the variations are found only in the modes of travelling. Having in this manner cleared the issues, there must be something said of the end and the way thereto.

There is a great experiment possible in this life and there is a great crown of the experiment, but in the nature of things it is not to be bought cheaply, for it demands the whole man. It has been said that the life of the mystic is one of awareness of God, and as to this we must remember that we are dealing with a question of life and a life-problem. But what is awareness of God? It is a certain inward realization, a consciousness of His Divine -not only without us but within. The word awareness is therefore good and true, but it is one of those intimations which -as I have suggested already- are of the path and not of the end. It is of the learner and not of the scientist. The proof can be put in a nutshell by an appeal to the perfect analogy of that experience which is human love. Can we say to the human over that an awareness of the beloved must content him here and now? But that which he seeks is possession, after the manner of all in all- possession which is reciprocal and mutual. In Divine Things the word is realization, and mystical realization is the state of being possessed and possessing. Otherwise, it is God in us and we in God: O' state of the ineffable, beyond all words and thoughts, deeper than tears of the heart and higher than all its raptures. The science of the mystic is that of the peculiar life-cultus, life-practice, or quest of life which leads to this state. In respect both of path and state the word is love. That kind of loving is summarized in the grand old counsel: "With all thy heart and with all thy soul." The rewards of love are not those which can be earned by divided allegiance. There is also another saying -about the desire of a certain house having eaten one up. There is no eye on two worlds in this and no Sabbath dedication except in the long Sabbath of undivided life. Here, too, is no art of making the best of both worlds and especially of this one, as if with one eye on the dollars and another on God. In this kind of dedication the world goes by and the pageants of all its temples: there are no half-measures respecting it. The motto of the path is *sub specie adernitatis,* and it connotes the awakening and subsequent activity of a particular inward faculty. We know well enough by experience the power of a ruling passion, and it may happen to be one that is lawful. The man who is ruled thereby is living *sub specie ilia;* it colors all his ways and days: it is the very motive of his life. Now, if we postulate in certain persons a ruling passion for God, it is then *sub ilia specie* that they live and move and have their being.

As regards this state and as regards its gifts and fruits, even at the early stages, I testify that the Divine in the universe answers to the Divine in man. There does take place that which maintains and feeds the passion. A life which is turned to the keynote of the eternal mode knows of the things that are eternal. It knows very soon that it is not on a false quest: that God is and that He recompenses those who seek Him out is verified by valid experience. It grows from more to more, an ever-expanding equipment in Lightest sanity of mind. Two things are certain: (1) apart from this high passion there can be no practical mystic; but (2) no one can teach another how to acquire it. Once it has been kindled in the heart, the secret of the path is its maintenance, and many devices have been tried-among others those of the ascetics. The only excellent way is that of love in its activity towards all in God and God in all. This is the sense of St. Augustine's Love and do what you will. Hatred is a canker in the heart and eats up this passion. Universal love maintains the passion for God till that time when God enters and takes over the work; it is then the beginning of the end, and that end is the still activity of union in the Eternal Centre. It is inevitable that vocation must be postulated, but this signifies an inward possibility of response to an ever-recurring call. It is thus that the divine passion is kindled which -as I have said- no one can communicate to another. There is something in the individual fount by which some are poets and some are called to the priesthood. For the same inscrutable reason there are some who receive and answer the call to mystic life. It may be a consequence of antecedent lives or of hidden leading from spiritual spheres: I do not know. It follows that the mystic life is reserved to those who can lead it, but unlike all other sciences the only technique connected with it is the technique of love; the apprenticeship is that of love; the science is love; and the end is love's guerdon. All this being so, I am sure that there are more true mystics than we can dream, and yet they are few enough. They will grow from more to more, for love always conquers. But as to when this science of love can appeal to all classes I make no pretense of knowing: it is for those who are able to acquire it; and so are the questions answered.

CLOUD UPON THE SANCTUARY
Introduction

Apart from "The Cloud upon the Sanctuary," Eckartshausen is a name only to the Christian Transcendentalists of England. He wrote much, and at his period and in his place, he exercised some considerable influence; but his other works are practically unknown among us, while in Germany the majority at least seem forgotten, even among the special class to which some of them might be assumed to appeal. "The Cloud upon the Sanctuary" has, I believe, always remained in the memory of a few, and is destined still to survive, for it carries with it a message of very deep significance to all those who look beneath the body of religious doctrine for the one principle of life which energizes the whole organism. This translation has offered it for the first time to English readers, and it enters here upon the third phase of its existence. It appeared originally in the pages of "The Unknown World," a magazine devoted to the deeper understanding of philosophical and mystical religion, and it was afterwards republished in volume form, of which edition this is a new issue. It has attracted very considerable attention and deserved it; it has even been translated into French, under the auspices of the late Countess of Caithness, for the pages of *L'Aurore*. These few words of bibliography are not unnecessary because they establish the fact that there has been some little sentiment of interest working within a restricted circle, as one may hope, towards a more general diffusion and knowledge of a document which is at once suggestive from the literary standpoint and profoundly moving from other and higher considerations.

It encourages me to think that many persons who know and appreciate it now, or may come under its influence in the future, will learn with pleasure the little that I can tell them of its author, the Councilor Eckartshausen, and of certain other books not of his writing, which, as I think, connect therewith, and the study of which may help us to understand its message.

Perhaps the most interesting thing that I can say at the beginning concerning Eckartshausen is that he connects with that group of Theosophists of which Lavater was so important a figure, the Baron Kirchberger an accomplished and interesting recorder, and Louis Claude de Saint-Martin a correspondent in France and a certain source of leading. In his letters to Saint-Martin, Kirchberger says that Eckartshausen, with whom he was in frequent communication, was a man of immense reading and wonderful fertility; he regarded him in other respects as an extraordinary personage, "whatever way providence may have led him." It would appear that at this period, namely, in 1795, Eckartshausen was looking for and obtaining his chief light from the mystical study of numbers, but was also, to use the veiled and cautious language of the correspondence, in enjoyment of more direct favors. Saint-Martin confesses on his own part that he was more interested in Eckartshausen than he could express. Kirchberger must have held him in even higher estimation, and undertook a journey to the Swiss frontier actually for the purpose of receiving from him the personal communication of the Lost Word; but the illness of the proposed communicator frustrated this project. The point is important because it establishes the pretensions of Eckartshausen. As to the Councilor of Berne so to us, he comes speaking with authority; and whatever may be our opinion as to the kind of sacramentalism or economy which was conveyed in a proposal to communicate the incommunicable name, there are some of us who know, at least within certain limits, that the little book which I am here introducing is not one of vain pretension. Saint-Martin acknowledges that part of the numerical system of Eckartshausen was in astonishing agreement with things that he had learned long ago in his own school of initiation— that of Martines de Pasqually. Altogether the French mystic had formed the best opinion possible of his German brother, and his Swiss correspondent further tells us that Eckartshausen, although a courtier, walked in the narrow way of the inner life. In a letter to Kirchberger dated March 19th, 1795, Eckartshausen bears witness to his own personal experience and instructions received from above, his consciousness of a higher presence, the answers which he had received and the visions, with the steps by which he had advanced even to the attainment of what he terms "the Law in its fullness." I have thought it well to give these data derived from private correspondence, the publication of which was never designed or expected at the time, because they constitute a sketch of Eckartshausen taken to some extent unawares, when there could be the least reason to suppose that he was adopting an attitude. Let us now compare the very strong claim which they incorporate with that of "The Cloud upon the Sanctuary" itself, and the little analysis which I shall give here will, I think, be otherwise serviceable to readers as a summary of the chief purport of the work. It is possible by seeking inwardly to approach the essential wisdom, and this wisdom is Jesus Christ who is also the essence of love within us. The truth of this statement can be experimentally proved by any one, the condition of the experience being the awakening within us of a spiritual faculty cognizing spiritual objects as objectively and naturally as the outward senses perceive natural phenomenon. This organ is the intuitive sense of the transcendental world, and its awakening, which is the highest object of religion, takes place in three stages: (*a*) morally, by the way of inspiration; (*b*) intellectually, by the way of illumination; (*c*) spiritually, by the way of revelation. The awakening of this organ is the lifting of the cloud from the sanctuary, enabling our hearts to become receptive of God, even in this world. The knowledge of these mysteries has been always preserved by an advanced school, illuminated inwardly by the Savior, and continued from the beginning of things to the present time. This community is the Invisible Celestial Church, founded immediately after the Fall, and receiving a first-hand revelation for the raising of humanity. But the weakness of men as they multiplied necessitated an external society, namely, the Outward Church, which, in the course of time, became separated from the Inner Church, also through human weakness. The external church was originally consecrated in Abraham, but received its highest perfection in the mystery of Jesus Christ. The Interior Church is invisible and yet governs all; it is perpetuated in silence but in real activity, "and united the science of the temple of the ancient alliance with the spirit of the Savior," or of the interior alliance. This community of light is the reunion of all those capable of receiving light, and is known as the Communion of Saints. It possesses its school, its chair, its doctor, and a rule for students, with forms and objects of study, and in short a method by which they study, together with degrees for successive development to higher altitudes. We must not, however, regard it as a secret society, meeting at certain times, choosing its elders and members, and united by special objects; for even the chief does not invariably know all the members, and those who are ripe are joined to the general members when they thought least likely, and at a point of which they knew nothing. The society forms a theocratic republic, which one day will be the Regent-Mother of the whole world. Its members are exactly acquainted with the innermost of religions and of the Holy Mysteries, but these treasures are concealed in so simple a manner that they baffle unqualified research.

This doctrine of the interior church must be interpreted by everyone after his own lights; it is presented by Eckartshausen as one having full knowledge and ambassadorial powers, as one speaking from the center. My purpose is solely to show that he was sincere, and this sincerity furnishes us with one more proof, out of many which are to be derived from other and independent sources, that there is a great experiment possible, and that some have performed it. The sincerity of which I speak is I think illustrated by his life, which I will now summarize briefly. Carl Von Eckartshausen was born on June 28th, 1752, at the Castle of Haimbhausen in Bavaria, and was the natural son of Count Carl of Haimbhausen by Marie Anne Eckhart, the daughter of the overseer of the estates. His mother died in giving birth to him, and he appears to have been the subject of the most solicitous affection on the part of his father, being educated with the utmost pains. However, from the earliest years, his illegitimacy is said to have filled him with perpetual melancholy and an inclination to retire from the world, characteristics which at the same time endeared him to his family and friends. Through all his life he remained less or more a prey to the painful consequences of his original disqualification. He was destined notwithstanding to a career of some public importance. His first education was received at the college of Munich, and he afterwards proceeded to Ingoldsladt for the study of philosophy and law, which he pursued with marked success. His university course at an end, his father procured him the title of Aulic Councilor; and in 1780 he was appointed censor of the library at Munich. This, in spite of the rectitude and goodness which characterized him, made him many enemies, but the favor of the Elector Carl Theodore sustained him against all combinations. In 1784 he was nominated Keeper of the Archives of the Electoral House, an appointment said to have been conferred upon him through the desire of the Elector to keep him near his person. He published in all some sixty-nine works, embracing many classes of literature, including science, the fine arts, the drama, politics, religion, history, and, in particular, certain contributions of great merit to the occult sciences. As already indicated, the majority of these are now forgotten, though some of his plays seem to have been successful in their day. "The Prejudice of Birth " in particular, his first published drama, is described as abounding in felicitous situations and interest. He even attempted a comedy, and this also received considerable approbation. One only of his books, under the title "God is the Purest Love," commanded wide popularity. Sixty editions are said to have been published in Germany, and it was translated into most languages of Europe, as well as into Latin. It is a small collection of Catholic prayers and meditations on the fear of God, the love of God, the elevation of man's sentiments towards his Creator, the knowledge of the Eternal, etc. There are also devotional exercises for use at Mass, before and after Confession, and at Communion, with acts of penance and adoration to the Blessed Virgin. In a word, I fail to see wherein or how far it differs from the innumerable manuals of piety which have been produced during the last two or three centuries for the use of the Catholic laity. I believe, however, that it still circulates in Germany, and perhaps even in France; it is said to have a wonderful charm, though its intense mysticism is also stated to have puzzled some of its admirers; it has indeed been described as speaking the language and expressing the soul of Fenelon. Eckartshausen, however, as already indicated, wrote other and very different books, some on magic and some on the properties of numbers, and he is even accredited with a certain knowledge of Alchemy. Finally, he was the author of "The Cloud upon the Sanctuary," though the biographers to whom I am indebted almost for the words of this notice have scarcely mentioned this last and crowning production of his intellectual life. In his private capacity he was exceedingly amiable and charitable, devoting every month the result of his economies to the poor, and his whole time to the practice of virtue. He was married three times, and left several children. He died on May 13th, 1813, after a painful illness. The monographs of his period mention him as one of the best writers of Bavaria.

There are two matters to which before concluding I wish to draw attention briefly, and, as regards the first, in a very particular manner. The point of view from which "The Cloud upon the Sanctuary" should be regarded is important from the claim which it makes. What is this inner church of which Eckartshausen speaks, is a question which readers must answer for themselves, according to their best direction. One thing which it is not has been indicated by Eckartshausen himself. It is not any corporate body existing merely within the church and controlling and leading it from a specific local center. This possibility being negatived by the best of all authority on the subject, I should like on my own responsibility to negative also its most direct and clearest antithesis. It does not answer to the collective mind or oversoul of the most advanced members of the visible church, nor is it the *consensus omnium sanctorum* which, according to the old church maxim, is *sensus spiritus Sancti.* Despite the absence of all corporate bonds, there is in the claim itself too direct a suggestion of conscious association occurring somehow in this present physical life. We must take the key which Eckartshausen himself offers, namely, that there is within all of us a dormant faculty, the awakening of which within us gives entrance, as it develops, into a new world of consciousness, which is one of the initial stages of that state which he, in common with all other mystics, terms union with the Divine. In that union, outside all formal sects, all orthodox bonds of fellowship and veils and webs of symbolism, we shall form or do form actually a great congregation, the first fruits of immortality, and in virtue of the solidarity of humanity, and in virtue of the great doctrine of the communication of all things holy with all that seeks for holiness, the above and the below, this congregation is, in very truth, the leader of the visible church of faith, aspiration and struggle, the church triumphant over- watching the church militant, and the channel through which the graces and the benedictions of the holy and glorious Zion are administered to the Zion which is on earth.

The second point concerns certain books which I have promised to mention as connecting with the claim of Eckartshausen, and perhaps in some measure assisting us to get in touch with that claim. Unfortunately, in this restricted notice, I can do little more than name them. The first is "The Mystery of the Cross," originally published in 1732, anonymously, in the French language, but evidently written by a foreigner. It is a profound and beautiful work which, unknown to the world at large, has in private, if I may so speak, influenced many to their advancement, and to the deeper understanding and fruition of the hidden truth. Strongly embedded in this book will be found several of the governing ideas and aspirations of schools of mystic thought which became illustrious in later years. I may add that I am acquainted with the existence of a translation made many years ago, but still remaining in manuscript. The next books which I would note come at first sight a little strangely in the professed connection, but they enter none the less into the series; they are the two dramatic poems of the German poet, Werner, namely, "The Templars in Cyprus" and "The Brothers of the Cross." They are the work of a man who was intimately acquainted with the occult movement of his period—that of the French Revolution—and a participant therein. After all his experience he carried his great genius and exceptional knowledge into the fold of the Latin Church and became a priest. His two plays convey many moving suggestions of a guiding but unknown hand leading the Christian Church. The next book is of Russian origin, but was translated into French and published in Paris in 1801; of this translation a reprint was issued recently at Lyons. It is entitled "Some Characteristics of the Interior Church." It connects the point of view which is met with in "The Mystery of the Cross" with that of Eckartshausen, and is interesting on account of its origin, and also for certain Martinistic associations, but it is less suggestive and less profound. Finally, there is a very remarkable and I may add a very rare series of works published at Berleburg in the province of Westphalia in seven volumes, dated 1738. It is entitled "New Spiritual Discourses on various matters of the Interior Life and the Doctrines of the Christian Religion, or testimony of a Child of Truth concerning the Ways of the Spirit." These discourses occupy three volumes; two others contain a commentary on the Apocalypse; the sixth volume is a literal and mystical explanation of the epistle to the Romans, with some supplementary papers and a catechism of the science of Christian religion. The seventh volume is another commentary, verse for verse, on the first three chapters of Genesis. The collection as a whole may perhaps be best described as an appeal from external creeds with their differences, their arguments and their justifications, to the witness of the heart itself. It is an appeal also to the mystical doctors of the church, and it cites many of the great mystics from Tauler and Ruysbroek to Engelbrecht, Antoinette de Bourignon and Madame de Guyon. The discourses on the union of the Church of Christ and the spiritual union of the children of God, as also on a new church, in the second volume, will be found very interesting to students of Eckartshausen. There are also extraordinary analogies with Saint-Martin, Eckartshausen and the "Mystery of the Cross" to be found in the third volume, and having regard to the proximity of the date of publication to that of the last work, I incline to the opinion that there may have been some connection also in the authorship. When all these works have been studied, not in the letter but in the spirit, along with "The Cloud upon the Sanctuary," the spiritual truths which Eckartshausen has to some extent veiled, and his motives for doing so, will not be beyond discernment, nor the line of his experiences in all cases beyond pursuit. I should add that, so far as I can trace, Eckartshausen always remained in loyal communication with the external church in which he was originally trained, and did not therefore regard apostasy and rebellion as among the first evidences of personal illumination. Perhaps, like one of the Eastern teachers, he thought that some things could be changed from within, and essentially, without altering outward names and forms.

Letter I

There is no age more remarkable to the quiet observer than our own. Everywhere there is a fermentation in the minds of men; everywhere there is a battle between light and darkness, between exploded thought and living ideas, between powerless wills and living active force; in short everywhere is there war between animal man and growing spiritual man.

It is said that we live in an age of light, but it would be truer to say that we are living in an age of twilight; here and there a luminous ray pierces through the mists of darkness, but does not light to full clearness either our reason or our hearts. Men are not of one mind, scientists dispute, and where there is discord, truth is not yet apprehended.

The most important objects for humanity are still undetermined. No one is agreed either on the principle of rationality or on the principle of morality, or on the cause of the will. This proves that though we are dwelling in an age of light, we do not well understand what emanates from our hearts—and what from our heads. Probably we should have this information much sooner if we did not imagine that we have the light of knowledge already in our hands, or if we would cast a look on our weakness, and recognize that we require a more brilliant illumination. We live in the times of idolatry of the intellect, we place a common torchlight upon the altar and we loudly proclaim the aurora, that now daylight is really about to appear, and that the world is emerging more and more out of obscurity into the full day of perfection, through the arts, sciences, cultured taste, and even from a purer understanding of religion.

Poor mankind! To what standpoint have you raised the happiness of man? Has there ever been an age which has counted so many victims to humanity as the present? Has there ever been an age in which immorality and egotism have been greater or more dominant than in this one? The tree is known by its fruits. Mad men! With your imaginary natural reason, from whence have you the light by which you are so willing to enlighten others? Are not all your ideas borrowed from your senses which do not give you the reality but merely its phenomena? Is it not true that in time and space all knowledge is but relative? Is it not true that all which we call reality is but relative, for absolute truth is not to be found in the phenomenal world. Thus your natural reason does not possess its true essence, but only the appearance of truth and light; and the more this appearance increases and spreads, the more the *essence of light* inwardly fades, and the man confuses himself with this appearance and gropes vainly after the dazzling phantasmal images he conjures.

The philosophy of our age raises the natural intellect into independent objectivity, and gives it judicial power, she exempts it from any superior authority, she makes it voluntary, converting it into divinity by closing all harmony and communication with God; and this god

Reason, which has no other law but its own, is to govern Man and make him happy! ...

... Darkness able to spread light!

... Death capable of giving Life!

... The truth leads man to happiness. Can you give it?

That which you call truth is a form of conception empty of real matter, the knowledge of which is acquired from without and through the senses, and the understanding co- ordinates them by observed synthetic relationship into science or opinion.

You abstract from the Scriptures and Tradition their moral, theoretical and practical truth; but as individuality is the principle of your intelligence, and as egotism is the incentive to your will, you do not see, by your light, the moral law which dominates, or you repel it with your will. It is to this length that the light of today has penetrated. Individuality under the cloak of false philosophy is a child of corruption.

Who can pretend that the sun is in full zenith if no bright rays illuminate the earth, and no warmth vitalizes vegetation? If wisdom does not benefit man, if love does not make him happy, but very little has been done for him on the whole.

Oh! if only natural man, that is, sensuous man, would only learn to see that the source of his intelligence and the incentive of his will are only his individuality, he would then seek interiorly for a higher source, and he would thereby approach that which alone can give this true element, because it is *wisdom in its essential substance.*

Jesus Christ is that Wisdom, Truth, and Love. He, as Wisdom, is the Principle of reason, and the Source of the purest intelligence. As Love, He is the Principle of morality, the true and pure incentive of the will.

Love and Wisdom beget the spirit of truth, interior light; this light illuminates us and makes supernatural things objective to us.

It is inconceivable to what depths of error a man falls when he abandons simple truths of faith by opposing his own opinions.

Our century tries to decide by its (brain) intelligence, wherein lies the principle or ground of reason and morality, or the ground of the will; if the scientists were mindful, they would see that these things are better answered in the heart of the simplest man, than through their most brilliant casuistry. The practical Christian finds this incentive to the will, the principle of all morality, really and objectively in his heart; and this incentive is expressed in the following formula:—"Love God with all thy heart, and thy neighbor as thyself."

The love of God and his neighbor is the motive for the Christian's will, and the essence of love itself is Jesus Christ in us.

It is in this way the principle of reason is wisdom in us; and the essence of wisdom, wisdom in its substance, is again Jesus Christ, the light of the world. Thus we find in Him the principle of reason and of morality.

All that I am now saying is not hyperphysical extravagance; it is reality, absolute truth, that everyone can prove for himself by experience, as soon as he receives in himself the principle of all reason and morality—Jesus Christ, being wisdom and love *in essence*.

But the eye of the man of sensuous perception only is firmly closed to the fundamental basis of all that is true and to all that is transcendental.

The intelligence which many would fain raise to legislative authority is only that of the senses, whose light differs from that of transcendental reason, as does the phosphorescent glimmer of decayed wood from the glories of sunshine.

Absolute truth does not exist for sensuous man; it exists only for interior and spiritual man who possesses a suitable sensorium; or, to speak more correctly, who possesses an interior sense to receive the absolute truth of the transcendental world, a spiritual faculty which cognizes spiritual objects as objectively and naturally as the exterior senses perceive external phenomena.

This interior faculty of the man spiritual, this sensorium for the metaphysical world, is unfortunately not known to those who cognize only outside of it—for it is a mystery of the kingdom of God.

The current incredulity towards everything which is not cognized objectively by our senses is the explanation for the misconception of truths which are, of all, most important to man.

But how can this be otherwise? In order to see one must have eyes, to hear, one must have ears. Every apparent object requires its appropriate senses. So it is that transcendental objects require their sensorium—and this said sensorium is closed in most men. Hence men judge the metaphysical world through the intelligence of their senses, even as the blind imagine colors and the deaf judge tones— without suitable senses.

There is an objective and substantial ground of reason, an objective and substantial motive for the will. These two together form the new principle *of life*, and morality is there essentially inherent. This pure substance of reason and will, re-uniting in us the divine and the human, is Jesus Christ, the light of the world, who must enter into direct relationship with us, to be really recognized.

This real knowledge is actual faith, in which everything takes place in spirit and in truth. Thus one ought to have a sensorium fitted for this communication, an organized spiritual sensorium, a spiritual and interior faculty able to receive this light; but it is closed to most men by their senses.

This interior organ is the intuitive sense of the transcendental world, and until this intuitive sense is effective in us we can have no certainty of more lofty truths.

This organism is naturally inactive since the Fall, which degraded man to the world of physical senses alone. The gross matter which envelops this interior sensorium is a film which veils the internal eye, and therefore prevents the exterior eye from seeing into spiritual realms. This same matter muffles our internal hearing, so that we are deaf to the sounds of the metaphysical world; it so paralyses our spiritual speech that we can scarcely stammer words of sacred import, *words we fully pronounced once*, and by virtue of which we held authority over the elements and the external world.

The opening of this spiritual sensorium is the mystery of the New Man—the mystery of Regeneration, and of the vital union between God and man—it is the noblest object of religion on earth, that religion whose sublime goal is none other than to unite men with God in Spirit and in Truth.

We can therefore easily see by this how it is that religion tends always towards the subjection of the senses. It does so because it desires to make the spiritual man dominant, in order that the spiritual or truly rational man may govern the man of sense. Philosophy feels this truth, only its error consists in not apprehending the true source of reason, and because she would replace it by individuality by sensuous reason.

As man has internally a spiritual organ and a sensorium to receive the true principle of divine wisdom, or a true motive for the will or divine love, he has also exteriorly a physical and material sensorium to receive the *appearance* of light and truth. As external nature can have no absolute truth, but only phenomenally relative, therefore, human reason cannot cognize pure truth, it can but apprehend through the appearance of phenomena, which excites the lust of the eye, and in this as a source of action consists the corruption of sensuous man and the degradation of nature.

This exterior sensorium in man is composed of frail matter, whereas the internal sensorium is organized fundamentally from incorruptible, transcendental, and metaphysical substance.

The first is the cause of our depravity and our mortality, the second the cause of our incorruptibility and of our immortality.

In the regions of material and corruptible nature mortality hides immortality, therefore all our trouble results from corruptible mortal matter. In order that man should be released from this distress, it is necessary that the immortal and incorruptible principle, which dwells within, should expand and absorb the corruptible principle, so that the envelope of the senses should be opened, and man appear in his pristine purity.

This natural envelope is a truly corruptible substance found in our blood, forming the fleshly bonds binding our immortal spirits under the servitude of the mortal flesh.

This envelope can be rent more or less in every man, and this places him in greater spiritual liberty, and makes him more cognizant of the transcendental world.

There are three different degrees in the opening of our spiritual sensorium.

The first degree reaches to the moral plane only, the transcendental world energizes through us in but by interior action, called inspiration.

The second and higher degree opens this sensorium to the reception of the spiritual and the intellectual, and the metaphysical world works in us by interior *illumination*.

The third degree, which is the highest and most seldom attained, opens the whole inner man. It breaks the crust which fills our spiritual eyes and ears; it reveals the kingdom of spirit, and enables us to see objectively, metaphysical, and transcendental sights; hence all visions are explained fundamentally.

Thus we have an internal sense of objectivity as well as externally. Only the objects and the senses are different. Exteriorly animal and sensual motives act in us and corruptible sensuous matter energizes. Interiorly it is metaphysical and indivisible substance which gains admittance within, and the incorruptible and immortal essence of our Spirit receives its influence. Nevertheless, generally things pass much in the same way interiorly as they do externally. The law is everywhere the same. Hence, as the spirit or our internal man has quite other senses, and quite another objective sight from the rational man; one need not be surprised that it (the spirit) should remain an enigma for the scientists of our age, for those who have no objective sense of the transcendental and spiritual world. Hence they measure the supernatural by the measurement of the senses. However, we owe a debt of gratitude towards the philosopher Kant for his view of the truths we have promulgated.

Kant has shown incontestably that the natural reason can know absolutely nothing of what is supernatural, and that it can never understand analytically or synthetically, neither can it prove the possibility of the reality of Love, Spirit, or of the Deity.

This is a great truth, lofty and beneficial for our epoch, though it is true that St Paul has already enunciated it (1 Cor. i. 2–24). But the Pagan philosophy of Christian scientists has been able to overlook it up to Kant. The virtue of this truth is double. First, it puts insurmountable limits to the sentiment, to the fanaticism and to the extravagance of carnal reason.

Then it shows by dazzling contrast the necessity and divinity of Revelation. It proves that our human reason, in its state of unfoldment, *has no other* objective source for the supernatural than revelation, the only source of instruction in Divine things or of the spiritual world, the soul and its immortality; hence it follows that without revelation it is absolutely impossible to suppose or conjecture anything regarding these matters.

We are, therefore, indebted to Kant for proving philosophically now-a-days, what long ago was taught in a more advanced and illuminated school, *that without revelation no knowledge of God, neither any doctrine touching the soul, could be at all possible.*

It is therefore clear that a universal Revelation must serve as a fundamental basis to all mundane religion.

Hence, following Kant, it is clear that the transmundane knowledge is wholly inaccessible to natural reason, and that

God inhabits a world of light, into which no speculation of the unfolded reason can penetrate. Thus the rational man, or man of human reason, has no sense of transcendental reality, and therefore it was necessary that it should be revealed to him, for which faith is required, because the means are given to him by faith whereby his inner sensorium unfolds, and through which he can apprehend the reality of truths otherwise incapable of being understood by the natural man.

It is quite true that with new senses we can acquire sense of further reality. This reality exists already, but is not known to us, because we lack the organ by which to cognize it. One must not lay the fault to the percept, but on the receptive organ.

With, however, the development of the new organ we have a new perception, a sense of new reality. Without it the spiritual world cannot exist for us, because the organ rendering it objective to us is not developed.

With, however, its unfoldment, the curtain is all at once raised, the impenetrable veil is torn away, the cloud before the Sanctuary lifts, a new world suddenly exists for us, scales fall from the eyes, and we are at once transported from the phenomenal world to the regions of truth.

God alone is *substance*, absolute truth; He alone is He who *is*, and we are what He has made us. For Him, all exists in Unity; for us, all exists in multiplicity.

A great many men have no more idea of the development of the inner sensorium than they have of the true and objective life of the spirit, which they neither perceive nor foresee in any manner. Hence it is impossible to them to know that one can comprehend the spiritual and transcendental, and that one can be raised to the supernatural, even to vision.

The great and true work of building the Temple consists solely in destroying the miserable Adamic hut and in erecting a divine temple; this means, in other words, to develop in us the interior sensorium, or the organ to receive God. After this process, the metaphysical and incorruptible principle rules over the terrestrial, and man begins to live, not any longer in the principle of self-love, but in the Spirit and in the Truth, of which he is the Temple.

The moral law then evolves into love for one's neighbor in deed and in truth, whereas for the natural man it is but a simple attitude of thought; and the spiritual man, regenerated in spirit, sees all *in its essence*, of which the natural man has only the forms void of thought, mere empty sounds, symbols and letters, which are all dead images without interior spirit. The lofty aim of religion is the intimate union of man with God; and this union is possible in this world; but it only can be by the opening of our inner sensorium, which enables our hearts to become receptive to God.

Therein are mysteries that our philosophy does not dream of, the key to which is not to be found in scholastic science.

Meanwhile, a more advanced school has always existed to whom this deposition of all science has been confided, and this school was the community illuminated interiorly by the Savior, the society of the Elect, which has continued from the first day of creation to the present time; its members, it is true, are scattered all over the world, but they have always been united in the spirit and in one truth; they have had but one intelligence and one source of truth, but one doctor and one master; but in whom resides substantially the whole plenitude of God, and who alone initiates them into the high mysteries of Nature and the Spiritual World.

This community of light has been called from all time the invisible celestial Church, or the most ancient of all communities, of which we will speak more fully in our next letter.

Letter II

It is necessary, my dear brothers in the Lord, to give you a clear idea of the interior Church; of that illuminated Community of God which is scattered throughout the world, but which is governed by one truth and united in one spirit.

This enlightened community has existed since the first day of the world's creation, and its duration will be to the last day of time.

This community possesses a School, in which all who thirst for knowledge are instructed by the Spirit of Wisdom itself; and all the mysteries of God and of nature are preserved in this School for the children of light. . . . Perfect knowledge of God, of nature, and of humanity are the objects of instruction in this school. It is from her that all truths penetrate into the world, she is the School of the Prophets, and of all who search for wisdom, and it is in this community alone that truth and the explanation of all mystery is to be found. It is the most hidden of communities yet possesses members from many circles; of such is this School. From all time there has been an exterior school based on the interior one, of which it is but the outer expression. From all time, therefore, there has been a hidden assembly, a society of the Elect, of those who sought for and had capacity for light, and this interior society was called the interior Sanctuary or Church. All that the external Church possesses in symbol ceremony or rite is the letter expressive outwardly of the spirit of truth residing in the interior Sanctuary.

Hence this Sanctuary composed of scattered members, but tied by the bonds of perfect unity and love, has been occupied from the earliest ages in building the grand Temple through the regeneration of humanity, by which the reign of God will be manifest. This society is in the communion of those who have most capacity for light, *i.e.*, the Elect. The Elect are united in truth, and their Chief is the Light of the World himself, Jesus Christ, the One Anointed in light, the single mediator for the human race, the Way, the Truth, and the Life—Primitive light, wisdom, and the only *medium* by which man can return to God.

The interior Church was formed immediately after the fall of man, and received from God at first-hand the revelation of the means by which fallen humanity could be again raised to its rights and delivered from its misery. It received the primitive charge of all revelation and mystery; it received the key of true science, both divine and natural.

But when men multiplied, the frailty of man and his weakness necessitated an exterior society which veiled the interior one, and concealed the spirit and the truth in the letter. Because many people were not capable of comprehending great interior truth, and the danger would have been too great in confiding the most Holy to incapable people. Therefore, interior truths were wrapped in external and perceptible ceremonies, so that men, by the perception of the outer, which is the symbol of the interior, might by degrees be enabled safely to approach the interior spiritual truths.

But the inner truth has always been confided to him who in his day had the most capacity for illumination, and he became the sole guardian of the original Trust, as High Priest of the Sanctuary.

When it became necessary that interior truths should be enfolded in exterior ceremony and symbol, on account of the real weakness of men who were not capable of bearing the

Light of Light, then exterior worship began. It was, however, always the type and symbol of the interior, that is to say, the symbol of the true homage offered to God *in spirit* and *in truth*.

The difference between spiritual and animal man, and between rational and sensual man, made the exterior and interior imperative. Interior truth passed into the external wrapped in symbol and ceremony, so that sensuous man could observe, and be gradually thereby led to interior truth. Hence external worship was symbolically typical of interior truths, and of the true relationship between man and God before and after the Fall, and of his most perfect reconciliation. All the symbols of external worship are based upon the three fundamental relations—the Fall, the Reconciliation, and the Complete Atonement.

The care of the external service was the occupation of priests, and every father of a family was in the ancient times charged with this duty. First fruits and the first born among animals were offered to God, symbolizing that all that preserves and nourishes us comes from Him; also that animal man must be killed to make room for rational and spiritual man.

The external worship of God would never have been separated from interior service but for the weakness of man which tends too easily to forget the spirit in the letter, but the spirit of God is vigilant to note in every nation those who are able to receive light, and they are employed as agents to spread the light according to man's capacity, and to revivify the dead letter.

Through these divine instruments the interior truths of the Sanctuary were taken into every nation, and modified symbolically according to their customs, capacity for instruction, climate, and receptiveness. So that the external types of every religion, worship, ceremonies and Sacred Books in general have more or less clearly, as their object of instruction, the interior truths of the Sanctuary, by which man, but only in the latter days, will be conducted to the universal knowledge of the one Absolute Truth.

The more the external worship of a people has remained united with the spirit of esoteric truth, the purer its religion; but the wider the difference between the symbolic letter and the invisible truth, the more imperfect has become the religion; even so far among some nations as to degenerate into polytheism. Then the external form entirely parted from its inner truth, when ceremonial observances without soul or life remained alone.

When the *germs* of the most important truths had been carried everywhere by God's agents, He chose a certain people to raise up *a vital symbol* destined by Him to manifest forth the means by which He intended to govern the human race in its present condition, and by which it would be raised into complete purification and perfection.

God Himself communicated to this people its exterior religious legislation, He gave all the symbols and enacted all the ceremonies, and they contained the impress, as it were, of the great esoteric truth of the Sanctuary.

God consecrated this external Church in Abraham, gave commandments through Moses, and it received its highest perfection in the double message of Jesus Christ, existing personally in poverty and

46

suffering, and by the communication of His Spirit in the glory of the Resurrection.

Now, as God Himself laid the foundation of the external Church, the whole of the symbols of external worship formed the science of the Temple and of the Priests in those days, because the mysteries of the most sacred truths became external through revelation alone. The scientific acquaintance of this holy symbolism was the science to unite fallen man once more with God, hence religion received its name from being the science of rebinding man with God, to bring man back to his origin.

One sees plainly by this pure idea of religion in general that unity in religion is within the inner Sanctuary, and that the multiplicity of external religions can never alter the true unity which is at the base of every exterior.

The wisdom of the ancient temple alliance was preserved by priests and by prophets.

To the priests was confided the external,—the letter of the symbol, hieroglyphics. The prophets had the charge of the inner truth, and their occupation was to continually recall the priest to the spirit in the letter, when inclined to lose it. The science of the priests was that of the knowledge of exterior symbol.

That of the prophets was experimental possession of the truth of the symbols. In the interior the spirit lived. There was, therefore, in the ancient alliance a school of prophets and of priests, the one occupying itself with the spirit in the emblem, the other with the emblem itself. The priests had the external possession of the Ark, of the shewbread, of the candlesticks, of the manna, of Aaron's rod, and the prophets were in interior possession of the inner spiritual truth which was represented exteriorly by the symbols just mentioned.

The external Church of the ancient alliance was visible, the interior Church was always invisible, must be invisible, and yet must govern all, because force and power are alone confided to her.

When the divine external worship abandoned the interior worship, it fell, and God proved by a remarkable chain of circumstances that the letter could not exist without the spirit, that it is only there to lead to the spirit, and it is useless and even rejected by God if it fails in its object.

As the spirit of nature extends to the most sterile depths to vivify and preserve and cause growth in everything susceptible to its influence, likewise the spirit of light spreads itself interiorly among nations to animate everywhere the dead letter by the living spirit.

This is why we find a Job among idolaters, a Melchizedek among strange nations, a Joseph with the Egyptian priests, a Moses in the country of Midian, as living proofs the interior community of those who are capable of receiving light was united by one spirit and one truth in all times and in all nations.

To these agents of light from the one inner community was united the Chief of all agents, Jesus Christ Himself, in the midst of time as *royal priest* after the order of Melchizedek.

The divine agents of the ancient alliance hitherto represented only specialized perfections of God; therefore a powerful movement was required which should show all at once—*all in one*. A universal type appeared, which gave the real touch of perfect unity to the picture, which opened a fresh door, and destroyed the number of the slavery of humanity.

The law of love began when the image emanating from wisdom itself showed to man all the greatness of his being, vivified him anew, assured him of his immortality, and raised his intellectual status to that of being the true temple for the spirit.

This Chief Agent of all, this Savior of the World and universal Regenerator, claimed man's whole attention to the primitive truth, whereby he can preserve his existence and recover his former dignity. Through the conditions of His own abasement He laid the base of the redemption of man, and He promised to accomplish it completely one day through His Spirit. He showed also truly in part among His apostles all that should come to pass in the future to all the Elect.

He linked the chain of the community of light among the Elect, to whom He sent the spirit of truth, and confided to them the true primitive instruction in all divine and natural things, as a sign that He would never forsake His community.

When the letter and symbolic worship of the external Church of the ancient alliance had been realized by the Incarnation of the Savior, and verified in His person, new symbols became requisite Tor external use, which showed us through the letter the future accomplishment of universal redemption.

The rites and symbols of the external Christian Church were formed after the pattern of these unchangeable and fundamental truths, announcing things of a strength and of an importance impossible to describe, and revealed only to those who knew the innermost Sanctuary.

This Sanctuary remains changeless, though external religion receives in the course of time and circumstances varied modification, entailing separation from the interior spirit which can alone preserve the letter. The profane idea of wishing to "secularize" all that is Christian, and to Christianize all that is political, changed the exterior edifice, and covered with the shadow of death all that was interior light and life. Hence divisions and heresies, and the spirit of Sophistry ready to expound the letter when it had already lost the essence of truth.

Current incredulity increased corruption to its utmost point, attacking the edifice of Christianity in its fundamental parts, and the sacred interior was mingled with the exterior, already enfeebled by the ignorance of weak man.

Then was born Deism; this brought forth materialism, which looked on the union of man with superior forces as imaginary; then finally came forth, partly from the head and partly from the heart, the last degree of man's degradation— Atheism.

In the midst of all this, truth reposes inviolable in the inner Sanctuary.

Faithful to the spirit of truth, which promised never to abandon its community, the members of the interior Church lived in silence, but in real activity, and united the science of the temple of the ancient alliance with the spirit of the great savior of man—the spirit of the interior alliance, waiting humbly the great moment when the Lord will call them, and will assemble his community in order to give every dead letter external force and life.

This interior community of light is the reunion of all those capable of receiving light as Elect, and it is known as the *Communion of Saints*. The primitive receptacle for all strength and truth, confided to it from all time—it alone, says St Paul, is in the possession of the science of the Saints.

By it the agents of God were formed in every age, passing from the interior to the exterior, and communicating spirit and life to the dead letter as already said.

This illuminated community has been through time the true school of God's spirit, and considered as school, it has its Chair, its Doctor, it possesses a rule for students, it has forms and objects for study, and, in short, a method by which they study.

It has, also, its degrees for successive development to higher altitudes.

The first and lowest degree consists in the moral good, by which the single will, subordinated to God, is led to God by the pure motive of willing with and to Jesus Christ, which it does through faith. The means by which the spirit of this school acts are called inspirations.

The second degree consists in the rational intellectuality, by which the understanding of the man of virtue, who is united to God, is crowned with wisdom and the light of knowledge, and the means which the spirit uses to produce this is called interior illumination.

The third and highest degree is the entire opening of our inner sensorium, by which the inner man perceives objectively and really, metaphysical verities. This is the highest degree when faith passes into open vision, and the means the spirit uses for this are real visions.

These are the three degrees of the school for true interior wisdom—that of the illuminated Society. The same spirit which ripens men for this community also distributes its degrees by the co-action of the ripened subject.

This school of wisdom has been forever most secretly hidden from the world, because it is invisible and submissive solely to divine government.

It has never been exposed to the accidents of time and to the weakness of man. Because only the most capable were chosen for it, and the spirits who selected made no error.

Through this school were developed the germs of all the sublime sciences, which were first received by external schools, then clothed in other forms, and hence degenerating.

This society of sages communicated, according to time and circumstances, unto the exterior societies their symbolic hieroglyphs, in order to attract man to the great truths of their interior.

But all exterior societies subsist through this interior one giving them its spirit. As soon as external societies wish to be independent of the interior one, and to transform a temple of wisdom into a political edifice, the interior society retires and leaves only the letter without the spirit. It is thus that secret external societies of wisdom were nothing but hieroglyphic screens, the truth remaining inviolable in the sanctuary so that she might never be profaned.

In this interior society man finds wisdom and with her—All—not the wisdom of this world which is but scientific knowledge, which revolves round the outside but never touches the center (in which is contained all strength), but true wisdom and men obeying her.

All disputes, all controversies, all the things belonging to the false cares of this world, fruitless discussions, useless germs of opinions which spread the seeds of disunion, all error, schisms, and systems are banished. Neither calumny nor scandal are known. Every man is honored. Satire, that spirit which loves to make its neighbor smart, is unknown. Love alone reigns.

Want and feebleness are protected, and rejoicings are made at the elevation and greatness which man acquires.

We must not, however, imagine this society resembles any secret society, meeting at certain times, choosing its leaders and members, united by special objects. All societies, be what they may, can but come after this interior illuminated circle. This society knows none of the formalities which belong to the outer rings, the work of man. In this kingdom of power all outward forms cease.

God himself is the Power always present. The best man of his times, the chief himself, does not always know all the members, but the moment when it is the Will of God that he should accomplish any object, he finds them in the world with certainty to work for that purpose.

This community has no outside barriers. He who may be chosen by God is as the first, he presents himself among the others without presumption, and he is received by the others without jealousy.

If it be necessary that real members should meet together, they find and recognize each other with perfect certainty.

No disguise can be used, neither hypocrisy nor dissimulation could hide the characteristic qualities of this society, they are too genuine. All illusion is gone, and things appear in their true form.

No one member can choose another, unanimous choice is required. All men are called, the called may be chosen, if they become ripe for entrance.

Anyone can look for the entrance, and any man who is within can teach another to seek for it; but only he who is fit can arrive inside.

Unprepared men occasion disorder in a community, and disorder is not compatible with the Sanctuary. This thrusts out all who are not homogeneous.

Worldly intelligence seeks this Sanctuary in vain, fruitless also will be the efforts of malice to penetrate these great mysteries; all is undecipherable to him who is not ripe, he can see nothing, read nothing in the interior.

He who is ripe is joined to the chain, perhaps often where he thought least likely, and at a point of which he knew nothing himself.

Seeking to become ripe, should be effort of him who sees wisdom.

But there are methods by which ripeness is attained, for in this holy communion is the primitive storehouse of the most ancient and original science of the human race, with the primitive mysteries also of all science. It is the unique and really illuminated community which is absolutely in possession of the key to all mystery, which knows the center and source of all nature and creation. It is a society which unites superior strength to its own, and counts its members from more than one world. It is the society whose members form a theocratic republic, which one day will be the Regent Mother of the whole World.

Letter III

The absolute truth lying in the center of Mystery is like the sun, it blinds ordinary sight and man sees only the shadow. The eagle alone can gaze at the dazzling light, likewise only the prepared soul can bear its luster. Nevertheless the great *Something* which is the inmost of the Holy Mysteries has never been hidden from the piercing gaze of him who can bear the light.

God and nature have no mysteries for their children. They are caused by the weakness of our nature, unable to support light, because it is not yet organized to bear the chaste light of unveiled truth.

This weakness is the Cloud that covers the Sanctuary; this is the curtain which veils the Holy of Holies.

But in order that man may recover the veiled light, strength and dignity, Divinity bends to the weakness of its creatures, and writes the truth that is interior and eternal mystery on the *outside of things*, so that man can transport himself through this to their spirit.

These letters are the ceremonies or the rituals of religion, which lead man to the interior life of union with God.

Mystic hieroglyphs are these letters also; they are sketches and designs holding interior and holy truth.

Religion and the Mysteries go hand in hand to lead our brethren to truth, both have for object the reversing and renewing of our natures, both have for the end the rebuilding of a temple inhabited by Wisdom and Love, or God with man.

But religion and the Mysteries would be useless phenomena if Divinity had not also accorded means to attain these great ends.

But these means are only in the innermost of the sanctuary. The Mysteries are required to build a temple to Religion, and religion is required to unite Man with God.

Such is the greatness of religion, and such the exalted dignity of the Mysteries from all time.

It would be unjust to you, beloved brothers, that we should think that you have *never* regarded the Holy Mysteries in this *real* aspect, the one which shows them as the only means able to preserve in purity and integrity the doctrine of the important truths concerning God, nature, and man. This doctrine was couched in holy symbolic language, and the truths which it contained having been gradually translated among the outer circle into the ordinary languages of man, became in consequence more obscure and unintelligible.

The Mysteries, as you know, beloved brothers, promise things which are and which will remain always the heritage of but a small number of men; these are the mysteries which can neither be bought nor sold publicly, and can only be acquired by a heart which has attained to wisdom and love.

He in whom this holy flame has been awakened lives in true happiness, content with everything and in everything free. He sees the cause of human corruption and knows that it is inevitable. He hates no criminal, he pities him, and seeks to raise him who has fallen, and to restore the wanderer, because he feels notwithstanding all the corruption, in the *whole* there is no taint.

He sees with a clear eye the underlying truth in the foundation of all religion, he knows the sources of superstition and of incredulity, as being caused by *modifications* of truth which have not attained perfect equilibrium.

We are assured, my esteemed brothers, that you consider the true Mystic from this aspect, and that you will not attribute to *his royal art*, that which the misdirected energy of some isolated individuals have made of this art.

It is, therefore, with these views, which accord exactly with ours, that you will compare religion, and the mysteries of the holy schools of Wisdom, to loving sisters who have watched over the good of mankind since the necessity of their birth.

Religion divides itself into exterior and interior religion, exterior signifying ceremony; and interior, worship in spirit and in truth; the outer

54

schools possessing the letter and the symbol, the inner ones, the spirit and meaning—but the outer schools were united to the inner ones by ceremonies, as also the outer schools of the mysteries were linked with the inner one by means of symbol.

Thus religion can never be *merely* ceremony, but hidden and holy mysteries penetrate through symbol into the outer worship to prepare men properly for the worship of God in spirit and in truth.

Very soon the night of symbol will disappear, the light will bring forth the day and the mysteries no longer veiled will show themselves in the splendor of full truth.

The vestibule of nature, the temple of reason and the sanctuary of Revelation, will form but one Temple. Thus the great edifice will be completed, the edifice which consists in the re-union of man, nature, and God.

A perfect knowledge of man, of nature, and of God will be the lights which will enable the leaders of humanity to bring back from every side their wandering brothers, those who are led by the prejudices of reason, by the turbulence of passions, to the ways of peace and knowledge.

We are approaching the period of light, and the reign of wisdom and love, that of God who is the source of light; Brothers of light, there is but one religion whose simple truth spreads in all religions like branches, returning through multiplicity into the unity of the tree.

Sons of truth, there is but one order, but one Brotherhood, but one association of men thinking alike in the one object of acquiring the light. From this center misunderstanding has caused innumerable Orders, but all will return from the multiplicity of opinions, to the only truth and to the true Order, the association of those who are able to receive the light, the *Community of the Elect*.

With this measure all religions and all orders of man must be measured. Multiplicity is in the ceremony of the exterior; truth only in the interior. The trend of these brotherhoods is in the variety of explanation of the symbols caused by the lapse of time, needs of the day, and other circumstances. The true Community of Light can be only one.

The exterior symbol is only the sheath which holds the inner; it may change and multiply, but it can never weaken the truth of the interior; moreover, it was necessary; we ought to seek it and try to decipher it to discover the meaning of the spiritual interior.

All errors, divisions, all misunderstandings in Religion and in secret societies only concern the letter. What rests behind it remains always pure and holy.

Soon the time for those who seek the light will be accomplished, for the day comes when the old will be united to the new, the outer to the inner, the high with the low, the heart with the brain, man with God, and this epoch is destined for the present age. Do not ask, beloved brothers, . . . why the present age? . . .

Everything has its time for beings subject to time and space. It is in such wise according to the unvarying law of the Wisdom of God, who has coordinated all in harmony and perfection.

The elect should first labor to acquire both wisdom and love, in order to earn the gift of power, which unchangeable Divinity gives only to those who *know* and those who *love*.

Morning follows night, and the sun rises, and all moves on to full mid-day, where all shadows disappear in his vertical splendor. Thus, the letter of truth must exist; then comes the practical explanation, then the truth itself; *only truth can comprehend truth;* then alone can the spirit of truth appear which sets the seals closing the light. He who now can receive the truth will understand. It is to you, much loved brothers, you who labor to reach truth, you who have so faithfully preserved the glyph of the holy mysteries in your temple, it is to you that the first ray of truth will be directed; this ray will pierce through the cloud of mystery, and will announce the full day and the treasure which it brings.

Do not ask *who* those are who write to you; look at the spirit not the letter, the thing, not at persons.

Neither pride, nor self seeking, neither does any unworthy motive, exist in our retreats; we know the object and the destination of man, and the light which lights us works in all our actions.

We are especially called to write to you, dear brothers of light; and that which gives power to our commission is the truth which we possess, and which we pass on to you on the least sign, and according to the measure of the capacity of each.

Light is apt for communication, where there is reception and capacity, but it constrains no one, and waits its reception tranquilly.

Our desire, our aim, our office is to revivify the dead letter, and to spiritualize the symbols, turn the passive into the active, death into life; but this we cannot do *by ourselves*, but through the spirit of light of Him who is Wisdom and the Light of the world.

Until the present time the Inner Sanctuary has been separated from the Temple, and the Temple beset with those who belong only to the precincts; but the time is coming when the Innermost will be re-united with the Temple, in order that those who are in the Temple can influence those who are in the outer courts, so that the outer pass in.

In our sanctuary all the hidden mysteries are preserved intact, they have never been profaned.

This sanctuary is invisible, as is a force which is only known through its action.

By this short description, my dear brothers, you can tell who we are, and it will be superfluous to assure you that we do not belong to those restless natures who seek to build in this common life an ideal after their own fantastic imaginations. Neither do we belong to those who wish to play a great part in the world, and who promise miracles that they themselves do not understand. We do not represent either that class of minds, who, resenting the condition of certain things, have no object but the desire of dominating others, and who love adventure and exaggeration.

We can also assure you that we belong to no other sect or association than the one true and great one of those who are able to receive the light. We are not also of those who think it their right to mold all after their own model, the arrogance to seek to re-model all other societies; we assure you faithfully that we know *exactly* the innermost of religion and of the Holy Mysteries; and that we possess with absolute certainty, all that has been surmised to be in the Adytum, and that this said possession gives us the strength to justify our commission, and to impart to the dead letter and hieroglyphic everywhere both spirit and life. The treasures in our sanctuary are many; we understand the spirit and meaning of all symbols and all ceremony which have existed since the day of Creation to the present time, as well as the most interior truths of all the Holy Books, with the laws and customs of primitive people.

We possess a light by which we are anointed, and by means of which we read the hidden and secret things of nature.

We possess a fire which feeds us, and which gives us the strength to act upon everything in nature. We possess *a key to open* the gate of mystery, and a *key to shut* nature's laboratory. We know of the existence of a bond which will unite us to the Upper Worlds, and reveal to us their sights and their sounds. All the marvels of nature arc subordinate to our will by *its* being united with Divinity.

We have mastered the science which draws directly from nature, whence there is no error, but truth and light only.

In our School we are instructed in all things because our Master is the Light itself and its essence. The plenitude of our scholarship is the knowledge of this tie between the divine and spiritual worlds and of the spiritual world with the elementary, and of the elementary world with the material world.

By these knowledges we are in condition to coordinate the spirits of nature and the heart of man.

Our science is the inheritance promised to the Elect; otherwise, those who are duly prepared for receiving the light, and the practice of our science is in the completion of the Divine union with the child of man.

We could often tell you, beloved brothers, of marvels relating to the hidden things in the treasury of the Sanctuary, which would amaze and astonish you; we could speak to you about ideas concerning which the profoundest philosophy is as removed as the earth from the sun, but to which we arc near being one with the light of the innermost.

But our object is not to excite your curiosity, but to raise your desires to seek the light at its source, where your search for wisdom will be rewarded and your longing for love satisfied, for wisdom and love dwell in our retreats. The stimulus of their reality and of their truth is our magical power.

We assure you that our treasures, though of infinite value, are concealed in so simple a manner that they entirely baffle the researches of opinionated science, and also though these treasures would bring to carnal minds both madness and sorrow, nevertheless, they are, and they ever remain to us the treasures of the highest wisdom.

My best blessing upon you, O my brothers, if you understand these great truths. The recovery of *the triple word* and of its power will be your reward.

Your happiness will be in having the strength to help to re-unite man with man, and with nature and with God, which is the real work of every workman who has not *rejected the Corner Stone.*

Now we have fulfilled our trust and we have announced the approach of full day, and the joining of the inner Sanctuary with the Temple; we leave the rest to your own free will.

We know well, to our bitter grief, that even as the Savior was not understood in his personality, but was ridiculed and condemned in his humility, likewise also His spirit which will appear in glory will also be rejected and despised by many. Nevertheless the coming of His Spirit should be announced in the Temples in order that these words should be fulfilled.

"I have knocked at your doors and you have not opened them to me; I have called and you have not listened to my voice; I have invited you to the wedding, but you were busy with other things."

May Peace and the light of the Spirit be with you!

Letter IV

As infinity in numbers loses itself in the unit, and as the innumerable rays of a circle are united in one single center only, it is likewise with the Mysteries; their hieroglyphics and infinite number of emblems have the object of exemplifying but one single truth. He who knows this has found the key to understand everything all at once.

There is but one God, but one truth, and one way which leads to this grand Truth. There is but one means of finding it.

He who has found this way possesses everything in its possession: all wisdom in one book alone, all strength in one force, every beauty in one single object, all riches in one treasure only, every happiness in one perfect felicity. And the sum of all these perfections is Jesus Christ, who was crucified and who lived again. Now, this great truth, expressed thus, is, it is true, only an object of faith, but it can become also one of *experimental knowledge*, as soon as we are instructed *how* Jesus Christ can be or become all this.

This great mystery was always an object of instruction *in the Secret School of the invisible and interior Church;* this great knowledge was understood in the earliest days of Christianity under the name of *Disciplina Arcana.* From this secret school are derived all the rites and ceremonies extant in the Outer Church. But the spirit of these grand and simple verities was withdrawn into the Interior, and in our day it is entirely lost as to the exterior.

It has been prophesied long ago, dear brothers, that all which is hidden shall be revealed in these latter days; but it has also been predicted that many false prophets will arise, and the faithful are warned not to believe every spirit, but to prove them if they really come from God, i John iv. 5. The apostle himself explains how this truth is ascertained. He says, "Hereby know ye the Spirit of God, every spirit which confesseth that Jesus Christ is come in the flesh is of God, and every spirit which confesseth not is not of God." That is to say, the spirit who separates in Him the Divine and human *is not from God.*

We confess that Jesus Christ is come in the flesh, and hence the spirit of truth speaks by us. But the mystery that Jesus Christ is come *in the flesh* is of wide extent and great depth, and in it is contained the knowledge of the divine- human, and it is this knowledge that we are choosing today as object for our instruction.

As we are not speaking to neophytes in matters of faith, it will be much easier for you, dear brothers, to receive the sublime truths which we will present to you, as without doubt you have already chosen as object for your holy meditation various preparatory subjects.

Religion considered scientifically is the doctrine of the re-union of man separated from God to man re- united to God. Hence its sole object is to unite every human being to God, through which union alone can humanity attain its highest felicity both temporally and spiritually.

This doctrine, therefore, of *re-union* is of the most sublime importance, and being a doctrine it necessarily must have a method by which it leads and teaches us. The first is the knowledge of the correct means of re-union, and secondly the teaching, after the knowledge of the correct means, how these means should be suitably coordinated to the end.

This grand concept of re-union, on which all religious doctrine is concentrated, could never have been known to man *without* revelation. It has always been altogether outside the sphere of scientific knowledge, but this very ignorance of man has made revelation absolutely necessary to us, otherwise we could, unassisted, never have found the means of rising out of this state of ignorance.

Revelation entails the necessity of faith in revelation, because he who has no experience or knowledge whatsoever of a thing must necessarily believe that he wishes to know and have experience. If faith fails, there is no desire for revelation, and the mind of man closes by itself, its own door and road for discovering the methods revealed by Revelation only. As action and re-action follow each other in nature, so also inevitably revelation and faith act and re-act. One cannot exist without the other, and the more faith a man has the more will revelation be made to him of matters which lie in obscurity. It is true, and very true, that all the veiled truths of religions, even those heavily veiled ones, the most difficult ones to us, will one day be revealed and justified before a tribunal of the most rigid Justice; but the weakness of men, the lack of penetration in perceiving the relation and correspondence between physical and spiritual nature, requires that the highest truths should only be imparted gradually. The holy obscurity of the mysteries is thus on account of *our* weakness, because our eyes are enabled only gradually to bear their full and dazzling light. In every grade at which the believer in Revelation arrives, he obtains clearer light, and this progressive illumination continues the more convincing, because every truth of faith so acquired becomes more and more vitalized, passing finally into conviction.

Hence faith is founded on our weakness, and also on the full light of revelation which will, in its communication with us, direct us according to our capabilities to the gradual understanding of things, so that in due order the cognizance of the most elevated truths will be ours.

Those objects which are quite unknown to human sense are necessarily belonging to the domain of faith.

Man can only adore and be silent, but if he wishes to demonstrate matters which cannot be manifested objectively, he necessarily falls into error.

Man should adore and be silent, therefore, until such time arrives when these objects in the domain of faith become clearer, and, therefore, more easily recognized. Everything proves itself by itself as soon as we have acquired the interior *experience* of the truths revealed through faith, so soon as we are led by faith to vision, that is to say, to full cognizance.

In all time have there been men illuminated of God who had this interior knowledge of the things of faith demonstrated objectively either in full or partly, according as the truths of faith passed into their understanding or their hearts. The first kind of vision was called *divine illumination*. The second was entitled *divine inspiration*.

The inner sensorium was opened in many to divine and transcendental vision, called ecstasy because this inner sensorium was so enlarged that it entirely dominated the outer physical senses.

But this kind of man is always inexplicable, and he must remain such always to the man of mere sense who has no organs receptive to the transcendental and supernatural, "the natural man receiveth not the things of the Spirit of God, for they are foolishness unto him and he cannot know them, because they are spiritually judged," 1 Cor. xi. 14, *i.e.*, because his spiritual senses are not open to the transcendental world, so that he can have no more objective cognizance of such world than a blind man has of color; thus the natural man has lost these interior senses, or rather, the capacity for their development is neglected almost to atrophy.

Thus mere physical man is, in general, spiritually blind, one of the further consequences of the Fall. Man then is doubly miserable; he not only has his eyes blindfolded to the sight of high truths, but his heart also languishes a prisoner in the bonds of flesh and blood, which confine him to animal and sensuous pleasures to the hurt of more elevated and genuine ones. Therefore, are we slaves to concupiscence, to the domination of tyrannical passions, and, therefore, do we drag ourselves as paralyzed sufferers supported on crutches; the one crutch being the weak one of mere human reason, and the other, sentiment—the one daily giving us appearance instead of reality, the other making us constantly choose evil, imagining it to be good. This is, therefore, our unhappy condition.

Men can only be happy when the bandage which intercepts the true light falls from their eyes, and when the fetters of slavery are loosened from their hearts. The blind must see, the lame must walk, before happiness can be understood. But the great and all-powerful law to which the felicity or happiness of man is indissolubly attached is the one following— "Man, let reason rule over your passions!"

For ages has man striven to teach and to preach, with, however, the result, after so many centuries, of but the blind always leading the blind; for in all the foolishness of misery into which we have fallen, we do not yet see that man wants more than man to raise us from this condition.

Prejudices and errors, crimes and vices, only change from century to century; they are never extirpated from humanity; reason without illumination flickers faintly in every age, in the heavy air of spiritual darkness; the heart, exhausted with passions, is also the same century after century.

There is but One who can heal these evils, but One who is able to open our inner eyes, but One who can free us from the bonds of sensuality.

This One is Jesus Christ, the *Savior of Man*, the *Savior* because He wishes to obliterate from us all the consequences which follow as result from the blindness of our natural reason, or the errors arising from the passions of ungoverned hearts.

Very few men, beloved brothers, have a true and exact conception of the *greatness* of the idea meant by the Redemption of Man; many suppose that Jesus Christ the Lord has only redeemed or rebought us by His Blood from *damnation, otherwise the eternal separation* of man from God; but they do not believe that He could also deliver all those who are bound in Him and confide in Him, from all the miseries of this earth plane!

Jesus Christ is the Savior of the World; He is the deliverer from all human wretchedness, and He has redeemed us from death and sin; how could He be all that, if the world must languish perpetually in the shades of ignorance and in the bonds of passions? It has been already very clearly predicted in the Prophets that the time of the Redemption of His people, the first Sabbath of time, *will come*. Long ago ought we to have acknowledged this most consolatory promise; but the *want* of the true knowledge of God, of man, and of nature has been the real hindrance which has always obstructed our sight of the great Mysteries of the faith.

You must know, my brothers, that there is a dual nature, one pure, spiritual, immortal, and indestructible, the other impure, material, mortal, and destructible. The pure nature was before the impure. This latter originated solely through the disharmony and disproportion of substances which form destructible nature. Hence nothing is permanent until all disproportions and dissonances are eradicated, so that all remains in harmony.

The incorrect conception regarding spirit and matter is one of the principal causes which prevent many verities of faith from shining in their true luster.

Spirit is a substance, an essence, an absolute reality. Hence its properties are indestructibility, uniformity, penetration, indivisibility, and continuity. Matter is not a substance, it is *an aggregate*. Hence it is destructible, divisible, and subject to change.

The metaphysical world is one *really existing* perfectly pure and indestructible, whose Centre we call Jesus Christ, and whose inhabitants are known by the names of Angels and Spirits.

The physical world is that of phenomena, and it possesses no absolute truth, all that we call truth here is but relative, the shadow and phenomena only of truth.

Our reason here borrows all its ideas from the senses, hence they are lifeless and dead. We draw everything from external objectivity, and our reason is like an ape who imitates what nature shows him outwardly. Thus the light of the senses is the principle of our earthly reason, sensuality the motive for our will, tending therefore to animal wants and their satisfaction. It is true, however, that we feel higher motives imperative, but up to the present we do not know either where to seek or where to find.

In this world everything is corruptible; it is useless to seek here for a pure *principle* of reason and morality or motive for the Will. This must be sought for in a more exalted world—there, where all is pure and indestructible, where there reigns a Being all wisdom and all love. Thus the world neither can nor will become happy until this Real Being can be received by humanity in full and become its All in All.

Man, dear brothers, is composed of indestructible and metaphysical substance, as well as of material and destructible substance, but in such a manner that the indestructible and eternal is, as it were, *imprisoned* in the destructible matter.

Thus two contradictory natures are comprehended in the same man. The destructible substance enchains us to the sensible, the other seeks to deliver us from these chains, and to raise us to the spiritual. Hence the incessant combat between good and evil.

The fundamental cause of human corruption is to be found in the corruptible matter from which man is formed. For this gross matter oppresses the action of the transcendental and spiritual principle, and is the true cause, hence, of the blindness of our understanding, and the errors of our inclinations.

The fragility of a china vessel depends upon the clay from which it is formed. The most beautiful form that clay of any sort is able to receive must always remain fragile because the matter of which it is formed is also fragile. Thus do men remain likewise frail notwithstanding all our external culture.

When we examine the causes of the obstacles keeping the natural man in such deep abasement, they are found in the grossness of the matter in which the spiritual part is, as it were, buried and bound.

The inflexibility of fibers, the immovability of temperaments, that would wish to obey the refined stimulation of the spirit, are, as it were, the material chains which bind them, preventing in us the action of the sublime functions of which the spirit is capable.

The nerves and fluidity of the brain can only yield us rough and obscure notions derived from phenomena, and not from truth and the things themselves; and as we cannot, by the strength of our thinking powers alone, have sufficient balance to oppose representations strong enough to counteract the violence of external sensation, the result is that we are governed by our sensations, and the voice of reason which speaks softly internally is deafened by the tumultuous noise of the elements which keep our mechanism going.

It is true that reason strains to raise itself above this uproar, and wishes to decide the combat, seeking to restore order by the light and force of its judgment. But its action is only like the rays of the sun constantly hidden by clouds.

The grossness of all the matter in which material man consists, and the tissue of the whole edifice of his nature, is the cause of that disinclination which holds the soul in continual imperfection.

The heaviness of our thinking power in general is consequent upon dependence upon gross and unyielding matter, this same matter forming the true bonds of the flesh, and is the true source of all error and vice. Reason, which should be an absolute legislator, is continually slave to sensuality, which raises itself as regent and, governing the reason that is drooping in chains, follows its own desires.

This truth has been felt for long, and it has always been taught that reason should be sole legislator. It should govern the will and never be governed itself.

Great and small feel this truth; but no sooner is it desired to put it in execution than the animal will vanquishes reason, and then the reason subjugates the animal will; thus in every man the victory and defeat are alternate, hence this power and counter- power are the cause of this perpetual oscillation between good and evil, or the true and the false.

If man wishes to be led to the true in such manner that we can only act after the laws of reason, and from the purified will, it is absolutely necessary to constitute the pure reason sovereign in man. But how can this be done when the matter out of which many men is formed is more or less brutal, divisible and corruptible, hence misery, illness, poverty, death, want, prejudices, errors, and vices, the necessary consequence of the limitation of the immortal spirit in the bonds of brute and corruptible matter. Sensuality is bound to rule if reason be fettered.

Yes, friends and brothers, such is the general fate of man, and as this state of things is propagated from man to man, it may in all justice be called the hereditary corruption of man.

We observe, in general, that the powers of reason act upon the heart, but in relation only to the specific constitution of the matter of which man is made. Thus it is extremely remarkable when we think that the sun vivifies this animal matter according to the measure of the distance from this terrestrial body, that it makes it suitable to the functions of animal economy, but at one degree more or less raised from spiritual influence. Diversity of nations, their properties with regard to climate, the variety of character, passions, manners, prejudices and customs, even their virtues and their vices, depend entirely upon the specific constitution of the matter from which they are formed, and in which the imprisoned spirit operates accordingly. Man's capacity for culture is modified to this constitution, likewise his science, which can only affect people as far as there is matter present, susceptible to such modification, and in this modification consists the capacity for culture suitable to such people, which suitability depends partly on climate, partly on descent.

Generally, we find in each zone man much the same everywhere, weak and sensual, wise just in so far as his physical matter allows reason to triumph over the sensuous, or foolish if the sensuous obtains mastery over the more or less fettered spirit. In this lies the evil and the good specially belonging to each nation, as well as to each isolated individual. We find in the world at large the same corruption inherent in the matter from which man is made, only under various forms and modifications.

From the lowest animal condition of savage nature man rises to the idea of the social state, primarily through his wants and desires, strength and cunning, qualities especially animal, inherently his as the animal develops thence gradually into other forms.

The modifications of these fundamental animal tendencies are endless; and the highest degree to which human culture as acquired by the world, has attained, up to the present has not carried things further than the putting of a finer polish on the substance of his animal instincts. This means to say we are raised from the rank of the brute to that of the refined animal.

But this period was necessary, because on its accomplishment begins a new era, when the animal instincts being fully developed, there commences the stage of evolution of the more elevated desires towards light and reason.

Jesus Christ has written in our hearts in exceedingly beautiful words this great truth, that man must seek in his common clay for the cause of all his sorrows. When He said, "The best man, he who strives the most to arrive at truth, sins seven times a day," He wished to say by this, in the man of the finest organization, the seven powers of the spirit are still closed, therefore the seven sensuous actions surmount them daily after their respective fashions.

Thus the best man is exposed to error and passions; the best man is weak and sinful; the best man is not a free man, and, therefore, exempt from pain and trouble; the best man is subject to sickness and death, and why? Because all these are the natural inevitable consequences incidental to the qualities of the corrupt matter of which he is formed.

Therefore, there could be no hope of higher happiness for humanity so long as this corruptible and material forms the principal substantial part of his being.

The impossibility of mankind to transport itself, of itself, to true perfection, is a despairing thought, but, at the same time, one full of consolation, because, in consequence of this radical impossibility, and because of it, a more exalted and perfect being than man permitted himself to be clothed in this mortal and destructible envelope *in order* to make the mortal immortal, and the destructible indestructible; and in this object is to be sought the true reason for the Incarnation of Jesus Christ.

Jesus Christ, the Son of God, the actual substantial Word by which all is made, and which existed from the beginning, Jesus Christ, the Wisdom of God working in everything, was as the center of Paradise of the world and of light. He was the only real organism by which alone Divine strength could be communicated, and this organism is of immortal and pure nature, that indestructible substance which gives new life and raises all things to happiness and perfection. This pure incorruptible substance is *the pure element* in which spiritual man lived.

From this perfect element, which God only can inhabit, and the substance out of which the first man was formed, from it was the first man separated by the Fall. By the partaking of the Tree of Good and Evil, of the mixture, the good and incorruptible principle with the bad and corruptible one, he was self-poisoned, so that his immortal essence retreated interiorly, and the mortal, pressing forward, clothed him externally. Thus, then, disappeared immortality, happiness, and life, and mortality and death were the results of this change.

Many men cannot understand the idea of the Tree of Good and Evil; this tree was, however, the product of moveable but central matter, but in which destructibility had somewhat the superiority over the indestructible. The premature use of this fruit was that which poisoned Adam, robbing him of his immortality and enveloping him in this material and mortal clay, and thenceforward he fell a prey to the Elements *which originally he governed*. This unhappy event was, however, the reason why Immortal Wisdom, the pure metaphysical element, clothed itself with a mortal body and voluntarily sacrificed himself, so that the Interior Powers could penetrate into the center of the destruction, and could then ferment gradually, changing the mortal to the immortal.

Thus, when it came about quite naturally that immortal man became subject to mortality through the enjoyment of mortal matter, it also happened quite naturally that mortal man could only recover his former dignity through the enjoyment of Immortal Matter.

All passes naturally and simply under God's Reign, but in order to understand this simplicity it is requisite to have pure ideas of God, of nature, and of man. And if the sublimest Truths of faith are still, for us, wrapped in impenetrable obscurity, the reason for this is because we have up to the present dissolved the connection between God, nature, and man.

Jesus Christ has spoken to His most intimate friends when He was still on this earth, of the grand mystery of Regeneration, but all that He said was obscure to them, they could not then receive it; thus the development of these great Truths was reserved for latter days, for it is the greatest and the last Mystery of Religion, in which all the others retreat as to a Unity.

Regeneration is no other than a dissolution of, and a release from this impure and corruptible matter, which enchains our immortal essence, plunging into deathly sleep its obstructed vital force. Therefore, there must necessarily be a real method to eradicate this poisonous ferment which breeds so much suffering for us, and thereby to liberate the obstructed vitality.

There is, however, no other means to find this excepting by religion, for religion looked at scientifically being the doctrine which proclaims the re-union with God, it must of necessity show us how to arrive at this re-union.

Is not Jesus the life giving intelligence? He gives us the principal object of the Bible and of all the desires, hopes, and efforts of the Christians. Have we not received from our Lord and Master while still He walked with His disciples, the profoundest solutions of the most hidden truths? Did not our Lord and Master when He was with them in His glorified Body after His resurrection give them the highest revelation with regard to His Person, and did He not lead them still more deeply into central knowledge of truth?

Will He not realize that which He said in His Sacerdotal prayer, St. John xvii. 22, 23: "And the glory which thou hast given to me I have given unto them, that they may be one, even as We are one: I in them, and they in Me, that they may be perfected into One."

As the disciples of the Lord could not comprehend this great mystery of the new and last alliance, Jesus Christ transmitted it to the latter days, of the future now arriving, when He said, "And the glory which Thou hast given Me, I have given unto them, that they may be one even as We are One," St. John xvii. 22. This alliance is called the Union of Peace. It is then that the law of God will be engraven in the heart of our hearts; we shall all know the Lord; and we shall be His people, and He will be our God.

All is already prepared for this actual possession of God, this union with God really possible here below; and the holy element, the efficacious medicine for humanity, is revealed by God's Spirit. The table of the Lord is ready and everyone is invited; the " true bread of Angels " is prepared.

The holiness and the greatness of the Mystery which contains within itself every mystery here obliges us to be silent, and we are not permitted to speak more than concerning its effects.

The corruptible and destructible is destroyed, and replaced by the incorruptible and by the indestructible. The inner sensorium opens and links us on to the spiritual world. We are enlightened by wisdom, led by truth, and nourished with the torch of love. Unimagined strength develops in us wherewith to vanquish the world, the flesh and the devil. Our whole being is renewed and made suitable for the actual dwelling-place of the Spirit of God. Command over nature, intercourse with the upper worlds, and the delight of visible intercourse with the Lord are granted also!

The hoodwink of ignorance falls from our eyes, the bonds of sensuality break, and we rejoice in the liberty of God's children.

We have told you the chiefest and most important fact, if your heart having the thirst for truth has laid hold on the pure ideas that you have gathered from all this, and have received in its entirety the grandeur and the blessedness of the thing itself as object of desire, we will tell you further.

May the Glory of the Lord and the renewing of your whole being be meanwhile the highest of your hopes!

Letter V

In our last letter, my dear brothers (and sisters), you granted me your earnest attention to that highest of mysteries, *the real possession of God;* it is therefore necessary to give you fuller light on this subject.

Man, as we know, is unhappy in this world because he is made out of destructible matter that is subject to trouble and sorrow.

The fragile envelope—*i.e.*, his body—exposes him to the violence of the elements, pain, poverty, suffering, illnesses. This is his normal fate; his immortal spirit languishing in the bonds of sense. Man is unhappy, because he is ill in body and soul, and he possesses no true panacea either for his body or for his soul.

Those whose duty it is to govern and lead other men to happiness, are as other men, also weak and subject to the same passions and prejudices.

Therefore, what fate can humanity expect? Must the greater part of it be always unfortunate? Is there no salvation for all?

Brothers, if humanity as a whole is ever capable of being raised to a condition of true happiness, such state can only be possible under the following conditions:—

First, poverty, pain, illness and sorrow must become much less frequent. Secondly, passions, prejudices and ignorance must diminish.

Is this at all possible with the nature of man, when experience proves that, from century to century, suffering only assumes fresh form; that passions, prejudices and errors always cause the same evils; and when we realize that all these things only change shape, and that man in every age remains much the same weak man?

There is a terrible judgment pronounced upon the human race, and this judgment is—men can never become happy so long as they will not become wise; but they will never become wise, while sensuality governs reason, while the spirit languishes in the bonds of flesh and blood.

Where is the man that has no passions? Let him show himself. Do we not all wear the chains of sensuality more or less heavily? Are we not all slaves? All sinners?

This realization of our low estate excites in us the desire to be raised beyond it, and we lift up our eyes on high, and an angel's voice says—*the sorrows of man shall be comforted.*

Man being sick body and soul, this mortal sickness must have a cause, and *this cause* is to be found in the very matter out of which man is made.

The destructible imprisons the indestructible, the *ferment of sin* is in us, and in this ferment is human corruption, and its propagation and consequences form the perpetuation of original sin.

The healing of humanity is only possible through the destruction of this ferment of sin, hence we have need of a physician and a remedy that really can cure us. But an invalid cannot be cured by another; the man of destructible matter cannot re-make himself of indestructible matter; dead matter cannot awake other dead, the blind cannot lead the blind.

Only the Perfect can bring anything to perfection; only the Indestructible can make the destructible likewise; only the Living can wake the dead.

This Physician and this active Medicine cannot be found in death and destruction, only in superior nature where all is perfection and life!

The lack of the knowledge of the union of Divinity with nature, nature with man, is the true cause of all prejudice and error. Theologians, philosophers, moralists, all wish to regulate the world, and they fill it with endless contradictions.

Theologians do not see the union of God with nature and fall therefore into error.

Modern philosophers study only matter, and not the connection of pure nature with divine nature, and therefore announce the falsest opinions.

Moralists will not recognize the inherent corruption of human nature, and they expect to cure by words, when means are absolutely necessary.

Thus the world, man and God, continue in permanent dissension; one opinion drives out another; superstition and incredulity take turn about in dominating society, separating man from the word of truth when he has so much dire need of approaching her.

It is only in the true Schools of Wisdom that one can learn to know God, nature, and man; and in these, for thousands of years, has work been done in silence to acquire to the highest degree this knowledge,—the union of man with pure nature and with God.

This great object, God and Nature, to which everything tends, has been represented to man symbolically in every religion; and all the symbols and holy glyphs are but the letter by which man can gradually, step by step, recover the highest of all divine mysteries, natural and human, and learn the means of healing his unhappy condition, and of the union of his being with pure nature and with God.

We have attained this epoch solely under God's guidance. Divinity, next remembering its covenant with man, has given forth the means of cure for suffering mankind, and shown thereby how to raise man to his original dignity, uniting him to God, the Source of his happiness.

The knowledge of this method ensuring recovery is the science of Saints and of the Elect, and its possession the inheritance promised to God's children.

Now, my beloved brothers, I want you to grant me your most earnest attention to what I am about to say.

In our blood there is lying concealed a slimy matter (called the gluten) which has a nearer kinship to animal than to spiritual man. This gluten is the body of sin.

This material, this matter, can be modified in various manners, according to the stimulus of sense; and according to the kind of modification and change occurring in this body or matter of sin, so also vary the diverse sinful tendencies of man.

In its most violent expansion this matter produces pride; in its utmost contraction, avarice, self-will and selfishness; in its repulsion, rage and anger; in its circular movements levity and incontinence; in its eccentricity, greediness and drunkenness; in its concentricity, envy; in its essence, sloth.

This ferment of sin, as original sin, is more or less working in the blood of every man, and is transmitted from father to son, and the perpetual propagation of this baneful material, everlastingly hinders the simultaneous action of spirit with matter.

It is quite true that man by his will-power can put limits to the action of this body of sin, and can dominate it so that it becomes less active, but to destroy and annihilate it altogether is beyond his power. This then is the cause of the combat we are constantly waging between the good and the evil in us.

This body of sin which is in us, forms the ties of flesh and blood which, on the one side, bind us to our immortal spirit, and, on the other, to the tendencies of the animal man. It is as it were the allurements of the animal passions that smolder and take fire at last.

The violent reaction of this body of sin in us, on sensuous stimulation, is the reason why we choose, for the want of calm and tranquil judgment, rather the evil than the good, because the active fermentation of this matter impedes the quiet action of the spirit necessary to instruct and sustain the reason.

This same evil matter is also the cause of our ignorance, because, as its thick and inflexible substance surcharges the fine brain fibers, it prevents the co-action of reason, which is required to penetrate the objects of the understanding.

Thus falseness and all evils are the properties of this sinful matter, this body of sin, just as the good and the true are the essential qualities of the spiritual principle within us.

Through the recognition and thorough understanding by us of this body of sin we learn to see that we are beings morally ill, that we have need of a physician who can give us a medicine which will destroy and eradicate the evil matter always fermenting banefully within us, a remedy that will cure us and restore us to moral health.

We learn also clearly to recognize that all mere moralizing with words is of little use *when real means are necessary.*

We have been moralizing in varied words for centuries, but the world remains pretty much the same. A doctor would do but little good in talking only of his remedies, it is necessary for him actually to prescribe his medicines; he has, however, first to see the real state of the sick person.

The condition of humanity—the moral sickness of man—is a true case of poisoning, consequent upon the eating of the fruit of the tree in which corruptible matter had the superiority.

The first effect of this poison resulted thus: the incorruptible principle, the body of life as opposed to the body of sin or death, whose expansion caused the perfection of Adam, concentrated itself inwardly, and the external part was abandoned to the government of the elements. Hence a mortal matter gradually covered the immortal essence, and the loss of this central light was the cause subsequently of all man's sufferings.

Communication with the world of light was interrupted, the interior eye which had the power of seeing truth *objectively* was closed, and the physical eye opened to the plane of changing phenomena.

Man lost all true happiness, and in this unhappy condition he would have for ever lost all means of restoration to health were it not that the love and mercy of God, who had no other object in creation but the greatest happiness for its creatures, immediately afforded to fallen man a means of recovery. In this means, he, with all posterity, had the right to trust, in order that while still in his state of banishment, he might support his misfortune with humility and resignation, and, moreover, find in his pilgrimage the great consolation, that every corruptible thing in man could be restored perfectly through the love of a Savior.

Despair would have been the fate of man without such revelation.

Man, before the Fall, was the living Temple of Divinity, and at the time when this Temple was destroyed, the plan to rebuild the Temple was already projected by the Wisdom of God; and at this period begin the Holy Mysteries of every religion, which are all and each in themselves, after a thousand varying modes, according to time and circumstances, and method of conception of different nations, but symbols repeated and modified of one solitary truth, and this unique truth is—*regeneration, or the re- union of man with God.*

Before the Fall man was wise, he was united to Wisdom; after the Fall he was no longer one with Her, hence a true science through express Revelation became absolutely necessary.

The Revelation was the following:—

The condition of immortality consists in immortality permeating the mortal. Immortal substance is divine substance, and is no other than the magnificence of the Almighty throughout nature, the substance of the world and spirits, the infinity, in short, of God in whom all things move and have their being.

It is an immutable law, no creature can be truly happy when separated from the source of all happiness. This source, this *in whom*, is the magnificence of God Himself.

Through the partaking of destructible nourishment, man himself became destructible and material; matter, therefore, as it were places itself between God and man, that is to say, man is not directly penetrated and permeated by divinity, and, in consequence, he is thenceforth subject to, and falls under the dominion of, the laws regulating matter.

The divine in man, imprisoned by the bonds of this matter, is his immortal part, the part that should be at liberty, in order that its development should once again rule the mortal. Then once more does man regain his original greatness.

But a means for his cure, and a method to externalize what is now hidden and concealed within, is requisite. Fallen and unwise man of himself can neither know nor grasp this expedient; he cannot even recognize it, because he has lost pure knowledge and the light of true wisdom; he cannot take hold of it, because this remedy is enfolded in interior nature, and he has neither the strength or power to unlock this hidden force.

Hence Revelation to learn this means, and strength to acquire this power, are necessary to man.

This necessity for the salvation of man was the cause of the determination of Wisdom, or the Son of God, to give Himself to be known by man, *being the pure substance out of which* all has been made. In this pure substance all power is reserved to vivify all dead substance, and to purify all that is impure.

But before that could be done, and the inmost part of man, the divine in him, be once more penetrated and re-opened again, and the whole world be regenerated, it was requisite that this divine substance should incarnate in humanity and become human, and therein transmit the divine and regenerative force to humanity; it was necessary also that this divine human form should be killed, in order that the divine and incorruptible substance contained in the blood should penetrate into the recesses of the earth, and thenceforth work a gradual dissolution of corruptible matter, so that in due time a pure and regenerated earth will be presented to man, with the Tree of Life growing once more, so that by partaking of its fruit, containing the true immortal essence, mortality in us will be once more annihilated, and man healed by the fruit of the Tree of Life, just as he was once poisoned by the partaking of the fruit of death.

This fact is the first and most important revelation and it embraces all, and it has been carefully preserved from mouth to mouth among the Chosen of God up to this time.

Human nature required a Savior, this Savior was Jesus Christ, the Wisdom of God itself, reality from God. He put on the envelope of humanity, to communicate *directly* the divine and immortal substance once more to the world, which was nothing else *but Himself.*

He offered himself voluntarily, in order that the *pure essential force* in His blood could penetrate directly, bringing with it the potentiality of all perfection to the hidden recesses of the earth.

Himself, both as High Priest and as Victim at the same time, entered into the Holy of Holies, and after having accomplished all that was necessary, he laid the foundation of the Royal Priesthood of His Elect, and taught these through the knowledge of His person and of His powers; now they should lead, as the first born of the spirit, other men, their brethren, to universal happiness.

And here begin the Sacerdotal Mysteries of the Elect and of the Inner Church.

The Royal and Priestly Science is that of Regeneration. It is called *Royal Science* because it leads man to power and the dominion over Nature.

It is called Sacerdotal, because it sanctifies and brings all to perfection, spreading blessing and goodness everywhere.

This Science owes its immediate origin to the *verbal revelation* of God, it is always the Science of the Inner Church of Prophets and of Saints, and it recognized no other High Priest but Jesus Christ the Lord.

This Science has a triple object; first, regenerating the individual and isolated man, or the first of the Elect; second, many men; thirdly, all humanity.

Its exercise consists in the highest perfecting of itself and of everything in Nature.

This Science was never taught otherwise than by the Holy Spirit of God, and by those who were in unison with this Spirit, and it is beyond all other sciences, because it can alone teach the knowledge of God, of nature, and of man in a perfect harmony; while other sciences do not understand truly either God or nature, neither man nor his destination.

The capabilities of this Science are the powers to know God in man, and divinity in nature; these being, as it were, the Divine impression or seals, by which our inner selves can be opened and can arrive at union with Divinity.

Thus the re-union was the most exalted aim, and hence the Priesthood derived its name *religio, clerus regenerans.*

Melchizedek was the first Priest King; all true Priests of God and of Nature descend from him, and Jesus Christ himself was united with him as "priest" after the order of Melchizedek. This word is literally of the highest and widest significance and extent מלכיצ-דק- (MLKIZ-DQ). It means literally the introducing of the true substance of vital life, and the separation of this true vital substance from the mortal envelope which encloses it.

A priest is one who separates that which is pure nature from that which is of impure nature, a separator of the substance which contains all from the destructible matter which occasions pain and misery. The sacrifice or that which has been separated consists in bread and wine.

Bread means literally the substance which contains all; wine the substance which vitalizes everything.

Therefore, a priest after the order of Melchizedek is one who knows how to separate the all-embracing and vitalizing substance from impure matter, one who knows how to employ it as a real means of reconciliation and of re-union for fallen humanity, in order to communicate to him his true and royal privilege of power over nature, and the Sacerdotal dignity or the ability to unite himself by grace to the upper worlds.

In these few words is contained all the mystery of God's Priesthood, and the occupation and aim of the Priest.

But this royal Priesthood was only able to reach perfect maturity when Jesus Christ Himself as High Priest had fulfilled the greatest of all sacrifices, and had entered into the Holy Sanctuary.

Here we are now entering on new and great mysteries worthy, I entreat you, of your most earnest attention.

When, according to the wisdom and justice of God, it was resolved to save the fallen human race, the Wisdom of God had to choose the method which afforded in every aspect the most efficacious means for the consummation of this great object.

When man became so thoroughly poisoned by the fruit of evil, carrying in himself henceforth the ferment of death, all around him became subject to death and destruction, therefore, divine mercy was bound to establish a counter remedy, which could be partaken of, containing within itself the divine and revitalizing substance, so that by taking this immortal food, poisoned and death-stricken man could be healed and rescued from his suffering. But in order that this Tree of Life could be replanted, it was requisite beyond all things that the corruptible material in the center of the earth should be first regenerated, resolved and made capable of being again one day a universally vitalizing substance.

This capacity for new life, bringing about the dissolution of corruptible essence which is inherent in the center of the earth, was, however, possible to no other matter than divine vital substance enveloped in flesh and blood which could transmit the hidden forces of life to dead nature. This was done through the death of Jesus Christ. *The tinctural force* which flowed from His shed blood penetrated to the innermost parts of the earth, raised the dead, rent the rocks, and caused the total eclipse of the sun when it pressed from the center of the earth where the light penetrated the central darkness to the circumference, and there laid the foundation of the future glorification of the world.

Since the death of Jesus Christ, the divine force, driven to the earth's center by the shedding of His blood, works and ferments perpetually to press outward, and to fit and prepare all substances gradually for the great cataclysm which is destined for the world.

But the rebuilding of the world's edifice in general was not only the aim of Redemption. Man was the principal object for the shedding of Christ's blood, and to procure for him already in this material world the highest possible perfection by the amelioration of his being, Jesus Christ submitted to infinite suffering.

He is the Savior of the world and of man. The object and cause of His Incarnation was to rescue us from sin, misery, and from death.

Jesus Christ has delivered us from all evil by His flesh, which he sacrificed, and by His blood, which He shed for us.

In the clear understanding of what consists this *flesh* and this *blood* of Jesus Christ lies the true and pure knowledge of the real regeneration of man.

The mystery of being united with Jesus Christ, not only spiritually *but also corporeally*, is the greatest aim of the Inner Church. Become one with Him in spirit and in being is the fulfilling and plenitude of the efforts of the Elect.

The means for this real possession of God is hidden from the wise of this world, and revealed to the simplicity of children.

Vain philosopher, bend thyself before the grand and Divine Mysteries that thou in thy wisdom canst not understand, and for the penetration of whose secrets the feeble light of human reason darkened by sense can give thee no measure!

Letter VI and Last

God made Himself man to deify man. Heaven united itself with earth to transform earth into Heaven.

But in order that these divine transformations can take place, an entire change, a complete and absolute overturning and upsetting of our being, is necessary.

This change, this upsetting, is called rebirth. *To be born*, simply means to enter into a world in which the senses dominate, in which wisdom and love languish in the bonds of individuality.

To be *reborn* means to return to a world where the spirit of wisdom and love governs, and where animal-man obeys.

The rebirth is triple; first, the rebirth of our intelligence; second, of our heart and of our will; and, finally, the rebirth of our entire being.

The first and second kinds are called the spiritual, and the third the corporeal rebirth.

Many pious men, seekers after God, have been regenerated in the mind and will, but few have known the corporeal rebirth. This last has been attained to but by few men, and those to whom it has been given have only received it that they might serve as *agents* of God, in accordance with great and grand objects and intentions, and to bring humanity nearer to felicity.

It is now necessary, my dear brothers, to lay before you the true order of rebirth. God, who is all strength, wisdom, and love, works eternally in order and in harmony.

He who will not receive the spiritual life, he who is not born anew from the Lord, can not enter into heaven.

Man is engendered through his parents in original sin, that is to say, he enters into the natural life and not the spiritual.

The spiritual life consists in loving God above everything, and your neighbor as yourself. In this double- love consists the *principle* of the new life.

Man is begotten in evil, in the love of himself and of the things of this world. Love of himself! Self interest! Self gratification! Such are the substantial properties of evil. The good is in the love of God and your neighbor, in knowing no other love but the love of mankind, no interest but that affecting every man, and no other pleasure but that of the well-being of all.

It is by such sentiments that the spirit of the children of God is distinguished from the spirit of the children of this world.

To change the spirit of this world into the spirit of the children of God is to be regenerated, and it means to despoil the old man, and to re-clothe the new.

But no person can be reborn if he does not know and put in practice the following principle—that of truth becoming the object for our doing or not doing; therefore, he who desires to be reborn ought first to know what belongs to rebirth. He ought to understand, meditate, and reflect on all this. Afterwards he should act according to his knowledge, and the result will be a new life.

Now, as it is first necessary to know, and to be instructed in all that appertains to rebirth, a doctor, or an instructor is required, and if we know one, faith in him is also necessary, because of what use is an instructor if his pupil have no faith in him?

Hence, the commencement of rebirth is faith in Revelation.

The disciple should begin by believing that the Lord, the Son, is the Wisdom of God, that He is, from all Eternity from God, and that He came into the world to bring happiness to humanity. He should believe that the Lord has full power in heaven and on earth, and that all faith and love, all the true and the good, come from Him alone; that He is the Mediator, the Savior, and Governor of men.

When this most exalting faith has taken root in us, we shall think often of the Savior, and these thoughts turned towards Him develop, and by His grace reacting in us, the seven closed and spiritual powers are opened.

The way to happiness.—Do you wish, man and brother, to acquire the highest happiness possible? Search for truth, wisdom, and love. But you will not find truth, wisdom, and love, save in the unity of the Lord Jesus Christ, the Anointed of God.

Seek, then, Jesus Christ with all your strength, search Him from the fullness of your heart.

The beginning of His Ascension is the knowledge of His absence, and from the recognition of this knowledge is the desire for increased power to seek Him, which desire is the beginning of faith.

Faith gives confidence, but faith has also its order of progress. First comes historic faith, then moral, then divine, and finally *living* faith. The progression is as follows: Historical faith when we learn to believe the history of Jesus of Nazareth, and through this simple historical faith in the existence of Jesus, will evolve moral faith, whose development consists in the acquirement of virtue by its search and practice, so that we see and find real pleasure in all that is taught by this Man; we find that His simple doctrine is full of wisdom and His teaching full of love; that His intentions towards humanity are straight and true, and that He willingly suffered death for the sake of justice. Thus, faith in His Person will be followed by faith in His Divinity.

This same Jesus Christ tells us now that He is Son of God, and He emphasizes His words by instructing His disciples in the sacred mysteries of nature and religion.

Here natural and reasonable faith changes into divine faith, and we begin to believe that he was God made man. From this faith it results that we hold as true all that we do not yet understand, but which He tells us to believe. Through this faith in the Divinity of Jesus, and by that entire surrender to Him, and the faithful attention to His directions, is at last produced that living faith, by which we find *within ourselves* and true through *our own experience*, all that hitherto we have until now believed in merely with the confidence of a child; and this living faith proved by experience is the highest grade of all.

When our hearts, through living faith, have received Jesus Christ into them, then this Light of the World is born within us as in a humble stable.

Everything in us is impure, surrounded by the spider- webs of vanity, covered with the mud of sensuality.

Our will is the Ox that is under the yoke of its passions. Our reason is the Ass who is bound through the obstinacy of its opinions, its prejudices, its follies.

In this miserable and ruined hut, the home of all the animal passions, can Jesus Christ be born in us through faith.

The simplicity of our souls, is as the shepherds who brought their first offerings, until at last the three principal powers of our royal dignity, our reason, our will, and our activity * prostrate themselves before Him and offer Him the gifts of truth, wisdom, and love.

Little by little, the stable of our hearts changes itself into an exterior Temple, where Jesus Christ teaches, but this Temple is still full of Scribes and Pharisees.

Those who sell, Dives and the money changers, are still to be found, and these should be driven out, and the Temple changed into a House of Prayer.

Little by little Jesus Christ chooses all the good powers in us to announce Him. He heals our blindness, purifies our leprosy, raises the dead powers into living forces within us; He is crucified in us, He dies, and He is gloriously raised again Conqueror with us. Afterwards his personality lives in us, and instructs us in exalted mysteries, until He has made us complete and ready for the perfect Regeneration when

He mounts to heaven and thence sends us the Spirit of Truth.

84

But before such a Spirit can act in us we experience the following changes:—

First, the seven powers of our understanding are lifted up within us; afterwards, the seven powers of our hearts or of our will, and this exaltation takes place after the following manner. The human understanding is divided into seven powers; the first is that of looking at abstract objects— *intuitus*. By the second we perceive the objects abstractedly regarded—*apperceptio*. By the third, that which has been perceived is reflected upon—*reflexio*. The fourth is that of considering these objects in their diversity *fantasia, imaginatio*. The fifth is that of deciding upon some thing— *judicium*. The sixth co-ordinates all these according to their relationships—ratio. The seventh and last is the power of realizing the whole intellectual intuition—*intellectus*.

This last contains, so to say, the sum of all the others.

The will of man divides itself similarly into seven powers, which, taken together as a unit, form the will of man, being, as it were, its *substantial* parts.

The first is the capacity of desiring things apart from himself—*desiderium*. The second is the power to annex mentally things desired for himself—*appetitus*.

The third is the power of giving them form, realizing them so as to satisfy his desire—*concupiscentia*. The fourth is that of receiving inclinations, without deciding upon acting upon any, as in the condition of passion—*passio*. The fifth is the capacity for deciding for or against a thing, liberty— *libertas*. The sixth is that choice or a resolution actually taken—*electio*. The seventh is the power of giving the object chosen an existence—*voluntas*. This seventh power also contains all the others in one figure.

Now the seven powers of the understanding, like the seven powers of our heart and will, can be ennobled and exalted in a very special manner, when we embrace Jesus Christ, as being the wisdom of God, as principle of our reason, and His whole life, which was all love, for motive power of our will.

Our understanding is formed after that of Jesus Christ; First, when we have Him in view in everything, when He forms the only point of sight for all our actions—*intuitus*. Second, when we perceive His actions, His sentiments, and His spirit everywhere— *apperceptio*. Third, when in all our thoughts we reflect upon His sayings, when we think in everything as He would have thought—*reflexio*. Fourth, when we so comfort ourselves in such wise, that His thoughts and His wisdom are the only object for the strength of our imagination—*fantasia*. Fifth, when we reject every thought which would not be His, and when we choose every thought which could be His—*judicium*. Sixth, when in short we co- ordinate the whole edifice of our ideas and spirit upon the model of His ideas and spirit—*ratio*. Seventh, It is then will be born in us a new light, a more brilliant one, surpassing far the light of reason of the senses—*intellectus*. Our heart is also reformed in like manner, when in everything,— First, We lean on Him only—*desidare*. Second, We wish for Him only—*appetere*. Third, We desire only Him—*concupiscere*. Fourth, We love Him only— *amare*. Fifth, We choose only that which He is, so that we avoid all that He is not— *eligere*. Sixth, We live only in harmony with Him after His commandments and His institutions and orders— *subordinare*. By which in short, Seventh, is born a complete union of our will with His, by which union man is with Jesus Christ but as one sense, one heart; by which perfect union the new man is little by little born in us, and Divine wisdom and love unite to form in us the new spiritual man, in whose heart faith passes into sight, and in comparison to this living faith the treasures of India can be considered but as ashes.

This actual possession of God or Jesus Christ in us is the Centre towards which all the mysteries converge like rays to the circle eye; the highest of the mysteries is this consummation.

The Kingdom of God is a kingdom of truth, morality, and happiness. It operates in the saints from the innermost to the outside, and spreads itself gradually by the Spirit of Jesus Christ into all nations, to institute everywhere an Order by means of which the individual can reach as well as the race; our human nature can be raised to its highest perfection, and sick humanity be cured from all the evils of its weakness.

Thus the love and spirit of God will one day alone vivify all humanity; they will awake and rekindle all the strength of the human race, will lead it to the goals of Wisdom and place it in suitable relationships.

Peace, fidelity, domestic harmony, love between nations, will be the first fruits of this Spirit. Inspiration of good without false similitudes, the exaltation of our souls without too severe a tension, warmth in the heart without turbulent impatience, will approach, reconcile, and unite all the various parts of the human race, long separated and divided by many differences, and stirred up against each other by prejudices and errors, and in one Grand Temple of Nature, great and little, poor and rich, all will sing the praise of the Father of Love.

DISCOURSE ON THE FELLOWCRAFT DEGREE

Brethren of the Order, and those among you in particular who have been received recently among us, there is no period too early to conceive a just and commensurate notion of the great institution to which we belong, and in which we have been incorporated as a part of its living body. It is desirable, in the first place, that we should understand certain intimations which occur in the Grade of Neophyte and in that of Fellow Craft. They are open on their surface to misconstruction, and did we afterwards pursue our researches into the history of Emblematic Freemasonry, it might even be thought that they were untrue unless we carried them further than is done commonly. Moreover, in the absence of such researches, they might come to be regarded as so many figures of speech.

The Entered Apprentice is told at an early stage of his experience that the Order possesses great and inestimable privileges as well as those secrets and mysteries concerning which he is sworn to inviolable secrecy. You will observe that the privileges are enumerated separately from the secrets, though the latter stand also for privileges. Among these I will particularize the Signs and Words of the successive Degrees. The privileges imparted by these include the right of entrance to a Lodge, as a guest or subscribing member. They are the titles of our initiation and assuredly they are more than valuable after their own kind, but they do not respond in themselves to the very wide claim which I have mentioned. I conceive therefore that there are other privileges. These are not, however, to be identified with the things implied by the great principles of the Order, precious as are the latter to our hearts, and advantageous as it must ever be to dwell within a circle of fellowship which recognizes the principles of solidarity and will at need extend them in good will to us. They are not in the category of those things which we seek to reserve to worthy men alone. They are rather the marks, seals and characters which it is our sacred duty to display and by which Masonry is known all over the world in its practice of beneficence, benevolence and fraternity, by the love of moral truth and by the truth which abides in honor. I conclude, therefore, that the reference to inestimable privileges is itself in the nature of a mystery and covers things, which do not exactly appear on the literal side of our rituals. This is the first point which I am now seeking to commemorate.

The second is concerned more especially with the obligation of the Neophyte Grade in which the Candidate is pledged to hele, conceal and never reveal the secret art and hidden mysteries of Masonry. I believe that after a little reflection I shall carry with me the concurring voice of every Brother amongst us, if I say that this pledge, with the penalties attached thereto, must cover more than the simple signs, tokens, words and procedure which takes place in our Lodges, or too elaborate machinery may be thought to be put in motion than the-end appears to require. Hence again it seems certain that the reference to secret arts and hidden mysteries is itself in the nature of a mystery and covers things which do not precisely appear on the literal surface of our Rituals. This is the next point, which I am seeking to commemorate here.

For the third, we must pass from the Grade of Initiate or Neophyte to that of Fellow Craft, in which there is a brief but singularly pregnant account (1) of that which was attained by the Candidate when he was made an Entered Apprentice; and (2) of that which he is expected to perform in his new capacity as a Craftsman. In the one it is pointed out that he has made himself acquainted with the principles of moral truth and virtue. Now, this is literally true, subject to a single reserve: as one newly admitted, he was not intended to be tried beyond his strength: the principles which he is said to have acquired were in reality communicated to him without action on his own part, but he was left in the First Degree to reflect upon them. They are actually the root matter and sum total of moral truth and all natural virtue. It is otherwise in the Degree of Fellow Craft. There it is assumed that the Masonic horizon has opened before and about him, and that he is prepared to enter an almost immeasurable region. He is accordingly advised (1) that he is expected to make the liberal arts and sciences his future study, and (2) that he is permitted to extend his researches into the hidden mysteries of nature and science. Once again, this is an intimation which covers much more than appears on the literal surface and is a mystery which is expressed shortly but not explained in our Rituals. Here is the third point which I am now seeking to commemorate.

Let us see if there is any direction in which we can turn for a little light on these problems, and as it so happens we shall not have to go outside the Lodge itself.

On his first entrance into Freemasonry the newly received Brother will perceive that he has come into a world of emblems or symbolism, and that whatsoever takes place therein has a meaning behind it which is by no means indicated invariably on the surface. Sometimes, and indeed frequently, there is more than one inward meaning, depending on the point of view from which it is approached. The Lodge is an eloquent example of this truth. When its door opens for the Candidate he enters into an institution, which has its branches spread over the four quarters of the globe. It may be a very small Lodge: it may be a Lodge of poor Brothers only: but whosoever is received therein is recognized through the Masonic world, in all countries and among all peoples. But there is more even than this: however humble in its appointments and proportions, that Lodge is a Microcosm, a symbol, a speaking likeness of universal Freemasonry. It represents also and contains the life of Masonry, and the Ceremony of his initiation integrates the newly-made Brother in that peculiar quality of life which is the principle and essence of the Order. He becomes part of an organic whole. In the third place, the Lodge is held to represent the three dimensions of space--that is to say, the universe itself as a cosmos: in length from East to West, in breadth between North and South, in depth from the surface to the center, and even as high as the heavens.

It is therefore as if the Candidate on his initiation had been born anew into the universe, or that a door had opened to admit him into another cosmos. He comes with his eyes dim and with a restraint about him; he is kept for a considerable period in a state of darkness and bondage: ultimately he is instructed, and that which he finds about him is truly the symbolic representation of a new world. For him at that moment all things seem to be renewed, and it is very soon after this strange and wonderful experience that he is given a key to the meaning. He is told that he is the corner stone of a new foundation, from which he has to build up himself after another and higher manner. In other words, he has to remake his inward nature according to the perfection of the standard which is prescribed by Masonry. It is a moral standard in respect of his dealings with his Brethren and with mankind at large. It is a spiritual standard in respect of his duty towards God, and through obedience thereto it is hoped, held and known that he will ascend to the home of the spirit in the heavenly kingdom, by means of the ladder of Jacob, the successive rounds of which are called by many names, but chief among these are faith, hope and charity. It follows that he has a two-fold work to perform, but it is all in the training of himself. If he be successful, the result will be perfect in its parts and honorable to the builder. From this point of view, the just, perfect and regular Lodge is also a symbol of the man in that state which he is called to attain.

Now, the word initiate, with which we are so familiar in Masonry, signifies a person who has made a new beginning, who has entered a path of experience heretofore untraveled. Its equivalent in other orders and fraternities is the word Neophyte. The Neophyte is also one who has made a new beginning and the term, which is Greek in its origin, signifies him who is reborn, a new plant, one who is remade. In the old instituted mysteries, like those of Samothrace, of Egypt and of Eleusis, the Candidate was regenerated or reborn-- he was otherwise transferred or grafted--at the beginning of his experience, and afterwards he passed through successive stages of a new life till he attained the culminating Grade. It was the same experiment as that of Craft Masonry, in which the Candidate-- as an Entered Apprentice--lays the foundation stone of that new building which is himself, raises a super structure according to the law and order that Masonry has imposed upon him, continues the erection as a Craftsman, in which Degree the mysteries of Nature and science, recommended to his study, are mysteries of God and the estimation of His wonderful works till at last he puts on the capstone when the Lodge is open in the Sublime Grade of Master.

Our secret art is therefore an art of life, an art of perfection, an art of creation according to a prescribed standard recognized in Masonry: our hidden mysteries are those of our own relations to God, man and the universe, that we may be enabled to fulfill by Masonry the higher law of our being. The inestimable privileges of Masonry include those of its symbolism, the study of which is for our instruction in this high mode of self-building. The arts and mysteries which we are pledged to conceal from the profane are also those of the peculiar law of life in Masonry by which these ends can be reached. Those who are outside the Lodge must come within it, if they desire to share in that life. It is really incommunicable beyond the mystic circle, for the simple reason that it is life itself and not one of its substitutes. While therefore we are properly pledged concerning it, there is something which we could not impart even if we tried. In some of the old mysteries, from which we are indirectly descended, initiation and its sequels meant real instruction in this subject, and several of our most suggestive intimations are reflections from that remote source.

And seeing that the Grade of Master Mason is not so much a

reflection as the very root, essence and quintessence, of those mysteries, and may be shortly described as an experiment in the deep mystery by which the soul passes through mortal life towards that life in God which is the end of all the mysteries, it comes about in this manner, my Brethren, that we are incorporated with all the great orders and sodalities of the far past and are therefore justified when we say that the meaning of our Masonic Badge is more ancient than the Golden Fleece and that our honorable institution--though under many transformations--has subsisted from time immemorial.

THE IMPORTANCE OF CEREMONIAL MAGIC

The ordinary fields of psychological inquiry, largely in possession of the pathologist, are fringed by a borderland of occult and dubious experiment into which pathologists may occasionally venture, but it is left for the most part to unchartered explorers. Beyond these fields and this borderland there lies the legendary wonder-world of Theurgy, so called, of Magic and Sorcery, a world of fascination or terror, as the mind which regards it is tempered, but in either case the antithesis of admitted possibility. There all paradoxes seem to obtain actually, contradictions coexist logically, the effect is greater than the cause and the shadow more than the substance. Therein the visible melts into the unseen, the invisible is manifested openly, motion from place to place is accomplished without traversing the intervening distance, matter passes through matter. There two straight lines may enclose a space; space has a fourth dimension, and untrodden fields beyond it; without metaphor and without evasion, the circle is mathematically squared. There life is prolonged, youth renewed, physical immortality secured. There earth becomes gold, and gold earth. There words and wishes possess creative power, thoughts are things, desire realises its object. There, also, the dead live and the hierarchies of extra-mundane intelligence are within easy communication, and become ministers or tormentors, guides or destroyers, of man. There the Law of Continuity is suspended by the interference of the higher Law of Fantasia.

But, unhappily, this domain of enchantment is in all respects comparable to the gold of Faerie, which is presumably its medium of exchange. It cannot withstand daylight, the test of the human eye, or the scale of reason. When these are applied, its paradox becomes an anticlimax, its antithesis ludicrous; its contradictions are without genius; its mathematical marvels end in a verbal quibble; its elixirs fail even as purges; its transmutations do not need exposure at the assayer's hands; its marvel-working words prove barbarous mutilations of dead languages, and are impotent from the moment that they are understood; departed friends, and even planetary intelligences, must not be seized by the skirts, for they are apt to desert their draperies, and these are not like the mantle of Elijah.

The little contrast here instituted will serve to exhibit that there are at least two points of view regarding Magic and its mysteries--the simple and homogeneous view, prevailing within a charmed circle among the few survivals whom reason has not hindered from entering, and that of the world without, which is more complex, more composite, but sometimes more reasonable only by imputation. There is also a third view, in which legend is checked by legend and wonder substituted for wonder. Here it is not the Law of Continuity persisting in its formulae despite the Law of Fantasia; it is Croquemetaine explained by Diabolus, the runes of Elf-land read with the interpretation of Infernus; it is the Law of Bell and Candle, the Law of Exorcism, and its final expression is in the terms of the *auto-da-fé*. For this view the wonder-world exists without any question, except that of the Holy Tribunal; it is not what it seems, but is adjustable to the eye of faith in the light from the Lamp of the Sanctuaries; in a word, its angels are demons, its Melusines stryges, its phantoms vampires, its spells and mysteries the Black Science. Here Magic itself rises up and responds that there is a Black and a White Art, an Art of Hermes and an Art of Canidia, a Science of the Height and a Science of the Abyss, of Metatron and Belial. In this manner a fourth point of view emerges; they are all, however, illusive; there is the positive illusion of the legend, affirmed by the remaining adherents of its literal sense, and the negative illusion which denies the legend crassly without considering that there is a possibility behind it; there is the illusion which accounts for the legend by an opposite hypothesis, and the illusion of the legend which reaffirms itself with a distinction. When these have been disposed of, there remain two really important questions-- the question of the Mystics and the question of history and literature. To a very large extent the first is closed to discussion, because the considerations which it involves cannot be presented with profit on either side in the public assemblies of the reading world. So far as may be held possible, it has been dealt with already. As regards the second, it is the large concern and purpose of this inquiry, and the limits of its importance may therefore be stated shortly.

There can be no extensive literatures without motives proportionate to account for them. If we take the magical literature of Western Europe from the Middle Ages and onward, we shall find that it is moderately large. Now, the acting principles in the creation of that literature will prove to rule also in its history; what is obscure in the one may be understood by help of the other; each reacted upon each; as the literature grew, it helped to make the history, and the new history was so much additional material for further literature. There were, of course, many motive principles at work, for the literature and history of Magic are alike exceedingly intricate, and there are many interpretations of principles which are apt to be confused with the principles, as, for example, the influence of what is loosely called superstition upon ignorance; these and any interpretations must be ruled out of an inquiry like the present. The main principles are summed in the conception of a number of assumed mysterious forces in the universe which could be put in operation by man, or at least followed in their secret processes. In the ultimate, however, they could all be rendered secondary, if not passive, to the will of man; for even in astrology, which was the discernment of forces regarded as peculiarly fatal, there was an art of ruling, and sapiens dominabitur astris became an axiom of the science. This conception culminated or centred in the doctrine of unseen, intelligent powers, with whom it was possible for prepared persons to communicate; the methods by which this communication was attempted are the most important processes of Magic, and the books which embody these methods, called Ceremonial Magic, are the most important part of the literature. Here, that is to say, is the only branch of the subject which it is necessary to understand in order to understand the history. Had Magic been focussed in the reading of the stars, it would have possessed no history to speak of, for astrology involved intellectual equipments which, comparatively speaking, were possible only to the few. Had Magic centred in the transmutation of metals, it would never have moved multitudes, but would have remained what that still is, the quixotic hope which emerges at a far distance from the science of chemistry. We may take the remaining occult sciences collectively, but there is nothing in them of themselves which would make history. In virtue of the synthetic doctrine which has been already formulated, they were all magically possible, but they were all subsidiary to that which was head and crown of all--the art of dealing with spirits. The presumed possession of the secret of this art made Magic formidable, and made therefore its history. There was a time indeed when Ceremonial Magic threatened to absorb the whole circle of the occult sciences; it was the superior method, the royal road; it effected immediately what the others accomplished laboriously, after a long time. It had, moreover, the palmary recommendation that it was a conventional art, working by definite formulæ; above all, it was a process in words.

It was the fascination of this process which brought men and women-all sorts and conditions of both--to the Black Sabbath and to the White Sabbath, and blinded them to the danger of the stake. It was the full and clear acceptation of this process as effectual by Church and State which kindled the faggots for the magician in every Christian land.

Astrology was scarcely discouraged, and if the alchemist were occasionally tortured, it was only to extract his secret. There was no danger in these things, and hence there was no judgment against them, except by imputation from their company; but Magic, but dealing with spirits, was that which made even the peasant tremble, and when the peasant shakes at his hearth, the king is not secure in his palace nor the Pope at St. Peter's, unless both can protect their own. Moreover, in the very claim of Ceremonial Magic there was an implied competition with the essential claim of the Church.

The importance of Ceremonial Magic, and of the literature which embodies it, to the history of the occult sciences being admitted, there is no need to argue that this history is a legitimate and reasonable study; in such a case, knowledge is its own end, and there can be certainly no question as to the distinguished influence which has been exercised by the belief in Magic throughout the ages. In order, however, to understand the literature of Magic, it is necessary to obtain first of all a clear principle of regarding it. It will be superfluous to say that we must surrender the legends, as such, to those who work in legends, and dispute about their essential value. We need not debate whether Magic, for example, can really square the circle, as magicians testify, or whether such an operation is impossible even to Magic, as commonly would be objected by those who deny the art. We need not seriously discuss the proposition that the devil assists the magicians to perform a mathematical impossibility, or its qualified form, that the circle can be squared indifferently by those who invoke the angel Cassiel of the hierarchy of Uriel and those who invoke Astaroth. We shall see very shortly, as already indicated in the preface, that we are dealing with a bizarre literature, which passes, by various fantastic phases, through all folly into crime. We have to account for these characteristics.

The desire to communicate with spirits is older than history; it connects with ineradicable principles in human nature, which have been discussed too often for it to be necessary to recite them here; and the attempts to satisfy that desire have usually taken a shape which does gross outrage to reason. Between the most ancient processes, such as those of Chaldean Magic, and the rites of the Middle Ages, there are marked correspondences, and there is something of common doctrine, as distinct from intention, in which identity would more or less obtain, underlying them both. The doctrine of compulsion, or the power which both forms pretended to exercise even upon superior spirits by the use of certain words, is a case in point. In approaching the Ceremonial Magic of the Middle Ages, we must therefore bear in mind that we are dealing with a literature which, though modern in its actual presentation, embodies some elements of great antiquity. It is doubtful whether the presence of these elements can be accounted for on the principle that mankind in all ages works unconsciously for the accomplishment of similar intentions in an analogous way; a bizarre intention, of course, tends independently to be fulfilled in a bizarre manner, but in this case the similarity is so close that it is more easily explained by the perpetuation--sporadic and natural or concerted and artificial--of an antique tradition, for which channels could be readily assigned. There is one upon the face of the literature, and that is the vehicle of Kabalistic symbolism, though it cannot be held to cover the entire distance in time.

There have been two ways of regarding the large and imperfectly explored literature which embodies the Kabalah of the Jews, and these in turn will give two methods of accounting for the spurious and grotesque processes which enter so extensively into Ceremonial Magic. It is treated either as a barren mystification, a collection of supremely absurd treatises, in which obscure nonsense is enunciated with preternatural solemnity, or it is regarded as a body of theosophy, written chiefly in the form of symbolism. The first view is that which is formed, I suppose, almost irresistibly upon a superficial acquaintance, and there is not any need to add that it is the one which obtains generally in derived judgments, for here, as in other cases, the second-hand opinion issues from the most available source. It is just to add that it does not differ very seriously from the opinions expressed in the past by a certain section of scholarship. The alternative judgment is that which prevails among those students of the literature who have approached it with a certain preparation through acquaintance with other channels of the Secret Tradition. From the one it would follow that the Ceremonial Magic which at a long distance draws from the Kabalah, reproduces its absurdities, possibly with further exaggerations, or it is the subject-matter of the literature carried to its final results. Two erroneous views have issued from the other--an exaggerated importance attributed to the processes in question on the ground of their exalted connections, and--this, however, is rarely met with--an inclination to regard them also as symbolical writing.

There is no ground for the criticism of the first inference, which has arisen legitimately enough and is that which will be most acceptable to the majority of readers. Those who value Kabalistic literature as a storehouse of symbolism, the inner sense of which is or may be of importance, but see nothing in the processes of Ceremonial Magic to make them momentous in their literal sense or susceptible to interpretation, will be tempted to dismiss them as mediæval and later impostures, which must be carefully distinguished from the true symbolical tradition. In either case the ceremonial literature is disdainfully rejected, and it follows in this manner that alternatives which exclude one another both reach the truth as their term.

There is, however, yet another point of view, and it is of some moment, as it connects with that question of the Instituted Mysteries about which it has been already observed that very little has transpired. Most students of occultism are acquainted with intimations and rumours of the existence in modern times of more than one Occult as of more than one Mystical Fraternity, deriving, or believed to derive, from other associations of the past. There are, of course, many unaffiliated occultists, as most mystics are unaffiliated, but the secret Fraternities exist, and the keys of occult symbolism are said to be in their possession. From a variety of isolated statements scattered up and down the works of professed Occultists in recent years, it is possible to summarise broadly the imputed standpoint of these bodies in respect of Ceremonial Magic. I will express it in brief as follows. There is no extant Ritual, as there is no doctrine, which contains, or can possibly contain, the real secret of magical procedure or the essence of occult doctrine.

The reason--whatever may be said in the excess of some self-constituted exponents--is not because there is, or can be, any indicible process, but because the knowledge in question is in the custody of those who have taken effectual measures for its protection; and though, from time to time, some secrets of initiation, belonging to this order, have filtered through printed books into the world at large, the real mysteries have never escaped.

The literature of Magic falls, therefore, on this hypothesis, under three heads: (a.) The work of putative adepts, stating as much as could be stated outside the circle of initiation, and primarily designed to attract those who might be ripe for entrance. (b.) The speculations of independent seekers, who, by thought, study and intuition, sometimes attained veridic results without assistance. (c.) Travesties of occult doctrine, travesties of occult intention, travesties of occult procedure, complicated by filtrations from the superior source.

The opinions of professed occultists on any subject whatsoever are of no importance to myself, and are named only to establish a point of view; but most Ceremonial Magic belongs to the third class, on the assumption that it still exists, like some other paths of Satanism; the first, by its nature, is not represented, and the second only slightly.

In a word, Ceremonial Magic reflects mainly the egregious ambitions and incorporates the mad processes of mediæval sorcery--of the Sabbath above all. The additional elements are debased applications of various Kabalistic methods, seering processes current among country people and fantastic attempts to reduce magical legends to a formal practice.

Whichever of the above views the reader may prefer to adopt, it will be seen that the net result as regards the Rituals is not generically different, that they are of literary and historical interest, but nothing further. For the occultist they will possess, from their associations, an importance which will be of no moment to another student.

It is desirable that they should not be undervalued, as records of the past, because they have exercised an influence, and they are memorable as curiosities thereof; but it is more desirable still that the weak and credulous should be warned against acting like fools, and that those who are seeking spiritual certitude should be dissuaded from the science of the abyss.

EMBLEMATIC FREEMASONRY, BUILDING GUILDS AND HERMETIC SCHOOLS

As Emblematic Freemasonry is the Craft of Building moralized, it follows that intellectually, at least, our figurative and speculative art has arisen out of the Operative. Here is a first link in any chain of connection with the building world of the past. But it seems certain also that the Free and Accepted, or Speculative, Masons had Operative documents, such as the so-called Gothic Constitutions and Old Charges, for part of their heritage. The proof is that soon after the revival of 1717, these documents were put into the hands of Dr. James Anderson "*to digest . . . in a new and better method.*" They were things apparently in evidence, and he was not commissioned to search them out. Beyond this *omnia exeunt in mysterium.* Almost from Year to year our documentary knowledge of Constitutions, Charges, and Landmarks extends slowly. There is also new light cast from time to time on the general history of architecture in Christian times. But no light is shed on the antiquities of art of building moralized. The existence of such an art prior to 1717 remains almost as much a matter of speculation as the art itself is speculative. We are led almost irresistibly to infer that it anteceded this date and a few remain among us who believe that it may have been old in the year 1646, when Ashmole was made a Mason at Warrington, but there is no real evidence. So also there are zealous and capable writers by whom our knowledge is expanded from time to time, however slightly, on particular sides and respecting the archaeology of architectural history, on Roman Collegia, Dionysian artificers, and Comacines. They furnish at the same time many plausible and taking speculations. But they do not help us in respect of Freemasonry, as we now understand the term, because no evidence of building association is of service to our own purpose unless such association embodies our "*peculiar system of morality, veiled in allegory and illustrated by symbols.*"

The Hittites of Syria and Asia Minor may have been of "Hamitic descent" and may have built the Temple at Jerusalem; the Etruscans, from whom architecture was learned by the Romans, may, have been Hittites; at the downfall of Rome, the Roman Collegia may have settled in that island on Lake Como, which is familiar at the present day as Isola Comacina, and may have become Comacines; the Comacines may, in turn, have merged into the great Masonic guilds of the Middle Ages. But, if so, all this is part and parcel of the history of architecture and not of

100

Emblematical Building, unless and until we can show that, practical Masons as they were, their system of secret association included what is called in the Craft degrees a side of Speculative Masonry and in the appendant degrees an art of building spiritualized. But it is just this which is wanting, or we should have taken the closing long since in the lodge of our debate on the origin of Freemasonry. There are not unnatural sporadic vestiges, few and far between. It is said, that the Comacines had a motto affirming that their temple, was "one made without hands," and this reminds us assuredly of the Mark degree; but it is not to be called evidence for a developed speculative element prevailing amongst the old masters. Nor can I think with Brother Ravencroft, in his memorable series of papers contributed to *The Builder* in 1918, that the two pillars of Wurzburg Cathedral, once situated on either side of the porch and bearing respectively on their capitals the letters J and B, can be termed "*a good illustration of the way in which symbols were transmitted even from the temple of Solomon to the medieval craftsmen and thence to our Speculative Masonry.*" It seems to me simply that the Cathedral builders were acquaint with Holy Scripture.

The conclusion which is forced upon me is that only by the use of liberal supposition can the Comacines and those who preceded them be made to connect with our subject. We may take H. J. Da Costa as early authority in England for the Dionysian fraternity and his successor, Krause, for the links between Masons of the Middle Ages and the Roman Collegia. The views of both have been summarized ably by my friend, Brother Joseph Fort Newton, but that which valid therein belongs to the history of architecture. It was, I think, Krause who said that each Roman collegium was presided over by a Master and two decuriones or Wardens, each of whom bore the Master's commands to the brethren of his respective column. The word "decurio" is here translated "warden," to institute an analogy by force. According to Suetonius, the Latin office in question was that of a captain over ten men whether horse or foot, and was therefore military in character. The first authority on the Comacines is Leader Scott (who is Miss Lucy E. Baxter) in "The Cathedral Builders," a most fascinating romance of architecture, which contains also some great and valuable historical lights. Joseph Fort Newton described it as an attempt to bridge the gap "between the classical Roman style and the rise of Gothic art." Again, therefore, it is a question of architectural evolution and I must say personally that, taken as such, it is to be questioned whether the gulf is really spanned. I can understand on the hypothesis the development of Italian architecture, more or less degenerated from classical types, but not the genesis of the great schools of Gothic building. It is to be understood, however, that this question exceeds the warrants of my subject to connect any ritual mystery which obtained *ex hypothesi* in the old Collegia, or among Comacine lodges, with the living mystery of Speculative Masonry, of which she Speaks with derision, but evidently knows it only through an Italian source. As a student of the Secret Tradition in Christian times I could wish that the facts were otherwise in the great story of all these ancient guilds. I could have wished that their supposed pageants of secret initiation were, as the speculations say, Dionysian representations of mystical death and resurrection, and that they are reflected at a far distance in our Sublime degree. But if these stories are dreams, or still awaiting demonstration, we have to face the fact, and the question remaining over is whether we can look elsewhere. Now, it happens that there is one direction which has been regarded not unfavorably as a possible source of light. It is that of the Hermetic Schools in England, and these, speaking broadly, may be classified as three- Alchemical, Rosicrucian, and Kabalistic. They had a common bond of interest and tended here, as elsewhere, to merge one into another. There are evidences to show that the experiment of Alchemy in England is an exceedingly old pursuit, but in the early part of the seventeenth century it had sprung into greater prominence. The rumor of the Rosicrucian fraternity was also raising curiosity in Europe. Hermetic literature- not only with a modern accent but also for the time in vernacular language- extended greatly, and schools of theosophy sprang up in several countries. The root of the Rosicrucian movement was in Germany, but the impulse reached England and some of the most famous names connected with the subject are identified with this country. Hence came Alexander Seton and hence Eirenaeus Philalethes, who has been regarded as one of the great masters of Hermetic Art. Here also was Robert Fludd, who must, I think, be regarded as not only advocate and apologist in chief of the Rosicrucian art and philosophy, but as a fountainhead. Here, too, was Thomas Vaughan, mystic as well as alchemist. And here, in 1640, lived Elias Ashmole, alchemist and antiquary, founder also of the Ashmolean Museum at Oxford.

A section of Masonic opinion has looked in the past and a section looks still towards Elias Ashmole and his connections in some way, yet undetermined, as the representatives of this transition from Operative to Speculative Masonry. In France there has been practically no doubt on the subject from the days of Ragon, though concerning the value of his personal view I must speak with desirable plainness elsewhere in this paper. In America the distinguished name of Albert Pike can be cited in support of the thesis. After every allowance has been made for the position of such a speculation, still almost inextricable, it can be affirmed that it seems to offer a place of repose for all the tolerable views, because it harmonizes all- on the understanding that Ashmole and his consociates are not regarded personally but as typifying a leavening spirit introduced there and here, and at work during the period intervening between 1640 and the foundation of the first Grand Lodge In 1717. Pike was like Ragon unfortunately, a man of uncritical mind, and I summarize his findings under all needful reserve.

Among Masonic symbols which he identifies as used in common by Freemasons and Hermetic and Alchemical literature are the Square and Compasses, the Triangle, the Oblong Square, the Legend of the three Grand Masters, the idea embodied in a substituted word, which might well be the most important of all, together with the Sun, the Moon, and Master of the lodge. It was, moreover, his opinion, based on this and other considerations, that the philosophers- meaning the members of the Hermetic confraternities- became Freemasons and introduced into Masonry their own symbolism. He thinks finally that Ashmole was led to be made a Mason because others who were followers of Hermes had taken the step before him. However this may be, I have said elsewhere that the influence of the Rosicrucian fraternity upon that of the Masons has been questioned only by those who have been unfitted to appreciate the symbolism which they possess in common. It does not belong to the formative period of Emblematic Freemasonry, but to that of development and expansion. The nature of the influence is another matter and one, moreover, in which it may be necessary to recognize the simple principle of imitation up to a certain point. The influence has been exercised more especially in connection with other Rites, as to which it is impossible, for example, to question that those who instituted the eighteenth degree of the Scottish Rite either must have received something by transmission from the old German Brotherhood, or, alternatively, must have borrowed from its literature.

That Ashmole was connected with Rosicrucians, or otherwise with the representatives of some association which had assumed their name is an inference drawn from his life. His antiquarian studies led him more especially in the direction of Alchemy, but as regards this art he did not remain an antiquary or a mere collector of old documents on the subject. He was, to some extent, a practical student and, moreover, not simply an isolated inquirer. He had secured that assistance which has been regarded always as next but one to essential, namely, the instruction of a Master. The alternative is Divine Aid, which is, of course, a higher kind of Mastery. He was associated otherwise with many of the occult philosophers, alchemists, astrologers, and so forth, belonging to his period. The suggestion that he acted as an instrument of the Rosicrucian Brotherhood, or as a member thereof, in the transfiguration of Operative into Speculative Freemasonry is a matter of faith for those who have held or hold it. Of direct or indirect evidence there is not one particle. Supposing that such a design existed at the period, he is not an unlikely person to have been concerned in planning it on the part of himself and others or to have been delegated for such a purpose. But of the design there is again no evidence. It has been affirmed further in the interests of the claim that a meeting of an Alchemical- presumably Rosicrucian- society perceiving how working Masons were already outnumbered in membership by persons of education not belonging to the trade, believed that the time was ripe for a complete ceremonial revolution and that one founded on mystical tradition was drawn up thereon in writing, constituting the Entered Apprentice grade, approximately as it exists now. The grade of Fellow Craft was elaborated in 1648, and that of Master Mason in 1659.

These are the reveries of Ragon, categorical in nature, accompanied by specific details, all in the absence of one particle of fact in any record of the past. It seems to me, therefore, that no language would be too strong to characterize such mendacities and that they can belong only to the class of conscious lying, but the charge against Ragon is more especially that he elaborated the materials of a hypothesis which had grown up among successive inventors belonging to the type of Reghellini. If there were Rosicrucians in England at the date in question, it may be presumed that those who, according to Ashmole's own statement, communicated to him some portions, at least, of the Hermetic secrets would not have withheld the corporate mysteries of their Fraternity. But, on the other hand, there is at present no historical certainty that the Hermetic Order possessed any such corporate existence in England at that period. However this may be, in the memoirs of the life of Elias Ashmole, as drawn up by himself in the form of a diary, there is the following now well-known entry under date of 16th October, 1646:

I was made a Freemason at Warrington in Lancashire with Colonel Henry Mainwaring of Kartichan in Cheshire; the names of those that were then at the Lodge: Mr. Richard Penket, Warden; Mr. James Collier, Mr. Richard Sankey, Henry Littler, John Ellam, Richard Ellam, and Hugh Brewer.

The two noteworthy points in this extract, over and above the main fact which it designs to place on record, are that neither candidate was an operative by business and that the work of initiation was performed evidently by the brother who acted as Warden. At that period Elias Ashmole was under thirty years of age. His father was a saddler by trade, his mother was the daughter of a draper and he himself solicited in Chancery. But while still in his youth he tells us that he had entered into that condition to which he had aspired always, "that I might be able to live to myself and studies, without being forced to take pains for a livelihood in the world." The admissions of 16th October, 1646, are not required to prove the practice of initiating men of other business than that of Masonry and its connected crafts, or even of no business at all, but it should be observed that here- as in cases of earlier date- the reception was in the capacity of simple brothers and not of patrons.

The nature of those studies which were engrossing Ashmole about the time of his initiation may be learned by the publication, five years later, of his *Theatrum Chemicum Britannicum,* being a collection of metrical treatises written in English at various dates on the subject of the Hermetic Mystery and the Philosopher's Stone. They appear to be concerned only with what is called technically the physical work on metals and the physical medicine or elixir, not with those spiritual mysteries which have passed occasionally into expression under the peculiar symbolism of Alchemy. At the same time Ashmole is careful to explain his personal assurance that the transmutation of metals is only one branch of Hermetic practice:

As this is but a part, so it is the least share of that blessing which may he acquired by the Philosopher's materia, if the full virtue thereof were known. Gold, I confess, is a delicious object, a goodly light which we admire and gaze upon ut pueri in Junonis avem, but as to make gold is the chief intent of the Alchemists, so was it scarcely any intent of the ancient Philosophers and the

105

lowest use the Adeptio made of this materia. For they, being lovers of wisdom more than worldly wealth, drove at higher and more excellent operations; and certainly he to whom the whole course of Nature lies open rejoiceth not so much that he can make gold and silver or the devils be made subject to him as that he sees the heavens open, the angels of God ascending and descending and that his own name is fairly written in the Book of Life.

It should be added that this exposition is a faithful reflection of Rosicrucian doctrine as it is put forward, directly or indirectly, under the name of the Brotherhood in German books and pamphlets of the early seventeenth century. Supposing that circa 1650 there was an incorporated Rosicrucian School in England, no person is so likely to have been a member as Ashmole, and it is not possible to imagine him in separation therefrom. Indeed, I am by no means certain that his testimony is not thinly presumptive of membership, being so to the manner born of it in thought and figures of speech. But if we can tolerate- however tentatively- the Rosicrucian initiation of Ashmole, we may take it for granted that he did not stand alone. On the whole it seems barely possible that on 16th October, 1646, a Brother of the Rosy Cross was made a Mason, with or without an ulterior motive in view. It follows expressly from his frank and honorable testimony concerning himself that he was one who had only seen the end of adeptship, even within the measures that he conceived it, while as regards any other Rosicrucians to whom he may have been joined we know very little concerning them.

It will be seen that the Ashmole hypothesis is but a part of the wider claim of direct Rosicrucian influence on the foundation of Emblematic Freemasonry. I agree with the opinion that in so far as it has been advanced in the past this claim has lapsed. It affirms that the House of the Holy Spirit, being the Rosicrucian Brotherhood in Germany, had a Secret House in England, which either transfigured itself into the thing called Speculative Masonry or revolutionized the old Operative Craft along speculative lines for its own purposes, presumably that it might have recruiting centers available and more or less openly manifest. There is no evidence whatever to support this view. The Rosicrucian zeal of the occult philosopher and intellectual mystic, Robert Fludd, left no trace behind it, until the time came for it to influence in a rather indefinite manner the impassionable enthusiasm of Thomas Vaughan, and this also led to nothing. The first incorporated Rosicrucian Society in England of which we hear belongs to the early nineteenth century. In particular, Fludd's activities had no bearing on any Masonry of the early seventeenth century, even if Robertus de Fluctitus was the Mr. Flood who presented a *Book of Contitutions* to the Masons' Company, as recorded in an inventory taken before the Fire of London.

When the question at issue has been relieved from these reveries there remains the more reasonable suggestion that the Operative Brotherhood came gradually and not unnaturally under the influence of persons who belonged to both associations. It would attract also those who were simply Hermetic students, though isolated and unattached as such. Attached or otherwise, Ashmole is a case in point, though his place in Freemasonry of the mid-seventeenth century is a subject for very careful adjudication. The influence which in this manner would begin to be exercised, consciously or unconsciously, would be Hermetic in a general sense rather than Rosicrucian exclusively; but this is a distinction which will not be realized readily by those who are acquainted only at second-hand with the mystical and occult movements of the seventeenth century. As to the ritual side of the Operative Masonry in that century we know next to nothing, while of Rosicrucian ritual procedure- if any- we know nothing at all.

Such in rough outline is the case as it stands for the interference of two Hermetic Schools in Freemasonry, prior to the first historical evidence for the ritual of the Third Craft degree and apart from any long since exploded hypothesis which has sought to connect the Brotherhood with older Mysteries by means of direct transmission within their own bends. I have registered my feelings that some day it may assume a less uncertain aspect, in other words that sources of additional knowledge may become available. I know that the root-matter of the Third degree belongs to the Secret Tradition and is not only of the Hermetic Schools but of Schools thereunto antecedent. This is not a speculative question or one of simple persuasion. It is, moreover, no question of history and does not stand or fall with particular personalities and with claims made concerning them. As regards these there is work remaining to be done- that is to say, in the purely historic field, but unfortunately the subject has only a few sympathizers in England and among these a small proportion only who are qualified to work therein. In the meantime it remains that the position of Hermetic Schools, so far delineated, is not unlike that of speculation on Comacines, Roman Collegia, and Dionysian architects. When we pass, however, to the third Hermetic School the position is, I think, different.

The root-matter of much that is shadowed forth in the traditional history of the Craft, as regards the meaning of the Temple and the search for the Lost Word, is to be found in certain great texts known to scholars under the generic name of Kabalah. We find therein after what manner, according to mystic Israel, Solomon's Temple was spiritualized; we find profound meanings attached to the, two pillars J and B; we find how a Word was lost and under what circumstances the chosen people were to look for its recovery. It is an expectation for Jewish theosophy, as it is for the Craft Mason. It was lost owing to a certain untoward event, and although the time and circumstances of its recovery have been calculated in certain texts, there has been something amiss with the methods. Those who were keepers of the tradition died with their faces towards Jerusalem, looking for that time; but for Jewry at large the question has passed long since from the field of view, much as the quest is continued by Masons in virtue of a ceremonial formula but cannot he said to mean anything for those who undertake and pursue it officially. It was lost owing to the unworthiness of Israel, and the destruction of the First Temple was one consequence thereof. By the waters of Babylon, in their exile, the Jews are said to have remembered Zion, but the Word did not return into their hearts; and when Divine Providence inspired Cyrus to project the building of a second temple and the return of Israel into their own land, they went back empty of all recollection in this respect.

The Word to which reference is made in that Divine Name out of the consonants of which we have formed **Jehovah,** or, by another speculation, **Yahve.** When Israel fell into a state that is termed impenitence it is said in Zoharic symbolism that VAV and HE final were separated. The name was thus dismembered, and this is the first sense of loss which is registered concerning it. The second is that it has no proper vowel points, those of the name ELOHIM being substituted, or alternatively, of the name ADONAI. It is said, for example: "My name is written YHVH and read ADONAI." The epoch of restoration and completion is called, almost indifferently, that of resurrection, the world to come and the advent of Messiah. In such day the present separation between the letters will reach its term, once and forever.

It is also to this Kabalistic source, rather than to the variant account in the first book of Kings or in Chronicles, that we must have recourse for the important Masonic symbolism concerning the pillars J and B. There is very little in Holy Scripture to justify a choice of those objects as particular representatives of an art of building spiritualized. But in later Kabalism, in the texts called *The Garden of Pomegranates* and *The Gates of Light* there is a very full explanation of the strength which is attributed to B, the left hand pillar, and of that which is "established" in and by the right hand pillar, called J.

As regards the temple itself, I have explained elsewhere after what manner it is spiritualized in various Kabalistic and semi- Kabalistic texts, so that it appears as "the proportion of the height, the proportion of the depth, and the lateral proportion" of the created universe. It offers another aspect of the fatal loss to Israel and the world which is commented on in the Tradition. That which the temple symbolizes above all things is, however, a House of Doctrine, and as on the one hand the Zohar shows us how a loss and substitution were perpetuated through centuries, owing to the idolatry of Israel at the foot of Mount Horeb in the wilderness of Sinai, and illustrated by the breaking of the tables of stone on which the Law was inscribed, so does Speculative Masonry intimate that the Holy House, which was planned and begun after one manner, was completed after another and a word of death was substituted for a word of life.

But if these are among the sources of Craft Masonry, taken at its culmination in the Sublime degree, what manner of people were those who grafted so strange a speculation and symbolism on the Operative procedure of a building guild, even when this has been symbolized? The answer is that all about the period which represents what is called the "transition," and indeed between the sixteenth and eighteenth centuries many Latin-writing scholars of Europe were animated with zeal for an exposition of the tradition in Israel, with the result that memorable and even great books were produced on the subject. But this zeal for Kabalistic literature had more than a scholastic basis. It was believed that the texts of the Secret Tradition showed plainly, out of the mouth of Israel itself, that the Messiah had come. This is the first fact. The second is in Ceremonial Masonry itself, and, namely, that although the central event of the Third degree is the candidate's raising, it is not said in the legend that the Master Builder rose, thus suggesting that something remains to come after, which might at once complete the legend and conclude the quest. The third fact is that in an important high grade of a philosophical kind, now almost unknown, the Master Builder of the Third degree rises as Christ. The dismembered Divine Name is completed therein by insertion of the Hebrew letter SHIN, thus producing YEHESHUAH, the official restoration of the Lost Word in the Christian degrees of Masonry. It follows that although the opening and closing of the Third degree and the legend of the Master-Builder, with all their speaking Mysteries, may seem to come from very far away, they are not so remote that we cannot trace them to their source.

It is to be observed that the presence of a Kabalistic element in the traditional history of the Craft by no means connotes antiquity, and antiquity is a difficult thing to predicate of the Third degree, at least in its present form. By whomsoever created or developed, its author was a student of the Secret Tradition in Israel, and drew great lights therefrom, possibly at first hand, but much more probably perhaps from those Latin commentaries and synopses already mentioned. The bulk of these were already compiled, whether we place his work late in the seventeenth or early in the eighteenth century. Much of it was available previously, supposing that more considerable antiquity could be predicated of the Third degree. But we must cleave to that which is evidentially reasonable in this respect, until time or circumstances shall provide better warrants. For Speculative Masonry as a whole we may have to rest content also, if we cannot date it much further back than the close of the seventeenth century, recognizing that its present characteristic developments are to be sought in and about the Revival period. Such recognition puts an end to romantic hypotheses, but the great intimations of the Third degree remain a speaking pageant in Symbolism, however late its origin. The quest of the Word remains, with all Zoharic Theosophy behind it and all the rites of Christian Masonry in front. The mythos connects our Order with the figurative Mysteries of past ages, while the opening and closing of the lodge in that degree are much greater than anything in the memorials of Greece and Egypt.

I shall, therefore, reach a general conclusion on the Hermetic Schools and their alleged intervention for the transformation of an Operative Guild into an Emblematic Freemasonry and it shall be expressed in such a manner as will be without detriment to ourselves or our connections as loyal and devoted Masons. In Dionysian architects, Roman Collegia, Gomacines, and Building Guilds of the Middle Ages, I have failed to discover any traces of an art of building spritualized. I have taken the old Gothic Constitutions and have sought to digest them like Anderson "in a new and better method"; but, however they were passed and repassed through the mental alembic, they have yielded nothing corresponding to a "system of morality veiled in allegory and illustrated by symbols." Not even the Regius MSS. betray a single vestige, though I have followed Gould anxiously. As regards the Hermetic Schools, and speaking, if I may venture to say so, as one who knows the literature, the allegation of Albert Pike is true in respect of a few world-wide symbols which prove nothing and false in all things else. There is no legend of three Grand Masters in Alchemy; there is no Substituted Word; and there is no Master of the lodge, for there is no need of ritual procedure among all its cloud of witnesses. The witness of Alchemy to Masonry is the witness of Elias Ashmole, the sole alchemist in the seventeenth century whom we know to have become a Mason. The Rosicrucian influence I believe to have been marked in character and exercised for a considerable period, but we know it only in its developments which belong to the eighteenth century, and are, of course, beyond our scope. Provisionally, and under all reserve, I am inclined to hold that it began earlier, but more especially as an atmosphere belonging to the formative period of Emblematic Freemasonry. But the great Rosicrucian maxim cited by Robert Fludd about 1630 must be ruled out unfortunately. *Transmutemini, transmutemini de lapidibus mortuis in lapides vivos philosophicos,* does not signify that the Brothers of the Rosy Cross had either joined or invented our figurative and speculative art; it is rather a contract established between material and spiritual alchemy. For the present, at least, we are asked also to set aside the winning speculation concerning a secret school of Emblematic Masonry co-existent through several generations or centuries with the Operative Guild and sometimes identified with Rosicrucians. There are no Rosicrucian traces prior to 1578. Moreover, the alleged school is a notion arising out of a false construction of the Regius MS.

We are left in this manner with the Kabalistic element about which I have spoken plainly. But now, as a last point, supposing that there is no trace of Third degree prior to 1717, that after this epoch it was devised by a group of Masonic literati or alternatively by an anonymous brother, whether famous like Desaguliers, or obscure; what, then, is our position? My own at least is this: that the Third degree was formulated on the basis of the Ancient Mysteries and illustrated by the light of Kabalism: facts about which there is no open question; that it belongs as such to an old and secret tradition, though not in respect of time; that it stands on its own symbolical value and that, in the words of Martines de Pasqually: We must needs be content with what we have. As a student of the past, again

I could wish that it were otherwise; but in this, as in all else, the first consideration is truth. There are high grades of Masonry for which no one in his senses predicates antiquity, and yet they are great grades. They are even holy grades, which, from my point of view, carry on the work of the Craft towards something that stands for completion. I conclude, therefore, with an affirmation which I have made in other places, that antiquary *per se* is not a test of value. I can imagine a rite created at this day which would be much greater and more eloquent in symbolism than anything that we work and love under the name of Masonry. Yet, for what Masonic antiquity is, let us call it two hundred years, under all needful reserves, such an invention would not have the hallowed and beloved associations, which have grown about our Emblematic Craft. Here is the matter of antiquity, which really signifies: it is part of the life of the Order. And after all the fables and all the fond reveries, the false analogies and mythical identifications with other and immemorial Mysteries, it is again the life which counts, the life of that great world-wide Masonic organism, in which we ourselves live and move and have our Masonic being.

FAMA FRATERNITATIS

THE FAMA FRATERNITATIS OF THE MERITORIOUS ORDER OF THE ROSY CROSS, ADDRESSED TO THE LEARNED IN GENERAL, AND THE GOVERNORS OF EUROPE

The original edition of the "Universal Reformation" contained the manifesto bearing the above title, but which the notary Haselmeyer declares to have existed in manuscript as early as the year 1610, as would also appear from a passage in the Cassel edition of 1614, the earliest which I have been able to trace. It was reprinted with the "Confessio Fraternitatis" and the "Allgemeine Reformation der Ganzen Welt" at Franckfurt-on-the-Mayne in 1615. A Dutch translation was also published in this year, and by 1617 there had been four Franckfurt editions, the last omitting the "Universal Reformation," which, though it received an elaborate alchemical elucidation by Brotoffer, seems gradually to have dropped out of notice. "Other editions," says Buhle, "followed in the years immediately succeeding, but these it is unnecessary to notice. In the title-page of the third Franckfurt edition stands--*First printed at Cassel* in the year 1616. But the four first words apply to the original edition, the four last to this.

Fama Fraternitatis
or
A Discovery of the Fraternity of the Most Laudable Order of the Rosy Cross

Seeing the only wise and merciful God in these latter days hath poured out so richly His mercy and goodness to mankind, whereby we do attain more and more to the perfect knowledge of His Son Jesus Christ and of Nature, that justly we may boast of the happy time wherein there is not only discovered unto us the half part of the world, which was heretofore unknown and hidden, but He hath also made manifest unto us many wonderful and never-heretofore seen works and creatures of Nature, and, moreover, hath raised men, endued with great wisdom, which might partly renew and reduce all arts (in this our spotted and imperfect age) to perfection, so that finally man might thereby understand his own nobleness and worth, and why he is called *Microcosmos*, and how far his knowledge extends in Nature.

Although the rude world herewith will be but little pleased, but rather smile and scoff thereat; also the pride and covetousness of the learned is so great, it will not suffer them to agree together; but were they united, they might, out of all those things which in this our age God doth so richly bestow on us, collect *Librum Naturæ*, or, a Perfect Method of all Arts. But such is their opposition that they still keep, and are loath to leave, the old course, esteeming Porphyry, Aristotle, and Galen, yea, and that which hath but a mere show of learning, more than the clear and manifested Light and Truth. Those, if they were now living, with much joy would leave their erroneous doctrines; but here is too great weakness for such a great work. And although in Theology, Physics, and Mathematics, the truth doth oppose it itself, nevertheless, the old Enemy, by his subtilty and craft, doth shew himself in hindering every good purpose by his instruments and contentious wavering people.

To such an intention of a general reformation, the most godly and highly-illuminated Father, our Brother, C.R.C., a German, the chief and original of our Fraternity, hath much and long-time labored, who, by reason of his poverty (although descended of noble parents), in the fifth year of his age was placed in a cloister, where he had learned indifferently the Greek and Latin tongues, and (upon his earnest desire and request), being yet in his growing years, was associated to a Brother, P.A.L., who had determined to go to the Holy Land. Although this Brothers dyed in Ciprus, and so never came to Jerusalem, yet our Brother C.R.C. did not return, but shipped himself over, and went to Damasco, minding from thence to go to Jerusalem. But by reason of the feebleness of his body he remained still there, and by his skill in physic he obtained much favor with the Turks, and in the meantime he became acquainted with the Wise Men of Damcar in Arabia, and beheld what great wonders they wrought, and how Nature was discovered unto them.

Hereby was that high and noble spirit of Brother C.R.C. so stirred up, that Jerusalem was not so much now in his mind as Damasco; also he could not bridle his desires any longer, but made a bargain with the Arabians that they should carry him for a certain sum of money to Damcar.

He was but of the age of sixteen years when he came thither, yet of a strong Dutch constitution. There the Wise Men received him not as a stranger (as he himself witnesses), but as one whom they had long expected; they called him by his name, and shewed him other secrets out of his cloister, whereat he could not but mightily wonder.

He learned there better the Arabian tongue, se that the year following he translated the book M into good Latin, which he afterwards brought with him. This is the place where he did learn his Physick and his Mathematics, whereof the world hath much cause to rejoice, if there were more love and less envy.

After three years he returned again with good consent, shipped himself over *Sinus Arabicus* into Egypt, where he remained not long, but only took better notice there of the plants and creatures. He sailed over the whole Mediterranean Sea for to come unto Fez, where the Arabians had directed him.

It is a great shame unto us that wise men, so far remote the one, from the other, should not only be of one opinion, hating all contentious writings, but also be so willing and ready, under the seal of secrecy, to impart their secrets to others. Every year the Arabians and Africans do send one to another, inquiring one of another out of their arts, if happily they had found out some better things, or if experience had weakened their reasons. Yearly there came something to light whereby the Mathematics, Physic, and Magic (for in those are they of Fez most skillful) were amended. There is now-a-days no want of learned men in Germany, Magicians, Cabalists, Physicians, and Philosophers, were there but more love and kindness among them, or that the most part of them would not keep their secrets close only to themselves.

At Fez he did get acquaintance with those which are commonly called the Elementary inhabitants, who revealed unto him many of their secrets, as we Germans likewise might gather together many things if there were the like unity and desire of searching out secrets amongst us.

Of these of Fez he often did confess, that their Magia was not altogether pure, and also that their Cabala was defiled with their Religion; but, notwithstanding, he knew how to make good use of the same, and found still more better grounds for his faith, altogether agreeable with the harmony of the whole world, and wonderfully impressed in all periods of time. Thence proceeds that fair Concord, that as in every several kernel is contained a whole good tree or fruit, so likewise is included in the little body of man, the whole great world, whose religion, policy, health, members, nature, language, words, and works, are agreeing, sympathizing, and in equal tune and melody with God, Heaven, and Earth; and that which is disagreeing with them is error, falsehood, and of the devil, who alone is the first, middle, and last cause of strife, blindness, and darkness in the world. Also, might one examine all and several persons upon the earth, he should find that which is good and right is always agreeing with itself, but all the rest is spotted with a thousand erroneous conceits.

After two years Brother R.C. departed the city Fez, and sailed with many costly things into Spain, hoping well, as he himself had so well and profitably spent his time in his travel, that the learned in Europe would highly rejoice with him, and begin to rule and order all their studies according to those sure and sound foundations. He therefore conferred with the learned in Spain, shewing unto them the errors of our arts, and how they might be corrected, and from whence they should gather the true *Inditia* of the times to come, and wherein they ought to agree with those things that are past; also how the faults of the Church and the whole *Philosophia Moralis* were to be amended. He shewed them new growths, new fruits, and beasts, which did concord with old philosophy, and prescribed them new Axiomata, whereby all things might fully be restored. But it was to them a laughing matter, and being a new thing unto them, they feared that their great name would be lessened if they should now again begin to learn, and acknowledge their many years' errors, to which they were accustomed, and wherewith they had gained them enough. Who so loveth unquietness, let him be reformed (they said). The same song was also sung to him by other nations, the which moved him the more because it happened to him contrary to his expectation, being then ready bountifully to impart all his arts and secrets to the learned, if they would have but undertaken to write the true and infallible Axiomata, out of all faculties, sciences, and arts, and whole nature, as that which he knew would direct them, like a globe or circle, to the only middle point and *centrum*, and (as it is usual among the Arabians) it should only serve to the wise and learned for a rule, that also there might be a society in Europe which might have gold, silver, and precious stones, sufficient for to bestow them on kings for their necessary uses and lawful purposes, with which [society] such as be governors might be brought up for to learn all that which God hath suffered man to know, and thereby to be enabled in all times of need to give their counsel unto those that seek it, like the Heathen Oracles.

Verily we must confess that the world in those days was already big with those great commotions, laboring to be delivered of them, and did bring forth painful, worthy men, who brake with all force through darkness and barbarism, and left us who succeeded to follow them. Assuredly they have been the uppermost point in *Trygono igneo*, I whose flame now should be more and more brighter, and shall undoubtedly give to the world the last light.

Such a one likewise hath Theophrastus been in vocation and callings, although he was none of our Fraternity, yet, nevertheless hath he diligently read over the Book M, whereby his sharp ingenium was exalted; but this man was also hindered in his course by the multitude of the learned and wise-seeming men, that he was never able peaceably to confer with others of the knowledge and understanding he had of Nature. And therefore in his writings he rather mocked these busy bodies, and doth not shew them altogether what he was; yet, nevertheless, there is found with him well grounded the afore-named Harmonia, which without doubt he bad imparted to the learned, if he had not found them rather worthy of subtle vexation then to be instructed in greater arts and sciences. He thus with a free and careless life lost his time, and left unto the world their foolish pleasures.

But that we do not forget our loving Father, Brother C.R., he after many painful travels, and his fruitless true instructions, returned again into Germany, the which he heartily loved, by reason of the alterations which were shortly to come, and of the strange and dangerous contentions. There, although he could have bragged with his art, but specially of the transmutations of metals, yet did he esteem more Heaven, and men, the citizens thereof, than all vain glory and pomp.

Nevertheless, he built a fitting and neat habitation, in the which he ruminated his voyage and philosophy, and reduced them together in a true memorial. In this house he spent a great time in the mathematics, and made many fine instruments, *ex omnibus hujus artis partibus*, whereof there is but little remaining to us, as hereafter you shall understand.

After five years came again into his mind the wished for Reformation; and in regard [of it] he doubted of the aid and help of others, although he himself was painful, lusty, and unwearisome; howsoever he undertook, with some few adjoined with him, to attempt the same. Wherefore he desired to that end to have out of his first cloister (to the which he bare a great affection) three of his brethren, Brother G.V., Brother I.A., and Brother I.O., who had some mere knowledge of the arts than at that time many others had. He did bind those three unto himself, to be faithful, diligent, and secret, as also to commit carefully writing all that which he should direct and instruct them in, to the end that those which were to come, and through especial revelation should be received into this Fraternity, might not be deceived of the least syllable and word.

After this manner began the Fraternity of the Rosie Cross--first, by four persons only, and by them was made the magical language and writing, with a large dictionary, which we yet daily use to God's praise and glory, and do find great wisdom therein. They made also the first part of the Book M, but in respect that that labor was too heavy, and the unspeakable concourse of the sick hindered them, and also whilst his new building (called *Sancti Spiritus*) was now finished, they concluded to draw and receive yet others more into their Fraternity. To this end was chosen Brother R.C., his deceased father's brother's son; Brother B., a skillful painter; G.G., and. P.D., their secretary, all Germans except I.A., so in all they were eight in number, all bachelors and of vowed virginity, by whom was collected a book or volume of all that which man can desire, wish, or hope for.

Although we do now freely confess that the world is much amended within an hundred years, yet we are assured that our Axiomata shall immovably remain unto the world's end, and also the world in her highest and last age shall not attain to see anything else; for our ROTA takes her beginning from that day when God spoke *Fiat* and shall end when he shall speak *Pereat*; yet God's clock strikes every minute, where ours scarcely strikes perfect hours. We also steadfastly believe, that if our Brethren and Fathers had lived in this our present and clear light, they would more roughly have handled the Pope, Mahomet, scribes, artists, and sophisters, and showed themselves more helpful, not simply with sighs and wishing of their end and consummation.

When now these eight Brethren had disposed and ordered all things in such manner, as there was not now need of any great labor, and also that everyone was sufficiently instructed and able perfectly to discourse of secret and manifest philosophy, they would not remain any longer together, but, as in the beginning they had agreed, they separated themselves into several countries, because that not only their Axiomata might in secret be more profoundly examined by the learned, but that they themselves, if in some country or other they observed anything, or perceived some error, might inform one another of it.

Their agreement was this:--

First, That none of them should profess any other thing then to cure the sick, and that gratis.

Second, None of the posterity should be constrained to wear one certain kind of habit, but therein to follow the custom of the country.

Third, That every year, upon the day C., they should meet together at the house *Sancti Spiritus*, or write the cause of his absence.

Fourth, Every Brother should look about for a worthy person who, after his decease, might succeed him.

Fifth, The word R.C. should be their seal, mark, and character.

Sixth, The Fraternity should remain secret one hundred years.

These six articles they bound themselves one to another to keep; five of the Brethren departed, only the Brethren B. and D. remained with the Father, Brother R.C., a whole year. When these likewise departed, then remained by him his cousin and Brother I.O., so that he hath all the days of his life with him two of his Brethren. And although that as yet the Church was not cleansed, nevertheless, we know that they did think of her, and what with longing desire they looked for. Every year they assembled together with joy, and made a full resolution of that which they had done. There must certainly have been great pleasure to hear truly and without invention related and rehearsed all the wonders which God hath poured out here and there throughout the world. Every one may hold it out for certain, that such persons as were sent, and joined together by God and the Heavens, and chosen out of the wisest of men as have lived in many ages, did live together above all others in highest unity, greatest secrecy, and most kindness one towards another.

After such a most laudable sort they did spend their lives, but although they were free from all diseases and pain, yet, notwithstanding, they could not live and pass their time appointed of God. The first of this Fraternity which dyed, and that in England, was I.O., as Brother C. long before had foretold him; he was very expert, and well learned in Cabala, as his Book called H witnesses. In England he is much spoken of, and chiefly because he cured a young Earl of Norfolk of the leprosy. They had concluded, that, as much as possibly could be, their burial place should be kept secret, as at this day it is not known unto us what is become of some of them, yet every one's place was supplied with a fit successor. But this we will confess publicly by these presents, to the honor of God, that what secret so ever we have learned out of the book M, although before our eyes we behold the image and pattern of all the world, yet are there not shewn unto us our misfortunes, nor hour of death, the which only is known to God Himself, who thereby would have us keep in a continual readiness. But hereof more in our Confession, where we do set down thirty-seven reasons wherefore we now do make known our Fraternity, and proffer such high mysteries freely, without constraint and reward. Also we do promise more gold then both the Indies bring to the King of Spain, for Europe is with child, and will bring forth a strong child, who shall stand in need of a great godfather's gift.

After the death of I.O., Brother R.C. rested not, but, as soon as he could, called the rest together, and then, as we suppose, his grave was made, although hitherto we (who were the latest) did not know when our loving Father R.C. died, and had no more but the bare names of the beginners, and all their successors to us. Yet there came into our memory a secret, which, through dark and hidden words and speeches of the hundred years, Brother A., the successor of D. (who was of the last and second row of succession, and had lived amongst many of us), did impart unto us of the third row and succession; otherwise we must confess, that after the death of the said A., none of us had in any manner known anything of Brother C.R., and of his first fellow-brethren, then that which was extant of them in our philosophical BIBLIOTHECA, amongst which our AXIOMATA was held for the highest, ROTA MUNDI for the most artificial, and PROTHEUS for the most profitable. Likewise, we do not certainly know if these of the second row have been of like wisdom as the first, and if they were admitted to all things.

It shall be declared hereafter to the gentle reader not only what we have heard of the burial of Brother R.C., but also it shall be made manifest publicly, by the foresight, sufferance, and commandment of God, whom we most faithfully obey, that if we shall be answered discreetly and Christian-like, we will not be ashamed to set forth publicly in print our names and surnames, our meetings, or anything else that may be required at our hands.

Now, the true and fundamental relation of the finding out of the high-illuminated man of God, *Fra: C.R.C.*, is this:--After that A. in *Gallia Narbonensi* was deceased, there succeeded in his place our loving Brother N.N. This man, after he had repaired unto us to take the solemn oath of fidelity and secrecy, informed us *bona fide*, that A. had comforted him in telling him, that this Fraternity should ere long not remain so hidden, but should be to all the whole German nation helpful, needful, and commendable, of the which he was not in anywise in his estate ashamed. The year following, after he had performed his school right, and was minded now to travel, being for that purpose sufficiently provided with Fortunatus' purse, he thought (he being a good architect) to alter something of his building, and to make it more fit. In such renewing, he lighted upon the Memorial Table, which was cast of brass, and contained all the names of the Brethren, with some few other things. This he would transfer into another more fitting vault, for where or when Brother R.C. died, or in what country he was buried, was by our predecessors concealed and unknown unto us. In this table stuck a great nail somewhat strong, so that when it was with force drawn out it took with it an indifferent big stone out of the thin wall or plaster of the hidden door, and so unlooked for uncovered the door, whereat we did with joy and longing throw down the rest of the wall and cleared the door, upon which was written in great letters—

Post CXX Annos Patebo,

with the year of the Lord under it. Therefore we gave God thanks, and let it rest that same night, because first we would overlook our *Rota*--but we refer ourselves again to the Confession, for what we here publish is done for the help of those that are worthy, but to the unworthy, God willing, it will be small profit. For like as our door was after so many years wonderfully discovered, also there shall he opened a door to Europe (when the wall is removed), which already doth begin to appear, and with great desire is expected of many.

In the morning following we opened the door, and there appeared to our sight a vault of seven sides and seven corners, every side five foot broad, and the height of eight foot. Although the sun never shined in this vault, nevertheless, it was enlightened with another sun, which had learned this from the sun, and was situated in the upper part in the center of the siding. In the midst, instead of a tomb-stone, was a round altar, covered with a plate of brass, and thereon this engraved:--

A. C. R. C. *Hoc universi compendium unius mihi sepulchram feci.*

Round about the first circle or brim stood,

Jesus mihi omnia.

In the middle were four figures, enclosed in circles, whose circumscription was,

1. *Nequaquam Vacuum.*
2. *Legis Jugum.*
3. *Libertas Evangelii.*
4. *Dei Gloria Intacta.*

This is all clear and bright, as also the seventh side and the two heptagons. So we kneeled down altogether, and gave thanks to the sole wise, sole mighty, and sole eternal God, who hath taught us more than all men's wits could have found out, praised be His holy name. This vault we parted in three parts, the upper part or siding, the wall or side, the ground or floor. Of the upper part you shall understand no more at this time but that it was divided according to the seven sides in the triangle which was in the bright center; but what therein is contained you (that are desirous of our Society) shall, God willing, behold the same with your own eyes. Every side or wall is parted into ten squares, everyone with their several figures and sentences, as they are truly shewed and set forth *concentratum* here in our book. The bottom again is parted in the triangle, but because therein is described the power and rule of the Inferior Governors, we leave to manifest the same, for fear of the abuse by the evil and ungodly world. But those that are provided and stored with the Heavenly Antidote, do without fear or hurt, tread on and bruise the head of the old and evil serpent, which this our age is well fitted for. Every side or wall had a door for a chest, wherein there lay diverse things, especially all our books, which otherwise we had, besides the *Vocabulario* of Theophrastus Paracelsus of Hohenheim, and these which daily unfalsifieth we do participate. Herein also we found his *Itinerarium* and *Vita*, whence this relation for the most part is taken. In another chest were looking-glasses of diverse virtues, as also in other places were little bells, burning lamps, and chiefly wonderful artificial songs--generally all was done to that end, that if it should happen, after many hundred years, the Fraternity should come to nothing, they might by this only vault be restored again.

Now, as we had not yet seen the dead body of our careful and wise Father, we therefore removed the altar aside; then we lifted up a strong plate of brass, and found a fair and worthy body, whole and unconsumed, as the same is here lively counterfeited, with all the ornaments and attires. In his hand he held a parchment called T, the which next unto the Bible is our greatest treasure, which ought not to be delivered to the censure of the world. At the end of this book standeth this following *Elogium*.

Granum pectori Jesu insitum.

C.R.C. ex nobili atque splendida Germaniæ R.C. familia oriundus, vir sui seculi divinis revelationibus, subtilissimis imaginationibus, indefessis laboribus ad cœlestia atque humana mysteria; arcanavè admissus postquam suam (quam Arabico at Africano itineribus collejerat) plus quam regiam, atque imperatoriam Gazam suo seculo nondum convenientem, posteritati eruendam custodivisset et jam suarum Artium, ut et nominis, fides ac conjunctissimos heredes instituisset, mundum minutum omnibus motibus magno illi respondentem fabricasset hocque tandem preteritarum, præsentium, et futurarum, rerum compendio extracto, centenario major, non morbo (quem ipse nunquam corpore expertus erat, nunquam alios infestare sinebat) ullo pellente sed Spiritis Dei evocante, illuminatam animam (inter Fratrum amplexus et ultima oscula) fidelissimo Creatori Deo reddidisset, Pater delictissimus, Frater suavissimus, præceptor fidelissimus, amicus integerimus, a suis ad 120 annos hic absconditus est.

Underneath they had subscribed themselves,

1. *Fra.* I.A. *Fra.* C.H. *electione Fraternitatis caput.*
2. *Fra.* G.V.M.P.C.

3. *Fra. F.R.C., Junior hæres S. Spiritus.*
4. *Fra. F.B.M.P.A., Pictor et Architectus.*
5. *Fra. G.G.M.P.I., Cabalista.*

Secundi Circuli.

1. *Fra. P.A. Successor, Fra. I.O., Mathematicus.*
2. *Fra. A. Successor, Fra. P.D.*
3. *Fra. R. Successor Patris C.R.C., cum Christo triumphantis.*

At the end was written,

Ex Deo nascimur, in Jesu morimur, per Spiritum Sanctum reviviscimus.

At that time was already dead, Brother I.O. and Brother D., but their burial place where is it to be found? We doubt not but our *Fra. Senior* hath the same, and some especial thing laid in earth, and perhaps likewise hidden. We also hope that this our example will stir up others more diligently to enquire after their names (which we have therefore published), and to search for the place of their burial; the most part of them, by reason of their practice and physick, are yet known and praised among very old folks; so might perhaps our GAZA be enlarged, or, at least, be better cleared.

Concerning *Minutum Mundum*, we found it kept in another little altar, truly more finer then can be imagined by any understanding man, but we will leave him undescribed until we shall be truly answered upon this our true-hearted FAMA. So we have covered it again with the plates, and set the altar thereon, shut the door and made it sure with all our seals. Moreover, by instruction, and command of our ROTA, there are come to sight some books, among which is contained M (which were made instead of household care by the praiseworthy M.P.). Finally, we departed the one from the other, and left the natural heirs in possession of our jewels. And so we do expect the answer and judgment of the learned and unlearned.

Howbeit we know after a time there will now be a general reformation, both of divine and humane things, according to our desire and the expectation of others; for it is fitting, that before the rising of the Sun there should appear and break forth *Aurora*, or some clearness, or divine light in the sky. And so, in the meantime, some few, which shall give their names, may join together, thereby to increase the number and respect of our Fraternity, and make a happy and wished for beginning of our PHILOSOPHICAL CANONS, prescribed to us by our Brother R. C., and be partakers with us of our treasures (which never can fail or be wasted) in all humility and love, to be eased of this world's labors, and not walk so blindly in the knowledge of the wonderful works of God.

But that also every Christian may know of what Religion and belief we are, we confess to have the knowledge of Jesus Christ (as the same now in these last days, and chiefly in Germany, most clear and pure is professed, and is nowadays cleansed and void of all swerving people, heretics, and false prophets), in certain and noted countries maintained, defended, and propagated. Also we use two Sacraments, as they are instituted with all Forms and Ceremonies of the first and renewed Church. In *Politia* we acknowledge the Roman Empire and *Quartam Monarchiam* for our Christian head, albeit we know what alterations be at hand, and would fain impart the same with all our hearts to other godly learned men, notwithstanding our handwriting which is in our hands, no man (except God alone) can make it common, nor any unworthy person is able to bereave us of it. But we shall help with secret aid this so good a cause, as God shall permit or hinder us. For our God is not blind, as the heathen's Fortuna, but is the Churches' ornament and the honor of the Temple. Our Philosophy also is not a new invention, but as Adam after his fall hath received it, and as Moses and Solomon used it, also it ought not much to be doubted of, or contradicted by other opinions, or meanings; but seeing the truth is peaceable, brief, and always like herself in all things, and especially accorded by with *Jesus in omni parte* and all members, and as He is the true image of the Father, so is she His image, so it shall not be said, This is true according to Philosophy, but true according to Theology; and wherein Plato, Aristotle, Pythagoras, and others did hit the mark, and wherein Enoch, Abraham, Moses, Solomon, did excel, but especially wherewith that wonderful book the Bible agrees. All that same concurs together, and makes a sphere or globe whose total parts are equidistant from the center, as hereof more at large and more plain shall be spoken of in Christianly Conference (in den Boecke des Levens).

But now concerning, and chiefly in this our age, the ungodly and accursed gold-making, which hath gotten so much the upper hand, whereby under color of it, many runagates and roguish people do use great villainies, and cozen and abuse the credit which is given them; yea, nowadays men of discretion do hold the transmutation of metals to be the highest point and *fastigium* in philosophy. This is all their intent and desire, and that God would be most esteemed by them and honored which could make great store of gold, the which with unpremeditate prayers they hope to obtain of the all-knowing God and searcher of all hearts; but we by these presents publicly testify, that the true philosophers are far of another mind, esteeming little the making of gold, which is but a *paragon*, for besides that they have a thousand better things. We say with our loving Father C.R.C., *Phy. aurium nisi quantum aurum*, for unto him the whole nature is detected; he doth not rejoice that he can make gold, and that, as saith Christ, the devils are obedient unto him, but is glad that he sees the Heavens open, the angels of God ascending and descending, and his name written in the book of life.

Also we do testify that, under the name of *Chymia*, many books and pictures are set forth in *Contumeliam gloriæ Dei*, as we will name them in their due season, and will give to the pure-hearted a catalogue or register of them. We pray all learned men to take heed of these kind of books, for the Enemy never rests, but soweth his weeds until a stronger one doth root them out.

So, according to the will and meaning of *Fra.* C.R.C., we his brethren request again all the learned in Europe who shall read (sent forth in five languages) this our *Fama* and *Confessio*, that it would please them with good deliberation to ponder this our offer, and to examine most nearly and sharply their arts, and behold the present time with all diligence, and to declare their mind, either *communicato consilio*, or *singulatim* by print. And although at this time we make no mention either of our names or meetings, yet nevertheless everyone's opinion shall assuredly come to our hands, in what language so ever it be, nor any body shall fail, whoso gives but his name, to speak with some of us, either by word of mouth, or else, if there be some letter, in writing. And this we say for a truth, that whosoever shall earnestly, and from his heart, bear affection unto us, it shall be beneficial to him in goods, body, and soul; but he that is false-hearted, or only greedy of riches, the same first of all shall not be able in any manner of wise to hurt us, but bring himself to utter ruin and destruction. Also our building, although one hundred thousand people had very near seen and beheld the same, shall forever remain untouched, undestroyed, and hidden to the wicked world.

Sub umbra alarum tuarum, Jehova.

CONFESSIO FRATERNITATIS

THE CONFESSION OF THE ROSICRUCIAN FRATERNITY, ADDRESSED TO THE LEARNED OF EUROPE

The translation of this manifesto which follows the Fama in the edition accredited by the great name of Eugenius Philalethes is prolix and careless: being made not from the Latin original but from the later German version. As a relic of English Rosicrucian literature I have wished to preserve it, and having subjected it to a searching revision throughout, it now represents the original with sufficient fidelity for all practical purposes. The "Confessio Fraternitatis" appeared in the year 1615 in a Latin work entitled "Secretioris Philosophiæ Consideratio Brevio à Philippo à Gabella, Philosophiæ studioso, conscripta; et nunc primum unà cum Confessione Fraternitatis R.C.," in lucem edita, Cassellis, excudebat G. Wesselius, a 1615, Quarto." It was prefaced by the following advertisement:--

"Here, gentle reader, you shall find incorporated in our Confession thirty-seven reasons of our purpose and intention, the which according to thy pleasure thou mayst seek out and compare together, considering within thyself if they be sufficient to allure thee. Verily, it requires no small pains to induce any one to believe what doth not yet appear, but when it shall be revealed in the full blaze of day, I suppose we should be ashamed of such questionings. And as we do now securely call the Pope Antichrist, which was formerly a capital offence in every place, so we know certainly that what we here keep secret we shall in the future thunder forth with uplifted voice, the which, reader, with us desire with all thy heart that it may happen most speedily.

"FRATRES R.C."

Confessio Fraternitatis R.C. ad Eruditos Europæ.

CHAPTER I

Whatsoever you have heard, O mortals, concerning our Fraternity by the trumpet sound of the Fama R.C., do not either believe it hastily, or willfully suspect it. It is Jehovah who, seeing how the world is falling to decay, and near to its end, doth hasten it again to its beginning, inverting the course of Nature, and so what heretofore hath been sought with great pains and daily labor He doth lay open now to those thinking of no such thing, offering it to the willing and thrusting it on the reluctant, that it may become to the good that which will smooth the troubles of human life and break the violence of unexpected blows of Fortune, but to the ungodly that which will augment their sins and their punishments.

Although we believe ourselves to have sufficiently unfolded to you in the *Fama* the nature of our order, wherein we follow the will of our most excellent father, nor can by any be suspected of heresy, nor of any attempt against the commonwealth, we hereby do condemn the East and the West (meaning the Pope and Mahomet) for their blasphemies against our Lord Jesus Christ, and offer to the chief head of the Roman Empire our prayers, secrets, and great treasures of gold. Yet we have thought good for the sake of the learned to add somewhat more to this, and make a better explanation, if there be anything too deep, hidden, and set down over dark, in the Fama, or fur certain reasons altogether omitted, whereby we hope the learned will be more addicted unto us, and easier to approve our counsel.

CHAPTER II

Concerning the amendment of philosophy, we have (as much as at this present is needful) declared that the same is altogether weak and faulty; nay, whilst many (I know not how) allege that she is sound and strong, to us it is certain that she fetches her last breath.

But as commonly even in the same place where there breaks forth a new disease, nature discovers a remedy against the same, so amidst so many infirmities of philosophy there do appear the right means, and unto our Fatherland sufficiently offered, whereby she may become sound again, and new or renovated may appear to a renovated world.

No other philosophy we have then that which is the head of all the faculties, sciences, and arts, the which (if we behold our age) contains much of Theology and Medicine, but little of Jurisprudence; which searches heaven and earth with exquisite analysis, or, to speak briefly thereof, which doth sufficiently manifest the Microcosm man, whereof if some of the more orderly in the number of the learned shall respond to our fraternal invitation, they shall find among us far other and greater wonders then those they heretofore did believe, marvel at, and profess.

CHAPTER III

Wherefore, to declare briefly our meaning hereof, it becomes us to labor carefully that the surprise of our challenge may be taken from you, to shew plainly that such secrets are not lightly esteemed by us, and not to spread an opinion abroad among the vulgar that the story concerning them is a foolish thing. For it is not absurd to suppose many are overwhelmed with the conflict of thought which is occasioned by our unhoped graciousness, unto whom (as yet) be unknown the wonders of the sixth age, or who, by reason of the course of the world, esteem the things to come like unto the present, and, hindered by the obstacles of their age, live no otherwise in the world then as men blind, who, in the light of noon, discern nothing only by feeling.

CHAPTER IV

Now concerning the first part, we hold that the meditations of our Christian father on all subjects which from the creation of the world have been invented, brought forth, and propagated by human ingenuity, through God's revelation, or through the service of Angels or spirits, or through the sagacity of understanding, or through the experience of long observation, are so great, that if all books should perish, and by God's almighty sufferance all writings and all learning should be lost, yet posterity will be able thereby to lay a new foundation of sciences, and to erect a new citadel of truth; the which perhaps would not be so hard to do as if one should begin to pull down and destroy the old, ruinous building, then enlarge the fore-court, afterwards bring light into the private chambers, and then change the doors, staples, and other things according to our intention.

Therefore, it must not be expected that new comers shall attain at once all our weighty secrets. They must proceed step by step from the smaller to the greater, and must not be retarded by difficulties.

Wherefore should we not freely acquiesce in the only truth then seek through so many windings and labyrinths, if only it had pleased God to lighten unto us the sixth Candelabrum? Were it not sufficient for us to fear neither hunger, poverty, diseases, nor age? Were it not an excellent thing to live always so as if you had lived from the beginning of the world, and should still live to the end thereof? So to live in one place that neither the people which dwell beyond the Ganges could hide anything, nor those which live in Peru might be able to keep secret their counsels from thee? So to read in one only book as to discern, understand, and remember whatsoever in all other books (which heretofore have been, are now, and hereafter shall come out) hath been, is, and shall be learned out of them? So to sing or to play that instead of stony rocks you could draw pearls, instead of wild beast's spirits, and instead of Pluto you could soften the mighty princes of the world? O mortals, diverse is the counsel of God and your convenience, Who hath decreed at this time to increase and enlarge the number of our Fraternity, the which we with such joy have undertaken, as we have heretofore obtained this great treasure without our merits, yea, without any hope or expectation; the same we purpose with such fidelity to put in practice, that neither compassion nor pity for our own children (which some of us in the Fraternity have) shall move us, since we know that these unhoped for good things cannot be inherited, nor be conferred promiscuously.

CHAPTER V

If there be anybody now which on the other side will complain of our discretion, that we offer our treasures so freely and indiscriminately, and do not rather regard more the godly, wise, or princely persons then the common people, with him we are in no wise angry (for the accusation is not without moment), but with all we affirm that we have by no means made common property of our arcana, albeit they resound in five languages within the ears of the vulgar, both because, as we well know, they will not move gross wits, and because the worth of those who shall be accepted into our Fraternity will not be measured by their curiosity, but by the rule and pattern of our revelations. A thousand times the unworthy may clamor, a thousand times may present themselves, yet God hath commanded our ears that they should hear none of them, and hath so compassed us about with His clouds that unto us, His servants, no violence can be done; wherefore now no longer are we beheld by human eyes, unless they have received strength borrowed from the eagle.

For the rest, it hath been necessary that the Fama should be set forth in everyone's mother tongue, lest those should not be defrauded of the knowledge thereof; whom (although they be unlearned) God hath not excluded from the happiness of this Fraternity, which is divided into degrees; as those which dwell in Damcar, who have a far different politick order from the other Arabians; for there do govern only understanding men, who, by the king's permission, make particular laws, according unto which example the government shall also be instituted in Europe (according to the description set down by our Christianly Father), when that shall come to pass which must precede, when our Trumpet shall resound with full voice and with no prevarications of meaning, when, namely, those things of which a few now whisper and darken with enigmas, shall openly fill the earth, even as after many secret chafing of pious people against the pope's tyranny, and after timid reproof, he with great violence and by a great onset was cast down from his seat and abundantly trodden under foot, whose final fall is reserved for an age when he shall be torn in pieces with nails, and a final groan shall end his ass's braying, the which, as we know, is already manifest to many learned men in Germany, as their tokens and secret congratulations bear witness.

CHAPTER VI

We could here relate and declare what all the time from the year 1378 (when our Christian father was born) till now hath happened, what alterations he hath seen in the world these one hundred and six years of his life, what he left after his happy death to be attempted by our Fathers and by us, but brevity, which we do observe, will not permit at this present to make rehearsal of it; it is enough for those which do not despise our declaration to have touched upon it, thereby to prepare the way for their more close union and association with us. Truly, to whom it is permitted to behold, read, and thenceforward teach himself those great characters which the Lord God hath inscribed upon the world's mechanism, and which He repeats through the mutations of Empires, such an one is already ours, though as yet unknown to himself; and as we know he will not neglect our invitation, so, in like manner, we abjure all deceit, for we promise that no man's uprightness and hopes shall deceive him who shall make himself known to us under the seal of secrecy and desire our familiarity. But to the false and to impostors, and to those who seek other things then wisdom, we witness by these presents publicly, we cannot be betrayed unto them to our hurt, nor be known to them without the will of God, but they shall certainly be partakers of that terrible commination spoken of in our Fama, and their impious designs shall fall back upon their own heads, while our treasures shall remain untouched, till the Lion shall arise and exact them as his right, receive and employ them for the establishment of his kingdom.

CHAPTER VII

One thing should here, O mortals, be established by us, that God hath decreed to the world before her end, which presently thereupon shall ensue, an influx of truth, light, and grandeur, such as he commanded should accompany Adam from Paradise and sweeten the misery of man: Wherefore there shall cease all falsehood, darkness, and bondage, which little by little, with the great globe's revolution, hath crept into the arts, works, and governments of men, darkening the greater part of them. Thence hath proceeded that innumerable diversity of persuasions, falsities, and heresies, which makes choice difficult to the wisest men, seeing on the one part they were hindered by the reputation of philosophers and on the other by the facts of experience, which if (as we trust) it can be once removed, and instead thereof a single and self-same rule be instituted, then there will indeed remain thanks unto them which have taken pains therein, but the sum of the so great work shall be attributed to the blessedness of our age.

As we now confess that many high intelligences by their writings will be a great furtherance unto this Reformation which is to come, so do we by no means arrogate to ourselves this glory, as if such a work were only imposed on us, but we testify with our Savior Christ, that sooner shall the stones rise up and offer their service, then there shall be any want of executors of God's counsel.

CHAPTER VIII

God, indeed, hath already sent messengers which should testify His will, to wit, some new stars which have appeared in *Serpentarius* and *Cygnus*, the which powerful signs of a great Council shew forth how for all things which human ingenuity discovers, God calls upon His hidden knowledge, as likewise the Book of Nature, though it stands open truly for all eyes, can be read or understood by only a very few.

As in the human head there are two organs of hearing, two of sight, and two of smell, but only one of speech, and it were but vain to expect speech from the ears, or hearing from the eyes, so there have been ages which have seen, others which have heard, others again that have smelt and tasted. Now, there remains that in a short and swiftly approaching time honor should be likewise given to the tongue, that what formerly saw, heard, and smelt shall finally speak, after the world shall have slept away the intoxication of her poisoned and stupefying chalice, and with an open heart, bare head, and naked feet shall merrily and joyfully go forth to meet the sun rising in the morning.

CHAPTER IX

These characters and letters, as God hath here and there incorporated them in the Sacred Scriptures, so hath He imprinted them most manifestly on the wonderful work of creation, on the heavens, the earth, and on all beasts, so that as the mathematician predicts eclipses, so we prognosticate the obscurations of the church, and how long they shall last. From these letters we have borrowed our magick writing, and thence have made for ourselves a new language, in which the nature of things is expressed, so that it is no wonder that we are not so eloquent in other tongues, least of all in this Latin, which we know to be by no means in agreement with that of Adam and of Enoch, but to have been contaminated by the confusion of Babel.

CHAPTER X

But this also must by no means be omitted, that, while there are yet some eagle's feathers in our way, the which do hinder our purpose, we do exhort to the sole, only, assiduous, and continual study of the Sacred Scriptures, for he that taketh all his pleasures therein shall know that he hath prepared for himself an excellent way to come into our Fraternity, for this is the whole sum of our Laws, that as there is not a character in that great miracle of the world which has not a claim on the memory, so those are nearest and likest unto us who do make the Bible the rule of their life, the end of all their studies, and the compendium of the universal world, from whom we require not that it should be continually in their mouth, but that they should appropriately apply its true interpretation to all ages of the world, for it is not our custom so to debase the divine oracle, that while there are innumerable expounders of the same, some adhere to the opinions of their party, some make sport of Scripture as if it were a tablet of wax to be indifferently made use of by theologians, philosophers, doctors, and mathematicians. Be it ours rather to bear witness, that from the beginning of the world there hath not been given to man a more excellent, admirable, and wholesome book then the Holy Bible; Blessed is he who possesses it, more blessed is he who reads it, most blessed of all is he who truly understands it, while he is most like to God who both understands and obeys it.

CHAPTER XI

Now, whatsoever hath been said in the Fama, through hatred of impostors, against the transmutation of metals and the supreme medicine of the world, we desire to be so understood, that this so great gift of God we do in no manner set at naught, but as it bringeth not always with it the knowledge of Nature, while this knowledge bringeth forth both that and an infinite number of other natural miracles, it is right that we be rather earnest to attain to the knowledge of philosophy, nor tempt excellent wits to the tincture of metals sooner than to the observation of Nature. He must needs be insatiable to whom neither poverty, diseases, nor danger can any longer reach, who, as one raised above all men, hath rule over that which loth anguish, afflict, and pain others, yet will give himself again to idle things, will build, make wars, and domineer, because he hath of gold sufficient, and of silver an inexhaustible fountain. God judges far otherwise, who exalts the lowly, and casts the proud into obscurity; to the silent he sends his angels to hold speech with them, but the babblers he drives into the wilderness, which is the judgment due to the Roman impostor who now pours his blasphemies with open mouth against

Christ, nor yet in the full light, by which Germany hath detected his caves and subterranean passages, will abstain from lying, that thereby he may fulfil the measure of his sin, and be found worthy of the axe. Therefore, one day it will come to pass, that the mouth of this viper shall be stopped, and his triple crown shall be brought to naught, of which things more fully when we shall have met together.

CHAPTER XII

For conclusion of our Confession we must earnestly admonish you, that you cast away, if not all, yet most of the worthless books of pseudo chemists, to whom it is a jest to apply the Most Holy Trinity to vain things, or to deceive men with monstrous symbols and enigmas, or to profit by the curiosity of the credulous; our age doth produce many such, one of the greatest being a stage-player, a man with sufficient ingenuity for imposition; such doth the enemy of human welfare mingle among the good seed, thereby to make the truth more difficult to be believed, which in herself is simple and naked, while falsehood is proud, haughty, and colored with a luster of seeming godly and humane wisdom. Ye that are wise eschew such books, and have recourse to us, who seek not your moneys, but offer unto you most willingly our great treasures. We hunt not after your goods with invented lying tinctures, but desire to make you partakers of our goods. We do not reject parables, but invite you to the clear and simple explanation of all secrets; we seek not to be received of you, but call you unto our more than kingly houses and palaces, by no motion of our own, but (lest you be ignorant of it) as forced thereto by the Spirit of God, commanded by the testament of our most excellent Father, and impelled by the occasion of this present time.

CHAPTER XIII

What think you, therefore, O Mortals, seeing that we sincerely confess Christ, execrate the pope, addict ourselves to the true philosophy, lead a worthy life, and daily call, intreat, and invite many more unto our Fraternity, unto whom the same Light of God likewise appears? Consider you not that, having pondered the gifts which are in you, having measured your understanding in the Word of God, and having weighed the imperfection and inconsistencies of all the arts, you may at length in the future deliberate with us upon their remedy, co-operate in the work of God, and be serviceable to the constitution of your time? On which work these profits will follow, that all those goods which Nature hath dispersed in every part of the earth shall at one time and altogether be given to you, *tanquam in centro solis et lunæ*. Then shall you be able to expel from the world all those things which darken human knowledge and hinder action, such as the vain (astronomical) epicycles and eccentric circles.

CHAPTER XIV

You, however, for whom it is enough to be serviceable out of curiosity to any ordinance, or who are dazzled by the glistering of gold, or who, though now upright, might be led away by such unexpected great riches into an effeminate, idle, luxurious, and pompous life, do not disturb our sacred silence by your clamor, but think, that although there be a medicine which might fully cure all diseases, yet those whom God wishes to try or to chastise shall not be abetted by such an opportunity, so that if we were able to enrich and instruct the whole world, and liberate it from innumerable hardships, yet shall we never be manifested unto any man unless God should favor it, yea, it shall be so far from him who thinks to be partaker of our riches against the will of God that he shall sooner lose his life in seeking us, then attain happiness by finding us.

FRATERNITAS R.C.

THE THREEFOLD DIVISION OF MYSTICISM

PART I

A magazine which has been founded to represent, and that for the first time, the whole circle of knowledge which is included under the term occult, must obviously provide at the outset a clear notion of Mysticism- what it is, and how its branches are to be tabulated. In the popular mind the conception conveyed by the word is in all respects vague and confused. It is, nevertheless, difficult at the present day to meet with any tolerably educated person, whatever his pursuit in life, who does not confess ultimately to a certain curiosity about it. Not only in professedly intellectual circles but in the commercial world, and more singularly in that of finance, in the thronged center of the city of London, where the congestion of this money-getting age is greatest, where, as at all centers, the rush of motion is swiftest, the writer of this paper has received over and over again evidence the most indubitable that there is a spirit of inquiry abroad, and a very general sentiment of interest in places where one would have thought that it would be least expected. There may be nothing solid in this interest, or serious in that inquiry, but the feeling is there and the curiosity at least is there; both in a certain way are significant that the awakening of the new spirit has an operation far outside the circle which is its visible limit, and, considering the classes referred to, this significance is perhaps greater than is the testimony of literature at the moment and the tendency of speculative thought in precisely the same direction. The case has been cited here because it indicates the need for definition, and it leads immediately to the keynote of this paper, which is this- that however profound and abstruse in some of its branches is that which we call Mysticism, a clear elementary comprehension of what it is can be very easily established even in the most ordinary mind. There is no reason inherent in the subject for the existing uncertainty and vagueness.

Mysticism admits of being separated into three chief divisions, and these are Transcendental Science, Transcendental Philosophy, and Transcendental Religion. The term transcendental applies to anything which is outside the normal sphere of experience, whether in fact, or thought, or faith. Transcendental Science deals with the operation and effects of forces generally unknown. Transcendental Philosophy is that body of doctrine which explains the phenomenal universe in accordance with the science of its secret laws. Transcendental Religion is the application of universal law to the interior nature of man. But while these comprehensive definitions are perfectly correct and acceptable, the actual limits of Mysticism are usually somewhat narrower. The idea of Transcendental Science is generally confined to such operations of unknown law as have a direct bearing upon Transcendental Religion, and Transcendental Philosophy does not commonly concern itself with the whole economy of the universe so much as with the intimate relations subsisting between the universe and man.

A definition of Mysticism, independent of its natural classifications, will illustrate this point. It has been most rightly and philosophically defined as the endeavor of the human mind to grasp the divine essence or ultimate reality of all things, and to enjoy, while in this life and in this body, the blessedness of an immediate communion with the Highest. This being the end in view, Transcendental Science consists in the knowledge of those forces, and the laws governing the same, by which the union of man with the Divine is accomplished, and Transcendental Philosophy is the wisdom which can apply these forces once their knowledge has been given. In other words, it is a practical doctrine founded upon the experience of the Mystics. So, also, Transcendental Religion is the accomplishment of the union in question. But it is proposed by THE UNKNOWN WORLD to accept everything in its broadest sense, and to treat it from that standpoint.

PART II
TRANSCENDENTAL SCIENCE

In the matter of Transcendental Science, it will be understood that this includes the whole circle of methods and processes by which occultists in the past have made themselves acquainted with the secret forces resident in man and the universe. It is the exploration of the unknown in Nature, and it has passed; hitherto, under another term which there is no reason to conceal, notwithstanding that it has been abused and misinterpreted by its friends as well as by its enemies. This term is Magic, and it is mentioned here because one of its most illustrious exponents has given a definition concerning it which is not only admirable in itself, but exhibits it as interchangeable with the term Transcendental Science.

"Magic," says Eliphas Levi, "is the traditional science of the secrets of nature, which has come down to us from the Magi." Now, this traditional science has been perpetuated in two ways- 1) by a literature which, to a large extent, veils the secrets, and 2) by occult assemblies and fraternities. THE UNKOWN WORLD will successively acquaint it readers with all that is important in all branches of the literature, and with the Mysteries which underlie its symbolism. It will acquaint them as well, up to the fullest point of possibility, with the history of the secret societies in connection with Mysticism, though at the same time the writers who may be engaged upon this work will violate no confidence with which they may have been entrusted on such a subject. Transcendental Science has several broad divisions. There is, for example, Astrology, which is the appreciation of the celestial influences in their operation upon the nature and life of man. There is Esoteric Medicine, which consists in the application of occult forces to the healing of disease in man: it includes also a traditional knowledge of the medicinal properties resident in various substances which are disregarded by ordinary pharmacy. There is Alchemy, which is the subject of a special notice elsewhere in the present issue, and does not therefore require to be defined here. It is, however, one of the most important and attractive branches of occult science. There is Divination, a term which will be made use of in THE UNKNOWN WORLD to indicate all that vast variety of methods and processes by which lucidity was supposed to be operated in suitable subjects, whether in mundane matters for the discovery of things unknown to the operator and of events to come, or in matters which are extra mundane for clairvoyant communication with spirits. This last-mentioned branch of Divination is a part of what has sometimes been termed Practical Pneumatology, and for purposes of classification it must be distinguished from that department of Transcendental Science which is commonly known as Ceremonial Magic, consisting in the scrupulous fulfillment of certain archaic rites and the operation of numerous bizarre formulae, as a result of which the Magician, or Magus, was enabled; as it is claimed, to invoke angels, demons, elemental and elementary spirits, the phantasms of the dead, and the astral entities of still living beings. A certain virtue inherent in certain words and actions is supposed by Ceremonial Magic, as also a great uninvestigated power resident in the will of the Magician, but it is open to question whether the results produced were not of the clairvoyant order.

Each and all of these Transcendental Sciences are supposed to be liable to that species of abuse which is technically known as Black Magic. The celestial influences could be perverted in the malefic composition of talismans. The malpractice of Esoteric Medicine produced the Secret Science of Poisoning, and the destruction of health, reason, or life by unseen forces. The perversion of Alchemy resulted in the sophistication of metals, and on this subject there is quite an extensive literature still extant. In like manner, Divination was debased into Witchcraft, and Ceremonial Magic into dealing with devil, compacts with demons, and other forms of transcendental delusion and imposture. The actual principles which are at the basis of the Black Art, when interpreted from the standpoint of the occultist, will be explained from time to time in THE UNKNOWN WORLD, and some extremely rare rituals never before translated will be given upon the same subject. The precise bearings of Transcendental Science upon the true ends of Mysticism will also be developed, as occasion may arise, in a very full and intelligible manner.

PART III
TRANSCENDENTAL PHILOSOPHY

As already indicated, is the mystical explanation of the universe, on the one hand, while on the other it is an explanation of the correlation subsisting between that universe and man. Thus, it expounds the process of development which operated in the creation of the world, and it expounds also the special quality of evolution which is still proceeding in humanity. The writings attributed to Hermes Trismegistus and the extraordinary body of literature comprised in the Jewish Kabbalah are good instances of a transcendental philosophy of the cosmos. They are not the only instances which have become generally known in the West, while over and above all written record there is affirmed to be the unwritten record of esoteric investigation and experience transmitted from remote ages by the occult associations before referred to, and not beyond attainment at the present day by a properly qualified aspirant. The evidences which can be gleaned in connection with this important claim will be considered at a proper time in the pages of THE UNKNOWN WORLD. Concerning the evolution of humanity and the forces at work therein, as unfolded by mystic philosophy, it seems scarcely necessary to promise that this will have adequate treatment. It leads up to the end of all mysticism, the Divine Union, which also has already been mentioned. From the Hermetic standpoint, Man is the great subject; his origin, his nature, his potentialities, his destiny, constitute the one interest. There is nothing in Transcendental Science which is of any moment except in so far as it concerns him, and assists the mind of the philosopher to understand better what he is. If his destiny be written in the stars, then the stars are of moment, and Astrology is also of moment, but not otherwise does day speak unto day or night show knowledge to night, and there is no reason in all the starry depths except in their relation to the astronomer who gages them, or to the babe who is affected by their influence. All that interests a man is man. It is the same through the whole gamut. There is no intrinsic importance in that which heals. The assuaging herb in itself is nothing; the man whom it salves is all; but when he is present the herb itself borrows importance from the possibility of its ministration to him, and from the application of his mind to its properties. Then even the "flower in the crannied wall" can tell us "what God and man is." The visible universe becomes intelligent in man, as man becomes intelligible in God. So, also, the modes of Divination are puerile, but there is no puerility about the sage who interprets the etheral world from the analogies of things which are seen. Thus, man is the focus of everything, towards him all forces tend, in him all interests center; he is that point "through which the universe is continually passing."

The very hierarchies of heaven are to him as nothing except in so far as there is some side in their nature which can adjust itself to man, so that it can exhibit a likeness to man, and put out a point for communication with him. It is for this reason that God Himself must become man in order that He can be understood by man, and can, in other and bolder words, be of any moment or importance to man, and it is also for this reason that the unknowable Deity of Agnostics is a more monstrous idol than is possessed by any pantheon. God is that which man is eternally knowing in himself, and that God is ever becoming man is a truth which must always be recognized by Mystics. Finally, the religion which most directly and vividly realizes that God takes flesh in man, and that man puts off flesh in God, is the nearest to the heart of Mysticism. It need not be here said that this is Christianity or that this is Buddhism, but, more simply that this is true religion. Thus Transcendental Science with man for its pivot gives us Transcendental Philosophy as a circle within its circle, while Transcendental Philosophy, in its turn, converging more upon the center, leads us to Transcendental Religion.

PART IV
TRANSCENDENTAL RELIGION

Now there are many definitions of religion, but there is one which includes all, just as there are many religions and one underlying all. It follows the philology of the word and exhibits it as a rebinding. There is nothing, it may be gratefully added, that is new in this definition; it is realized by many people who consciously are not Mystics, and it is intellectually understood by a still greater number who are not religious at all. The term rebinding involves the idea of something which has been set loose or has broken away from another thing. Here the reference is to the mind of man the individual which has been loosed from man the universal- the essential nature of man from the essential nature of God. It does not matter how or why this separation has taken place. It may be accepted that the Mystic has much to learn before he can plumb that mystery. It may be true that no written Mysticism, and no unwritten tradition of the inner orders, can expound it; but the end of all Mysticism as of all religion, is to attain that reunion. The possibility is not merely the fundamental doctrine of Transcendental Religion; it is the one doctrine; all else is a question of processes. Some of them may be better than some others, as some methods of divination produce the hypnotic state more readily than the rest. Hence the religion of the Mystics is the most simple, the most easy of popular understanding, because it is the least encumbered. Begin where one may in the universe it affirms that all roads ultimately lead to God. The path of vice will lead there though it passes through perdition by the way. Soul and body may be destroyed in hell but the spirit must return to God who gave it. But it is well, if it be possible, to save the soul alive, that Psyche may be united to Eros. There is no reason therefore why Mysticism should fail in the common understanding. It sees the end and it claims to know the way, while the direction of that way has no insuperable difficulties. It does not lie far from any man's walk in life, and it will be the chief object of THE UNKNOWN WORLD to simplify as far as possible the instructions of Transcendental Religion.

THE KABBALISTIC CONCLUSIONS OF
PICO DELLA MIRANDOLA

PROLOGUE

Magical legend has availed itself of the name of Mirandola, and on the warrant of his Kabbalistic enthusiasm has accredited him with the possession of a familiar demon. His was the demon of Socrates which a late Cardinal Archbishop has brought within the limits of natural and clerical orthodoxy. His marvelous precocity has furnished a thesis to the ingenuity of M. Gabriel Delanne, for, as with the music of Mozart and as with the mathematics of Pascal, it remains a ground of speculation how this Italian Crichton acquired his enormous erudition. M. Delanne would assure us that he brought it with him at his birth, that it was an inheritance from a previous life, and that Pico della Mirandola Kabbalised in a college of Babylon. On the other hand, Catholic writers, for whom his studies are unsavory, affirm that he was swindled by an impostor who sold him sixty bogus manuscripts on the assurance that they had been composed by the Order of Esdras. "They contained only ridiculous Kabbalistic reveries." These manuscripts have been enumerated and described by Gaffarel, and his monograph on the subject will be found, among other places, in the great bibliography of Wolf. We are not concerned with these nor yet with the apocryphal stories of their original authorship and eventual sale. But as Mirandola, who was born on February 24, 1463, and died mentally exhausted in 1494, is the first true Christian student of the Kabbalah, it is important to know what he derived from his studies in this respect. Now, unfortunately, we are met at the outset with a difficulty only too common in such inquiries. Of the Kabbalistic conclusions arrived at by Pico della Mirandola, and actually bearing this name, there are two absolutely different versions extant; there is that which we find in the collected editions of his works, both late and early, reproduced in the collection of Pistorius with a voluminous commentary by Archangelus de Burgo Nuovo, and there is that which we find with another commentary, though curiously by the same writer, in a little volume, published at Bologna in 1564, and again at Basle in 1600. The evidence is in favor of the first version, though I have so far failed to meet with an alleged original edition said to have been published at Rome in 1486, and therefore in the lifetime of the author. We may accept either version without prejudice to the point which it is here designed to establish, and that is the nature of the enthusiasm which prompted Pico della Mirandola. In the first place, though he speaks of magic in terms which may be held to indicate that he possessed a tolerant and open mind as to some of its claims, and, like a learned man as he was, did not regard it after the vulgar manner, he cannot be considered as, in any real sense, an occult philosopher. The only department of occult science which he has treated at any length is astrology, and to this he devoted a long, savage and undermining criticism, which in some of its salient parts is as good reading as Agrippa's "Vanity of the Sciences," and on its special subject takes much the same point of view. We should not therefore expect that he betook himself to the esoteric speculations of Jewry because he was attracted by the transcendental powers attributed to the Divine Names, because he intended to compose talismans, or because he desired to evoke. I must not speak so confidently as to possible fascinations in the direction of Gematria and Temurah, for his was a subtle and curious intelligence which found green spots or rather enchanted cities of mirage in many deserts of the mind, and he might perhaps have discovered mysteries in beheaded words and achroamatica in acrostics. There is, however, no proof that he did. The bibliographical legend which represents him purchasing manuscripts on the assurance that the prophet Esdras had a hand in their production will disclose his probable views as to the antiquity of Kabbalistic literature. He took it, we may suppose, at its word, and the legend also indicates that he was persuaded easily; it was a common weakness in men of learning and enthusiasm at the period. On the other hand, it is more than certain that he did not regard this antiquity as a presumption that the Kabbalah was superior to Latin Christianity; the wisdom which he found in the Kabbalah was the wisdom of Christian doctrine; when he hung up his famous theses in Rome and offered to defray the expenses of every scholar who would dispute with him, those theses included his Kabbalistic Conclusions, but that which he sought to establish was a via media between Jewry and Christendom. When he turned the head of Pope Julius with the secret mysteries of the Torah, the enthusiasm which was communicated for a moment to the chair of Peter was, like Lully's, that of the evangelist. The servus servorum Dei found other zeal for his ministry, and the comet of the schools blazed itself out. The Kabbalistic Conclusions alone remain to tell that Rome had a strange dream in the evening of the fifteenth century. They lie in a small compass and, as I believe it will be of interest to show what Pico della Mirandola extracted from his sixty manuscripts, I will here translate them for the reader. I ought perhaps to premise that Eliphas Levi translated some of them in his own loose fashion and published them with a suggestive commentary, in La Science des Esprits, ascribing them to the collection of Pistorius but without mentioning the name of Mirandola. He also gave what purports to be the Latin originals, but these he has polished and pointed. To do justice to his genius they are much better than the quintessential Kabbalism of Pico, but as they are neither Pico nor the Kabbalah, I shall not have recourse to them for the purposes of the following version.

NOTE: We have seen that a rival series of Kabalistic Conclusions has been referred to Pico, and so also the number of the following series is occasionally extended to seventy. The collection of Pistorius contains only those which have been cited, and they are possibly intended to connect with the Fifty Gates of Understanding, less the one gate which was not entered by Moses (thus, 49 in total). To develop any system from these aphorisms would appear almost impossible, and this difficulty has occurred to earlier critics. Their source is also uncertain like their meaning, despite the labors of their commentator, Archangelus de Burgo-Nuovo, who was himself a Christian Kabbalist, but disputatious, verbose, and with predetermined theological motives.

KABBALISTIC CONCLUSIONS

I.

As man and the priest of inferior things sacrifices to God the souls of unreasoning animals, so Michael, the higher priest, sacrifices the souls of rational animals.

II.

There are nine hierarchies, and their names are *Cherubim, Seraphim, Chasmalim, Aralim, Tarsisim, Ophanim, Ishim, Malachim, and Elohim.*

III.

Although the ineffable name is the quality of clemency, it is not to be denied that it combines also the quality of judgment.

IV.

The sin of Adam was the separation of the kingdom from the other branches.

V.

God created the world with the tree of the knowledge of good and evil, whereby the first man sinned.

VI.

The great north wind is the fountain of all souls simply, as other days are of some and not all.

VII.

When Solomon said in his prayer, as recorded in the Book of Kings, "Hear, O Heaven," we must understand by heaven the green line which encircles all things.

VIII.

Souls descend from the third light to the fourth day, and thence issuing, they enter the night of the body.

IX.

By the six days of Genesis we must understand the six extremities of the building proceeding from Bereishit as the cedars come forth out of Lebanon.

X.

Paradise is more correctly said to be the whole building than the tenth part. And in the center thereof is placed the Great Adam, who is *Tiphereth*.

XI.

A river is said to flow out from Eden and to be parted into four heads signifying that the third numeration proceeds from the second, and is divided into the fourth, fifth, sixth, and tenth.

XII.

It is true that all things depend on fate, if we understand thereby the Supreme Arbiter.

XIII.

He who shall know the mystery of the Gates of Understanding in the Kabbalah shall know also the mystery of the Great Jubilee.

XIV.

He who shall know the meridional property in dextral co-ordination shall know why every journey of Abraham was always to the south.

XV.

Unless the letter *He* had been added to the name of Abram, Abraham would not have begotten.

XVI.

Before Moses all prophesied by the stag with one horn (*i.e.*, the unicorn).

XVII.

Wheresoever the love of male and female is mentioned in Scripture, there is exhibited mystically the conjunction of *Tiphereth* and *Chienset* (or *Cheneceth*) *Israel*, or *Beth* and *Tiphereth*.

XVIII.

Whosoever shall have intercourse with *Tiphereth* in the middle night shall flourish in every generation.

XIX.

The letters of the name of the evil demon who is the prince of this world are the same as those of the name of God— *Tetragrammaton* — and he who knows how to effect their transposition can extract one from the other.

XX.

When the light of the mirror which shines not shall be like the light of the shining mirror, the day shall become as the night, as David says.

XXI.

Whosoever shall know the quality which is the secret of darkness shall know why the evil demons are more hurtful in the night than in the day.

XXII.

Granting that the co-ordination of the chariots is manifold, nevertheless, in so far as concerns the mystery of the *Philaterios,* two chariots are prepared, so that one chariot is formed from the second, third, fourth, and fifth, and these are the four philateria which *Vau* assumes, and from the sixth, seventh, eighth, and ninth a second chariot is made, and these are the philateria which the *He* final assumes.

XXIII.

More than the quality of penitence is not to be understood (or applied) in the word (which signifies) "He said."

XXIV.

When Job said: "Who maketh peace in his highest places," he signified the austral water and boreal fire, and their leader, concerning which things there must be nothing said further.

XXV.

Bereishit—i.e., in the beginning He created, is the same as if it were said: "In Wisdom He created."

XXVI.

When Onkelos the Chaldean said: "*Buadmin*" —i.e., with or by the Eternals, he understood the Thirty-two Paths of Wisdom.

XXVII.

As the first man is the congregation of the waters, so the sea, to which all rivers run, is the Divinity.

XXVIII.

By the flying thing which was created on the fifth day we must understand angels of this world, which appear to men, and not those which do not appear, save in the spirit.

XXIX.

The name of God, composed of four letters, *Mem, Tsade, Pe*, and final *Tsade*, must be referred to the Kingdom of David.

XXX.

No angel with six wings is ever transformed.

XXXI.

Circumcision was ordained for deliverance from the impure powers wandering round about.

XXXII.

Hence circumcision was performed on the eighth day, because it is above the universal bride.

XXXIII.

There are no letters in the entire Law which do not show forth the secrets of the ten numerations in their forms, conjunctions, and separations, in their twisting and direction, their deficiency and superfluity, in their comparative smallness and largeness, in their crowning, and their enclosed or open form.

XXXIV.

He who comprehends why Moses hid his face and why Ezechias turned his countenance to the wall, the same understands the fitting attitude and posture of prayer.

XXXV.

No spiritual things descending below can operate without a garment.

XXXVI.

The sin of Sodom was the separation of the final branch.

XXXVII.

By the secret of the prayer before the daylight we must understand the quality of piety.

XXXVIII.

As fear is outwardly inferior to love, so love is inwardly inferior to fear.

XXXIX.

From the preceding conclusion it may be understood why Abraham was praised in Genesis for his fear, albeit we know by the quality of piety that all things were made from love.

XL.

Whensoever we are ignorant of the quality whence the influx comes down upon the petition which we put up, we must have recourse to the House of Judgment.

XLI.

Every good soul is a new soul coming from the East.

XLII.

Therefore Joseph was buried in the bones only and not in the body, because his bones were virtues and the hosts of the supernal tree, called *Zadith*, descending on the supernal earth.

XLIII.

Therefore also Moses knew no sepulchre, being taken up into the supernal jubilee and setting his roots above the jubilee.

XLIV.

When the soul shall comprehend all that is within its comprehension, and shall be joined with the supernal soul, it shall put off from itself its earthly garment and shall be rooted out from its place and united with Divinity.

XLV.

When prophecy by the spirit ceased, the wise men of Israel prophesied by the Daughter of the Voice.

XLVI.

A king of the earth is not manifested on the earth until the heavenly host is humbled in heaven.

XLVII.

By the word "ath," which twice occurs in the text, "In the beginning God created the heaven and the earth," I believe that Moses signified the creation of the intellectual and animal natures, which in the natural order preceded that of the heaven and the earth.

XLVIII.

That which is said by the Kabbalist, namely, that the green line encircles the universe, may be said also appropriately at the final conclusion which we draw from Porphyry.

XLIX.

Amen is the influence of numbers.

THE STONE OF THE PHILOSOPHERS

CHAPTER I
The Introduction

Because many have written of the Philosopher's Stone without any knowledge of the art; and the few books extent, written by our learned predecessors and true masters hereupon, are either lost or concealed in the collections of such (*however despised*) as are lovers and seekers of natural secrets, we have taken a resolution to communicate our knowledge in this matter, to the intent that those who are convinced the Philosophical Work is no fiction, but grounded in the possibility of Nature, may be faithfully directed in their studies, and have an undoubted criterion to distinguish between such authors as are genuine sons of science and those who are spurious, as writing by hearsay only.

We shall not on this occasion give a summary of their names who are undoubted masters in the art, but shall take occasion to introduce them, as it may be necessary, in the following chapters; and as their sense is often concealed under a studied ambiguity of expression, we shall, out of the gift which the Almighty hath dispensed to us, declare plainly, and without any reserve, the first matter of the Philosopher's Stone, the manner of proceeding through the whole process, both in the Vegetable and Metallic Tinctures, beginning with the Vegetable process first, as the most easy and simple, yet well worthy the attention of all ingenious persons, particularly the practical chemists and preparers of medicines.

CHAPTER II
Of the Vegetable Tincture, or the Process called the Lesser Circulation

Very few of the true philosophers have touched upon this subject, for it seemed trifling in respect to the great work, as the process in metals is generally termed; but there is a modern publication in English, a small thin duodecimo, without any author's name, having for its title: Aphorismi, seu Circulus majus et Circulus minus, wherein the whole process is plainly laid down.

This book is written by an undoubted master in the art; and no treatise, ancient or modern, is so explicit in the directions for conducting the great work. The directions are very short, but much to the purpose, provided the reader has an idea what part of the work is alluded to. The author, agreeable to his title, delivers his doctrine by way of aphorisms. But to return from this digression.

We proposed in this chapter to lay open the vegetable process, as a clue to the more important work in the mineral kingdom. A certain person, who is now living, and advertises balsam of honey, tincture of sage, etc, has turned his studies this way; and from his great abilities as a professed physician and botanist, has convinced all unprejudiced persons that noble tinctures may be extracted from vegetables. We hope this gentleman will not despise our free communication, both to him and the public, if we show the insufficiency of his method, though it is ingenious, while we establish the rationale of ours on the never-failing ground of truth and philosophy.

He observes, with a precision which can only result from numerous trials, that different herbs impart their tinctures in such proportions of alcohol as he has found out. It is allowed that the volatile spirit and balsamic sulphur are thus extracted; but there are the essential, or fixed, salt and sulphur of the herb yet left in the process. These require another management to extract, which he is either ignorant of, or is so disingenuous as to conceal from the public; but that so noble a secret may lie open to all for a general advantage, here follows a plain account of the vegetable work.

Take any herb which is potent in medicine, and either extract the tincture with spirit of wine, or distil in the common way; reserve the distilled water, or tincture, when separated from the feces, for use. Then take the feces, or Caput Mortuum, and calcine it to a calx. Grind this to powder.

That done, take the water, or tincture, and mix them together; distil again, and calcine, forcing the moisture over by a retort, in a wary process, calcining and cohobating the spirit on the salt till it attains a perfect whiteness and oily nature, like the finest alkali, commonly called Flemish.

As your salt requires it in the process, have in readiness more of the extracted tincture, or distilled spirit, that you may not work it, viz., the salt, too dry; and yet proceed cautiously, not adding too much of the moisture, so that the dealbating, or whitening, may keep visibly heightening at every repetition of the process. Frequent experiments may enable you to push it on to a redness, but a fine yellow is the best of all; for the process tends, in its perfection at this period, to a state of dryness, and must be managed with a strong fire. By following these directions, you have here the two tinctures in the Vegetable Kingdom, answering to the white and red tinctures in the mineral.

CHAPTER III
Of the Uses of the Vegetable Tinctures, with some general remarks on their great efficacy in medicine

You have, by carefully following our directions above, procured the tinctures, white or yellow, in the Vegetable Kingdom. The yellow is more efficacious if the work is well performed; either of them, by being exposed in the air, will soon run into a thick, essential oil, smelling very strong of the plant, and the virtues of any quantity may be concentrated by often repeating the circulation. But you have no need of this, unless for curiosity, there being in your tinctures a real permanent power to extract the essential virtues of any herb you may require on immersion only, where the essential salt and volatile spirit, together with the sulphureous oil, are all conjoined, floating on the top of your tincture, and the terrestrial feces precipitated to the bottom; not as in distillation, or extraction of the tincture with alcohol, while the stalk and texture of the plant are entire; no, this Vegetable Tincture devours the whole substance of the plant, and precipitates only the earthy particles acquired in its vegetation, which no degree of calcination could push to an alkali, without its essential salt.

Such is the virtue of our Vegetable Tincture; and if the operation be never so often repeated with different herbs, it loses nothing of its virtue, or quantity or quality, casting up the virtues of whatever herb is immersed, and precipitating the earth as before when both are easily separated and the medicine preserved for use.

Let a medicine, thus prepared, be examined, and the principles by which it is extracted, with the general methods of preparation; if the distilled water for instance, of any aromatical or balsamic herb, be took, common experience will convince us that nothing but its volatile parts come over the head; but take the Caput Mortuum, and it will calcine after this process, and afford an alkali, which proves itself to be an essential salt by its pungency, and will, in the air, run to an oil, which is its essential sulphur. If you take the tincture extracted with alcohol, it is the same, only the more resinous parts of some herbs may enrich the extract, and the volatile sulphur giving the color and scent, be retained, which escapes in distillation; but the potent virtue or soul of the herb, if we may be allowed the expression, goes to the dunghill. It is the same if the expressed juice of the herb is used; and if taken in powder, or substance, as it is sometimes prescribed, but little of its virtue, beyond its nourishing quality, can be communicated to the patient, except as a bitter or a vermifuge, in which cases, perhaps, it is best by way of infusion.

Let none despise the operation above laid down, because it is not to be found in the ordinary books of chemistry; but consider the possibility of Nature, who brings about wonderful effects by the most simple causes: neither let any imagine this process so easy as to perform it without some trials, patiently attending to her operations and endeavoring to account for any deficiency in the course of his work. For this reason it will be proper that the artist forms to himself an idea what the intention is to procure, how far Nature has prepared his matter to work upon, in what state she has left it, and how far it may be exalted above the ordinary point of virtue, which it could attain in the crude air, and this by the Philosophic Art assisting Nature, as a handmaid, with an administration of due heat, which is nutritive and not corrosive.

A recapitulation of the foregoing process, with some remarks on the different stages, will be sufficient here to explain our meaning above, and prepare the reader for what follows concerning the metallic tincture, or Stone of the Philosophers.

The virtues of herbs and simples are confessedly great and manifold; among these, some are poisonous and narcotic, yet of great use in medicine; none of them but want some preparation or correction. Now the common ways of doing this are defective; neither preserving the virtue entire, nor furnishing any menstruum capable of doing it with expedition and certainty. Alcohol, as was before observed, will extract a tincture and distillation a spirit. We reject neither of these methods in our work, as they are useful to decompound the subject; but we are not content with a part of its virtues.

To speak philosophically, we would have its soul, which is in its Essential Salt, and its spirit, which is in the Inflammable Sulphur. The body in which these resided we are not concerned for; it is mere earth, and must return from whence it came: whereas the soul and spirit are paradisiacal, if the artist can free them from their earthy prison without loss; but this can only be done by death. Understand us aright. Philosophically speaking, no more is meant than decomposition of the subject into its first principles, as the uniting them more permanently with an increase of virtue is most emphatically called a resurrection and regeneration. Now this decompounding is to be done with judgment, so as not to corrode or destroy, but divide the matter into its integral parts. At this period of the work the artist will consider what is further intended, keeping Nature in view, who, if she is properly assisted in her operations, produces from the dissolution of any subject something more excellent, as in a grain of corn, or any vegetable seed, which by cultivation may be pushed to a surprising produce; but then it must die first, as our Blessed Saviour very emphatically observes: and let this saying dwell upon the artist's imagination, that he may know what he generally intends; for the whole philosophical work, both in vegetables and minerals, is only a mortifying of the subject, and reviving it again to a more excellent life.

Now if the intention in the foregoing process was to increase simply any vegetable in its kind, the destruction and revivification must follow the ordinary course of vegetation by the medium of seed; and Nature can only be assisted by fertilizing the soil, together with a proper distribution of heat and moisture. Yet there are not wanting authors, and particularly Paracelsus, who boldly describe processes wherein the vital quality of the seed has been destroyed by calcination, and yet brought to life again at the pleasure of an artist. Such reveries are a scandal to philosophy, and a snare to the superficial reader, who is generally more struck with impossibilities, roundly asserted, than the modesty of true artists. These confess their operations are within the bounds of Nature, whose limits they cannot surpass.

The reader, then, will consider that our intention here is not to increase the seminal quality, but to concenter, in a little compass, the medicinal virtues of a herb. Nature is desirous of this in all her productions, but can only rise to such a point of perfection, in her ordinary course, through the crudity of the air and fixing power of the elements. Now if we take the vegetables at that point of perfection to which she has pushed them, and farther assist her in decompounding, purifying, uniting, and reviving the subject, we obtain, what she could not otherwise produce, a real permanent tincture, the quintessence, as it is called, or such a harmonious mixture of the four elementary qualities as constitutes a fifth, from thenceforth indissoluble, and not to be debased with any impurity.

But the virtue of this Vegetable Tincture is capable of improvement ad infinitum, in its own kind, by adding more of its spirit or extracted tincture, and repeating the circulation, which is every time more speedily finished, as there is a magnetical quality in the fixed salt, and essential oil, which assimilates to itself all the real virtues of what is added, only rejecting the feculent, earthy qualities; so that in a grain of the tincture much virtue may be concentered, not at all corrosive or ardent, but friendly to the animal life, and most powerful as a medicine for disorders which the herb is appropriated to cure. Nay, something of this nature was still sought for by the distillers of ardent spirits, when phlegm has been drawn away from the volatile sulphur, till it becomes proof spirit, as it is termed, which will burn dry, a plain indication that it contained nothing essential in it from the subject out of which it was extracted: for that which is essential cannot be destroyed by the fire, but is reddened to an alkaline salt, having in its center an Incombustible Sulphur, which, on exposing to the air, manifests itself both to the sight and touch. Now, if this Salt and Sulphur are purified, and the distilled spirit, or extracted tincture, added, Nature finds a subject wherein she can carry her operations to the highest limit, if an artist furnishes her with proper vessels, and a degree of heat suitable to her intentions.

CHAPTER IV
Of the Metallic Tincture

When we undertook a description of the vegetable process, it was chiefly with a view to familiarize the reader to a general idea of the Philosophic Work in metals, as both proceed upon the same principles, only the mercuries of metals are more difficult to extract, and stronger degrees of heat are required, as well as more of the artist's time and patience; neither can he succeed in the operation without frequent trials, and a constant consideration within his mind as to what is within the possibility of Nature.

For this purpose it is necessary to know the composition of metals, that he may know how to decompound and reduce them to their first principles, which is treated of very mysteriously by the philosophers, and purposely concealed, as the right key to unlock all the secrets of

Nature. We shall be more explicit on this head, for the time draws near when, as Sendivogius has observed, the confection of the Stone will be discovered as plainly as the making of cheese from rennet. But we warn the reader not to imitate Midas in the fable, by seeking the noble tincture in metals out of covetousness; for the true wise men seek only a medicine for human infirmities, and esteem gold but as it furnishes them with the means of independence and the exercise of universal beneficence. They communicate their talents, without vain glory or ostentation, to such as are worthy searchers of Nature, but concealing their names as much as possible, while living, as well as their knowledge of the mystery from the world.

We shall herein follow their example, and yet write more plainly of the Metallic Process than any of them has hitherto done, knowing that the providence of the Most High will effectually guard this Arcanum from falling into the hands of covetous gold seekers and knavish pretenders to the Art of Transmutation; because the first sort of men will, from their impatience, soon leave the simplicity of Nature for processes of more subtlety invented by the latter, and adapted to such avaricious views as the other have formed, who, judging of things by their own griping dispositions, know not the noble liberality of Nature, but imagine some gold must be advanced before she will replenish their heaps. This is well foreseen by those smoke sellers, who receive what they can catch, as if they were her proper agents; and, having no conscience to put a stop to their imposition, the deception is kept up till all vanishes in smoke.

Let it be observed, then, that all who have written on the art, from undoubted principles, assert that the genuine process is not expensive; time and fuel, with manual labour, being all allowed for. Besides, the matter to be wrought upon is easy to procure by the consent of all. A small quantity of gold and silver is, indeed, necessary when the stone is made, as a medium for its tinging either in the white or red tinctures, which such pretenders have urged from books of philosophers as a plausible pretense to rob the avaricious both of their time and money; but their pretenses are so gross that none can be sufferers in this respect, if they have not justly deserved it.

The reader may then rest assured that this process is not expensive, and reject all authors or practitioners who advance anything contrary to this established verity, remembering the simplicity of Nature in her operations, observing her frugal method in the production, and consummate wisdom in the dissolution of things; always endeavoring at something perfect in a new production. And because we are here proposing to help her in a metallic process, as before in the vegetable, let us consider a little how she forms the metals, in what state she has left them, and what need there is of the artist's skill to assist her in pushing them to that degree of perfection they are capable of attaining.

All true philosophers agree that the First Matter of metals is a moist vapor, raised by the action of the central fire in the bowels of the earth, which, circulating through its pores, meets with the crude air, and is coagulated by it into an unctuous water, adhering to the earth, which serves it for a receptacle, where it is joined to a sulphur more or less pure, and a salt more or less fixing, which it attracts from the air, and, receiving a certain degree of concoction from the central and solar heat, is formed into stones and rocks, minerals, and metals. These were all formed of the same moist vapor originally, but are thus varied from the different impregnations of the sperm, the quality of salt and sulphur with which it is fixed, and the purity of the earth which serves it for a matrix; for whatever portion of this moist vapor is taking along its impurities, is soon deprived of heat, both solar and central, and the grosser parts, forming a mucilaginous substance, furnish the matter of common rocks and stones. But when this moist vapor is sublimed, very slowly, through a fine earth, not partaking of a sulphureous unctuously, pebbles are formed; for the sperm of these beautiful, variegated stones, with marbles, alabasters, etc., separates this depurated vapor, both for their first formation and continual growth. Gems are in like manner formed of this moist vapor when it meets with pure salt water, with which it is fixed in a cold place. But if it is sublimed leisurely through places which are hot and pure, where the fatness of sulphur adheres to it, this vapor, which the philosophers call their Mercury, is joined to that fatness and becomes an unctuous matter, which coming afterwards to other places, cleansed by the afore-named vapors, where the earth is subtle, pure, and moist, fills the pores of it, and so gold is made.

But if the unctuous matter comes into places cold and impure, lead, or Saturn, is produced; if the earth be cold and pure, mixed with sulphur, the result is copper. Silver also is formed of this vapor, where it abounds in purity, but mixed with a laser degree of sulphur and not sufficiently concocted. In tin, or Jupiter, as it is called, it abounds, but in less purity. In Mars, or iron, it is in a lesser proportion impure, and mixed with an adjust sulphur.

Hence it appears that the First Matter of metals is one thing, and not many, homogeneous, but altered by the diversity of places and sulphurs with which it is combined. The philosophers frequently describe this matter.

Sendivogius calls it heavenly water, not wetting the hands; not vulgar, but almost like rain water. When Hermes calls it a bird without wings, figuring thereby its vaporous nature, is it well described. When he calls the sun its father and the moon its mother, he signifies that it is produced by the action of heat upon moisture. When he says the wind carries it in its belly, he only means that the air is its receptacle. When he affirms that which is inferior is like that which is superior, he teaches that the same vapor on the surface of the earth furnishes the matter of rain and dew, wherewith all things are nourished in the vegetable and animal kingdoms. This now is what the philosophers call their Mercury and affirm it to be found in all things, as it is in fact. This makes some suppose it to be in the human body, others in the dunghill, which has often bewildered such as are fond of philosophical subtleties, and fly from one thing to another, without any fixed theory about what they would seek, expecting to find in the Vegetable or Animal Kingdoms the utmost perfection of the Mineral. To this mistake of theirs, without doubt, the philosophers have contributed with an intention of hiding their First Matter from the unworthy; in which they were, perhaps, more cautious than is necessary, for Sendivogius declares that occasionally, in discourse, he had intimated the art plainly word by word to some who accounted themselves very accurate philosophers; but they conceived such subtle notions, far beyond the simplicity of Nature, that they could not, to any purpose, understand his meaning. Wherefore, he professes little fear of its being discovered but to those who have it according to the good pleasure and providence of the Most High.

This benevolent disposition has induced him to declare more openly the First Matter, and fix the artist in his search of it to the mineral kingdom; for, quoting Albertus Magnus, who wrote that, in his time, grains of gold were found betwixt the teeth of a dead man in his grave, he observes that Albertus could not account for this miracle, but judged it to be by reason of the mineral virtue in man, being confirmed by that saying of Morien: "And this matter, O King, is extracted from thee." But this is erroneous, for Morien understood those things philosophically, the mineral virtue residing in its own kingdom, distinct from the animal.

It is true, indeed, in the animal kingdom mercury, or humidity, is as the matter, and sulphur, or marrow in the bones, as the virtue; but the animal is not mineral, and vice versa. If the virtue of the animal sulphur were not in man, the blood, or mercury, could not be coagulated into flesh and bones; so if there were not a vegetable sulphur in the vegetable kingdom, it could not coagulate water, or the vegetable mercury, into herbs, etc. The same is to be understood in the mineral kingdom.

These three kingdoms do not, indeed, differ in their virtue, nor the three sulphurs, as every sulphur has a power to coagulate its own mercury; and every mercury has a power of being coagulated by its own proper sulphur, and by no other which is a stranger to it.

Now the reason why gold was found betwixt the teeth of a dead man is this: because in his lifetime mercury had been administered to him, either by unction, turbid, or some other way; and it is the nature of this metal to ascend to the mouth, forming itself an outlet there, to be evacuated with the spittle. If, then, in the time of such treatment, the sick man died, the mercury, not finding an egress, remained in his mouth between his teeth, and the carcass becoming a natural matrix to ripen the mercury, it was shut up for a long time, till it was congealed into gold by its own proper sulphur, being purified by the corrosive phlegm of the man's body; but this would never have happened if mineral mercury had not been administered to him.

CHAPTER V
Of the Second Matter, or Seed in Metals

All philosophers affirm, with one consent, that metals have a seed by which they are increased, and that this seminal quality is the same in all of them; but it is perfectly ripened in gold only, where the bond of union is so fixed that it is most difficult to decompound the subject, and procure it for the Philosophical Work. But some, who were adepts in the art, have by painful processes taken gold for their male, and the mercury, which they knew how to extract from the less compacted metals, for a female: not as an easier process, but to find out the possibility of making the stone this way; and have succeeded, giving this method more openly to conceal the true confection, which is most easy and simple. We shall, therefore, set before the reader a landmark, to keep him from tripping on this difficulty, by considering what is the seed wherein the metals are increased, that the artist may be no longer at a loss where to seek for it, keeping in view the writings of our learned predecessors on this subject.

The seed of metals is what the Sons of Wisdom have called their mercury, to distinguish it from quicksilver, which it nearly resembles, being the radical moisture of metals. This, when judiciously extracted, without corrosives, or fluxing, contains in it a seminal quality whose perfect ripeness is only in gold; in the other metals it is crude, like fruits which are yet green, not being sufficiently digested by the heat of the sun and action of the elements. We observed that the radical moisture contains the seed, which is true: yet it is not the seed, but the sperm only, in which the vital principle floats, being invisible to the eye. But the mind perceives it, and in a true artist, as a central point of condensed air, wherein Nature, according to the will of God, has included the first principles of life in everything, as well animal and vegetable as mineral; for in animals the sperm may be seen, but not the included principle of impregnation: this is a concentered point, to which the sperm serves only as a vehicle, till, by the action and ferment of the matrix, the point wherein Nature has included a vital principle expands itself, and then it is perceivable in the rudiments of an animal. So in any succulent fruit (*as, for instance, in an apple*), the pulp or sperm is much more in proportion than the seed included; and even that which appears to be seed is only a finer concoction of sperm, including the vital stamina; as also in a grain of wheat the flour is only the sperm, the point of vegetation is an included air, which is kept by its sperm from the extremes of cold and heat, till it finds a proper matrix, where the husk being softened with moisture, and warmed by the heat, the surrounding sperm putrefies, making the seed, or concentered air, to expand and to burst the husk carrying along in its motion a milky substance, assimilated to itself from the putrefied sperm. This the condensing quality of the air includes in a film and hardens into a germ, all according to the purpose of Nature.

"If this whole process of Nature, most wonderful in her operations, was not constantly repeated before our eyes, the simple process of vegetation would be equally problematical with that of the philosophers; yet how can the metals increase, nay, how can anything be multiplied without seed? The true artists never pretend to multiply metals without it, and can it be denied that Nature still follows her first appointment? She always fructifies the seed when it is put into a proper matrix. Does not she obey an ingenious artist, who knows her operations, with her possibilities, and attempts nothing beyond them? A husbandman

162

meliorates his ground with compost, burns the weeds, and makes use of other operations. He steeps his seed in various preparations, only taking care not to destroy its vital principle; indeed, it never comes into his head to roast it, or to boil it, in which he shows more knowledge of Nature than some would-be philosophers do. Nature, like a liberal mother, rewards him with a more plentiful harvest, in proportion as he has meliorated her seed and furnished a more suitable matrix for its increase.

"The intelligent gardener goes farther; he knows how to shorten the process of vegetation, or retard it. He gathers roses, cuts salads, and pulls green peas in winter. Are the curious inclined to admire plants and fruit of other climates? He can produce them in his stoves to perfection. Nature follows his directions unconstrained, always willing to obtain her end, viz., the perfection of her offspring.

"Open your eyes here, yet studious searchers of Nature! Is she so liberal in her perishing productions, how much more in those which are permanent, and can subsist in the fire? Attend, then, to her operations; if you procure the metallic seed, and ripen that by art which she is many ages in perfecting, it cannot fail but she will regard you with an increase proportioned to the excellency of your subject.

"The reader will be apt to exclaim here: "Very fine! All this is well; but how shall the seed of metals be procured, and whence comes it that so few know how to gather it?' To this it is answered that the philosophers have hitherto industriously kept that a profound secret; some out of selfish disposition, though otherwise good men. Others, who wished only for worthy persons to whom they might impart it, could not write of it openly, because covetousness and vanity have been governing principles in the world: and, being wise men, they knew that it was not the will of the most High to inflame and cherish such odious tempers, the genuine offspring of pride and self-love, but to banish them out of the earth, wherefore they have been withheld hitherto. But we, finding no restraint on our mind in that respect, shall declare what we know: and the rather because we judge the time is come to demolish the golden calf, so long had in veneration by all ranks of men, insomuch that worth is estimated by the money a man possesses; and such is the inequality of possessions that mankind are almost reducible to the rich, who are rioting in extravagance, and the poor, who are in extreme want, smarting under the iron hand of oppression. Now the measure of inequality among the rich hastens to its limit, and the cry of the poor is come before the Lord: "Who will give them to eat till they shall be satisfied?"

Hereafter the rich shall see the vanity of their possessions when compared with the treasures communicated by this secret; for the riches it bestows are a blessing from God, and not the squeezing of oppression. Besides, its chief excellence consists in making a medicine capable of healing all diseases to which the human body is liable, and prolonging life to the utmost limits ordained by the Creator of all things.

There want not other reasons for the manifestation of the process; for skepticism has gone hand in hand with luxury and oppression, insomuch that the fundamental truths of all revealed religion are disputed. These were always held in veneration by the possessors of this art, as may be seen from what they have left upon record in their books: and, indeed, the first principles of revealed religion are demonstrated from the whole process, for the seed of metals is shown in corruption, and raised in incorruption; it is sown a natural body, and raised a spiritual body; it is known to partake of the curse which came upon the earth for man's sake, having in its composition a deadly poison, which can only be separated by regeneration in water and fire; it can, when it is thoroughly purified and exalted, immediately tinge imperfect metals and raise them to a state of perfection, being in this respect a lively emblem of that seed of the woman, the Serpent Bruiser, who, through His sufferings and death, hath entered into glory, having thenceforth power and authority to redeem, purify, and glorify all those who come unto Him as a mediator between God and mankind.

Such being our motives, we can no longer be silent concerning the seed of metals, but declare that it is contained in the ores of metals, as wheat is in the grain; and the sottish folly of alchemists has hindered them from adverting to this, so that they have always sought it in the vulgar metals, which are factitious and not a natural production, therein acting as foolishly as if a man should sow bread and expect corn from it, or from an egg which is boiled hope to produce a chicken. Nay, though the philosophers have said many times the vulgar metals are dead, not excepting gold, which passes the fire, they could never imagine a thing so simple as that the seed of metals was contained in their ores, where alone it ought to be expected; so bewildered is human ingenuity, when it leaves the beaten track of truth and Nature, to entangle itself in a multiplicity of fine-spun inventions.

The searcher of Nature will rejoice greatly in this discovery, as grounded in reason and sound philosophy, but to fools it would be in vain, should even wisdom herself cry out in the streets. Wherefore, leaving such persons to hug themselves in their own imaginary importance, we shall go on to observe that the ores of metals are our First Matter, or sperm, wherein the seed is contained, and the key of this art consists in a right dissolution of the ores into a water, which the philosophers call their mercury, or water of life, and an earthy substance, which they have denominated their sulphur.

The first is called their woman, wife, Luna, and other names, signifying that it is the feminine quality in their seed; and the other they have designated their man, husband, Sol, etc., to point out its masculine quality.

In the separation and due conjunction of these with heat, and careful management, there is generated a noble offspring, which they have for its excellency called the quintessence or a subject wherein the four elements are so completely harmonized as to produce a fifth subsisting in the fire, without waste of substance, or diminution of its virtue, wherefore they have given it the titles of Salamander, Phoenix, and Son of the Sun.

CHAPTER VI
Of the Dissolution and Extraction of the Seed in Metals

The true Sons of Science have always accounted the dissolution of metals as the master key to this art, and have been particular in giving directions concerning it, only keeping their readers in the dark as to the subject, whether ores, or factitious metals, were to be chosen: nay, when they say most to the purpose, then they make mention of metals rather than the ores, with an intention to perplex those whom they thought unworthy of the art.

Thus the author of the "Philosophical Duet," or a dialogue between the stone, gold, and mercury, says:

"By the omnipotent God, and on the salvation of my soul, I here declare to you earnest seekers, in pity to your earnest searching, the whole Philosophical Work, which is only taken from one subject and perfected in one thing. For we take this copper, and destroy it crude and gross body;

we draw out its pure spirit, and after we have purified the earthy parts, we join them together, thus making a Medicine of a Poison."

It is remarkable that he avoids mentioning the ore, but calls his subject copper, which is what they call a metal of the vulgar, being indeed factitious, and not fit for the confection of our Stone, having lost its seminal quality in the fire; but in other respects it is the plainest discovery extant, and is accounted to be so by Sendivogius.

Yet the reader is not to suppose that the ore of copper is to be chosen in consequence of that assertion, as preferable to others. No, the mercury, which is the metallic seed, is attainable from all, and is easier to be extracted from lead, which is confirmed by the true adepts, advising us to seek for the noble child where it lies in a despised form, shut up under the seal of Saturn; and, indeed, let it be supposed, for an illustration of this subject, that any one would propose to make malt, he may effect his purpose in the other grains, but barley is generally chosen, because its germ is made to sprout by a less tedious process, which is to all intents and purposes what we want in the extraction of our mercury: neither are the proceeding different in both cases, if regard is had to the fixity of ores, and the ease with which barley gives forth its seminal virtue from the slight cohesion of its parts.

Let the artist remark how a maltster manages his grain by wetting, to loosen the cohesion of its parts, and leaves the rest to Nature, knowing that she will soon furnish the necessary heat for his purpose, if he does not suffer it to escape by mismanagement in his laying of his heap too thin, or raising the fermentation too high by a contrary proceeding, as it is well known actual fire may be kindled from the fermentation of vegetable juices when crude; and ripe corn, under such treatment, would soon be fit for nothing but hogs, or the dunghill. Now the intention is to raise such a fermentation only as will draw out the vegetable mercury without spoiling it, either for the earth, if it was cast there to fructify, or the kiln, if it is to be fixed at that precise point, by exhaling the Adventitious moisture, and thus preserving the whole strength of its seminal quality for the purposes of brewing, or making malt spirits.

Suppose, then, an artist would extract a mineral mercury from the ores, and chooses an ore for his subject. He can only assist Nature in the process by stirring up a central heat, which she includes in everything not already putrefied, as a root of its life, in which it is increased. The medium by which this central heat is put in motion is known to be putrefaction; but the ores of every kind are found to resist putrefaction in all known processes extant. They may, indeed, when they have been fluxed in the fire, contract a rust from the air, which is a gradual decomposition of their substance, but this is only the natural decay of a dead body, not the putrefaction of its sperm for the purposes of propagation; and we are sensible from the heat of furnaces which is required to flux the ores, and the slowness of their decay when deprived of their seminal qualities, by fluxation, that a heat which would destroy the seed in vegetables may be necessary in the first stages of putrefaction for the ores, as they will bear a red fire without being fluxed or losing anything but their sulphureous and arsenical impurities; in short, a matter in itself as much extraneous to the seed of metals, as the chaff to the wheat; wherefore, a careful separation of these by roasting, or otherwise, is deservedly reckoned among the first operations for the putrefaction of ores, and the rather because that which has been calcined, by having its pores opened, is rendered attractive, both of the air and other menstruums proper for its decomposition.

Let the artist, therefore, by fire and manual operation, separate the impure qualities from his subject, pounding, washing, and calcining, till no more blackness is communicated to his menstruum, for which pure rain water is sufficient. It will be seen on every repetition of this process, that what fouls the water is extraneous and the ore yet exists in its individual metallic nature, except it is fluxed by a too intense heat, in which case it is no longer fit for our purpose; therefore fresh ore is to be used.

The matter being thus prepared, its central fire will be awakened, if it is treated properly, according to the process for extracting quicksilver from its ores, by keeping it in a close heat, which is continued without admission of the crude air, till the radical moisture is elevated in the form of a vapor, and again condensed into a metallic water, analogous to quicksilver.

This is the true mercury of the Philosophers, and fit for all their operations in the Hermetic Art.

CHAPTER VII
Of the Separation and Further Treatment of our Philosophical Seed

The Putrefaction of our subject being thus completed, it exists under two forms; the moisture which was extracted, and the residuum, being our Philosophical Earth. The water contains its seminal virtue, and the earth is a proper receptacle, wherein it may fructify. Let the water, then, be separated and kept for use; calcine the earth, for an impurity adheres to it which can only be taken away by fire, and that, too, of the strongest degree; for here there is no danger of destroying the seminal quality, and our earth must be highly purified before it can ripen the seed. This is what Sendivogius means when he says: Burn the sulphur till it becomes Sulphur incombustible. Many lose in the preparation what is of most use in the art; for our mercury is corrected (*healed*) by the sulphur, else it would be of no use. Let, therefore, the earthy part be well calcined, and return the mercury on the calcined earth; afterwards draw it off by distillation; then calcine, cohere, and distill, repeating the process till the mercury is well corrected by the sulphur, and the sulphur is purified to a whiteness, and goes on to red, a sign of its complete purification, where you have the Philosophical Male and Female ready for conjunction.

This must now be managed with judgment, as the noble child may be yet strangled in the birth; but all things are easy to an ingenious artist, who knows the proportion of mixture required and accommodates his operations to the intention of Nature, for which purpose we shall faithfully conduct him according to our ability.

CHAPTER VIII
Of the Union or Mystical Marriage in the Philosophical Process

The seed and its earth being thus prepared, nothing remains but a judicious conjunction of them together; for it too much moisture prevails, the philosophical egg may burst before it can go through the heat necessary for its hatching. To speak without a figure. Our subject must now be enclosed in a small glass vial, made strong enough to bear a due heat, which is to be raised gradually to the highest degree: the best form for this vessel being that of an oil flask, with a long neck; but these are much too thin in substance for this operation. In such a vessel the mixture is to be sealed hermetically, and digested so long till it is fixed into a dry concretion; but, if, as we observed, the moisture should predominate, there is great danger of the vessel bursting, with a vapor which cannot be concentered by the fixing quality in the matter. The intention is, nevertheless, to fix our subject in the heat, and so render its future destruction impossible.

On the other hand, if the dry, fixing quality of the sulphur exceeds so as not to suffer an alternate resolution of its substance into vapors, and a re- manifestation of its fixing quality, by causing the whole to subside in the bottom of the vessel till the matter again liquefies and sublimes (*which Ripley has well described*), there is danger of the whole vitrifying; and thus you shall have only glass instead of the noble tincture. To avoid these two extremes it is very proper that the purified earth be reduced by manual operation to an impalpable fineness, and then its corrected mercury must be added, incorporating both together till the earth will imbibe no more. This operation will require time, with some degree of the artist's patience; for however the humidity may seem disproportionate, on letting it rest awhile, a dryness on the surface of your matter will show that it is capable of imbibing more, so that the operation is to be repeated till it is fully saturated, which may be known from its bearing the air without any remarkable change of surface from dry to humid; or, on the contrary, if so, the conjunction is well made, which is farther confirmed if a small portion be spread upon a thin plate if iron, heated till it flows gently like wax, casting forth the moisture with heat and again absorbing it when cold, so as to return to the former consistence; but if a clamminess ensures it is a sign you have exceeded in the quantity of humidity, which must be extracted by distilling again and repeating the process till it is right.

Your sulphur and mercury being thus united, put them into a glass vial, before described, in such a quantity as to take up one-third of its contents, leaving two-thirds, including the neck, for the circulation of your matter.

Secure the neck of your vial with a temporary luting at the first, and give a gentle heat, observing whether it sublimes and fixes alternately. If it easily sublimes and shows a disposition, at intervals, to subside at the bottom of the vessel, all is well conducted hitherto; for the moisture will first be predominant, which the sulphur can only perfectly absorb as the heat is increased for the perfect ripening of our Paradisiacal Fruit. Therefore, if it manifests a too early disposition for fixing, add more of the corrected mercury till Luna rises resplendent in her season; she will give place to the Sun in his turn. This would be the language of an adept on this occasion, only suggesting that the female quality in our prepared seed is first active, while the male is passive, and that it is afterwards passive while the male is active, such being the case in all vegetation; for every germ which is the first rudiments of a herb or tree, is predominant in moisture, and then only becomes fixed when it is fully concocted in the seed.

CHAPTER IX
Of the Further Treatment and Ripening of our Seed

This is deservedly called the Great Work of the Philosophers; and the artist having done his part hitherto, must seal up his glass hermetically, an operation which every maker of barometers knows how to perform.

The glass is then to be put into a furnace with a proper nest contrived for its reception, so as to give a continual heat from the first to the fourth degree, and to afford the artist an opportunity, from time to time, of inspecting every change which his matter assumes during the process, without danger of damping the heat and putting a stop to its perfect circulation. A heat of the first degree is sufficient at the first, for some months, in which method much time may be lost by a young practitioner, till he knows how to handle his matter from experience; but then he is not so liable to be disappointed with the bursting of his vessel or the matter vitrifying.

Thus you have arrived at the desired seed-time in our Philosophical Work, which, though it may appear in the artist's power to ripen, depends no less on the Divine blessing than the harvest, which a painful husbandman has not the presumption to expect otherwise than from God's beneficence.

There are many requisites to entitle anyone to the possession of our philosophical harvest, and the true laborers in it have sought for such persons to whom they might communicate it, by evident testimony of the senses, after which they account the confection of our Stone an easy process, manageable by women and children; but without such a communication, there is a necessity that those who would undertake it are endowed by Nature with an ingenious mind, patient to observe and accurate to investigate her ordinary appearances which, from their commonness, are less noticed than such phenomena as are more curious though of less importance; yet these for the most part employ the precious

170

time of those egregious triflers, the modern virtuosi. These smatterers in discovery of a shell or butterfly differently streaked from those of the same kind: and all the while water, air, earth, fire, with their continual changes and resolutions into one another, by the medium of our atmosphere, through the efficacy of the central and solar heat, are unstudied by these would-be philosophers; so that a sensible rustic has more real knowledge, in this respect, than a collector of natural rarities, and makes a much wiser use of the experiences he has acquired.

CHAPTER X
Of the Further Process to the Ripening of our Noble Seed

Supposing such dispositions in the artist as have been previously laid down, and the work well performed hitherto, for his direction herein we shall describe the changes which our subject undergoes during the second part of the process, commonly called the Great Work of the Philosophers.

Our vessel being warily heated at the first for fear of its cracking, an ebullition of the contained matter is brought on, so that the moisture is alternately circulated in white fumes above, and condensed below, which may continue for a month or two, nay longer, increasing the heat gradually to another degree, as your matter discovers a disposition for fixing, by the vapor continuing at longer intervals condensed, and rising in a lesser quantity, of an ash color, or other dark shades, which it will assume as a medium to perfect blackness, the first desirable stage in our harvest. Other colors may be exhibited in this part of the work without danger, if they pass transiently; but if a faint redness, like that of the corn poppy, continues, the matter is in danger of vitrifying, either from an impatient urging of the fire, or the moisture not being sufficiently predominant. An ingenious artist can remedy this by opening his vessel and adding more of the corrected mercury, sealing it up as before; but a novice would do much better to prevent it by governing his fire according to the appearances of his matter, with judgment and patience, increasing it if the moisture manifests its predominancy too long, and slacking if the dry prevails, till such time as the vapors become dark; and after they have continued for some time at rest, a pellicle or film on the matter shows its disposition for fixing, retaining the vapor captive for some time, till it breaks through at different places on its surface (much like the bituminous substance of coal in a soldering fire), with darker clouds, but quickly dissipated, and growing less in quantity, till the whole substance resembles molten pitch, or the aforesaid bituminous substance, bubbling less and less, resting in one entire black substance at the bottom of your glass. This is called the blackness of black, the head of the crow, etc., and is esteemed a desirable stage in our philosophical generation, being the perfect putrefaction of our seed, which will ere long show its vital principle by a glorious manifestation of Seminal Virtue.

CHAPTER XI
A Further Description of the Process

When the putrefaction of our seed has been thus completed, the fire may be increased till glorious colors appear, which the Sons of Art have called Cauda Pavonis, or the Peacock's Tail. These colors come and go, as heat is administered approaching to the third degree, till all is of a beautiful green, and as it ripens assumes a perfect whiteness, which is the White Tincture, transmuting the inferior metals into silver, and very powerful as a medicine. But as the artist well knows it is capable of a higher concoction, he goes on increasing his fire till it assumes a yellow, then an orange or citron color; and then boldly gives a heat of the fourth degree, till it acquires a redness like blood taken from a sound person, which is a manifest sign of its thorough concoction and fitness for the uses intended.

CHAPTER XII
Of the Stone and its Uses

Having thus completed the operation, let the vessel cool, and on opening it you will perceive your matter to be fixed into a ponderous mass, thoroughly of a scarlet color, which is easily reducible to powder by scraping, or otherwise, and in being heated in the fire flows like wax, without smoking, flaming, or loss of substance, returning when cold to its former fixity, heavier than gold, bulk for bulk, yet easy to be dissolved in any liquid, in which a few grains being taken its operation most wonderfully pervades the human body, to the extirpation of all disorders, prolonging life by its use to its utmost period; and hence it has obtained the appellation of "Panacea,"or a Universal Remedy. Therefore, be thankful to the Most High for the possession of such an inestimable jewel, and account the possession of it not as the result of your own ingenuity, but a gift bestowed, of God's mere bounty, for the relief of human infirmities, in which your neighbor ought to share jointly with you, without any grudging or sinister views, according to the charge delivered to the Apostles: Freely have you received, freely communicate, remembering at the same time not to cast your pearls before swine; in a word, to withhold the manifestations of Nature you are enabled to exhibit, by the possession of our Stone, from the vicious and unworthy.

CHAPTER XIII
Of the Transmutation

It is much to be lamented that the seekers of natural knowledge in this art propose, principally, the Science of Transmutation as their ultimate view, and overlooking the chief excellency of our Stone as a medicine.

Notwithstanding this groveling spirit, we shall commit the issue to His Providence, and declare the Transmutation (*which, indeed, the philosophers do*) openly, after which we shall describe the further circulation of our Stone for an increase of its virtues, and then make an end of our treatise.

When the artist would transmute any metal- for instance, lead- let a quantity be melted in a clean crucible, to which let a few grains of gold in filings be cast; and when the whole is melted, let him have in readiness a little of the powder, which will easily scrape off from his "stone," the quantity inconsiderable, and cast it on the metal while in fusion.

Immediately there will arise a thick fume, which carries off with it the impurities contained in the lead, with a crackling noise, and leaves the substance of the lead transmuted into most pure gold, without any kind of sophistication; the small quantity of gold added, previous to projection, serves only as a medium to facilitate the transmutation, and the quantity of your tincture is best ascertained by experience, as its virtue in proportioned to the number of circulations you have given after the first has been completed.

For instance: when you have finished the stone, dissolve it in our mercury again, wherein you have previously dissolved a few grains of pure gold. This operation is done without trouble, both substances readily liquefying. Put it into your vessel, as before, and go through the process. There is no danger in the management, but breaking your vessel; and every time it is thus treated its virtues are increased, in a ratio of ten to one hundred, a thousand, ten thousand, etc., both in medicinal and transmuting qualities; so that a small quantity may suffice for the purposes of an artist during the remaining term of his life.

MYSTICISM AND OCCULTISM

There are certain conventional terms which, on the one hand, do not accurately represent the construction placed upon them along a given line, but that construction has been accepted so long and so generally that the defect in the application may be regarded as partially effaced; and, on the other hand, there are also conventional terms between which a distinction has come into existence, although it is not justified by their primary significance. As regards the first class, the very general use of the term "occult movement" may be taken as an example. It is inexact after two manners: in involves at once too much and too little – too much, because it has served to represent a good deal that is not at all of the occult order; and too little, because a slight change in the point of view would bring within the range of its meaning, many things which nobody who now uses it would think of including therein. The doings of more than one great secret political organization might, in the full sense of the words, require to be classed as part of the occult movement, though no one will need to be informed that the latter is not political; while certain events which have occurred and are occurring in the open day, and have all along challenged the verdict of public opinion, cannot strictly be included in occultism, as they betray none of its external characteristics. I refer to the phenomena of animal magnetism, hypnotism, spiritualism and all that which is included in the field of psychical research.

In respect of the second class, a very clear differentiation now exists between the terms "occult" and "mystic," and it is one also which it is necessary to recognize, though, fundamentally speaking, the two words are identical, differing only in the fact that one of them is of Latin and the other of Greek origin. By the occultist we have come to understand the disciple of one or all of the secret sciences; the student, that is to say, of alchemy, astrology, the forms and methods of divination, and of the mysteries which used to be included under the generic description of magic. The mystic is, at the first attempt, perhaps more difficult to describe, except in the terminology of some particular school of thought; he has no concern as such with the study of the secret sciences; he does not work on materials or investigate forces which exist outside himself; but he endeavors, by a certain training and the application of a defined rule of life to reestablish correspondence with the divine nature from which, in his belief, he originated, and to which his return is only a question of time, or what is commonly understood as evolution. The distinction between the occultist and the mystic, however much the representative of physical science at the present day might be disposed to resent the imputation, is therefore, loosely speaking, and at least from one point of view, the distinction between the man of science and the man of introspection. The statement, as we shall see, is not exhaustive, and it is not indeed descriptive. It may be said more fully, in the words of the late Edward Maitland, that the occultist is concerned with "transcendental physics, and is of the intellectual, belonging to science," while the mystic "deals with transcendental metaphysics, and is of the spiritual, belonging to religion." Expressed in modern terms, this is really the doctrine of Plotinus, which recognizes "the subsistence of another intellect, different from that which reasons, and which is denominated rational." Thus, on the one hand, there are the phenomena of the transcendental produced on the external plane, capable of verification and analysis, up to a certain point; and, on the other, there is the transcendental life. "That which is without corresponds with that which is within," says the most famous Hermetic maxim; indeed, the connection suggested is almost that of the circumference with the center; and if there is a secret of the soul expressed by the term mysticism, the phenomena of the soul manifesting on the external plane must be regarded as important; but these are the domain of occultism. The importance must, of course, differ as the phenomena fall into higher and lower; the divinations of geomancy carry an appearance of triviality, while the design of ceremonial magic to establish communication with higher orders of extra-mundane intelligence wears a momentous aspect; but both are the exercise of seership, and this gift, as a testimony of the soul and her powers, is never trivial.

Assuming therefore a relationship subsisting between occult practice and the transcendental life of the soul, it seems worthwhile to contrast for a moment the work of the mystic with that of the disciple of occult science, so as to realize as accurately as possible the points of correspondence and distinction between Ruusbroeck, St. John of the Cross and Saint Martin, as types of the mystic school, and Arnaldus de Villa Nova and Martinez de Pasqually, as representing the school of occult science. The examples of such a contrast must naturally be sought in the past, because, although occult science is pursued at the present day, and by some ardently, it can scarcely be said to have votaries like those who were of old. The inquiry belongs also to the past in respect of the mystic, for, to speak plainly, the saint belongs to the past. So far as the life of the outside world is concerned, there is little opportunity amidst mundane distractions for the whole-hearted labors of the other centuries. The desire of the house is indeed among us, but the zeal of it is scarcely here, not, at least, in the sense of the past.

The distinction in question is more than that which is made between the man of action and the man of reflection; it is not that which we have come to regard as differentiating the man of science from the philosopher. There are many instances of synthetic occult philosophers – among them Cornelius Agrippa and Robert Fludd – who neither divined nor evoked – who were not alchemists, astrologers or theurgists – but rather interpreters and harmonizers; and yet these men were not mystics in the proper sense of the term. Nor is the distinction quite that which constitutes the essential difference between the saint and the specialist, though the occult student of the past was in most cases a specialist who was faithful to his particular branch. The activity and the strenuousness of the life was often greater with the mystic than in the case of the man who was dedicated to some particular division of occult knowledge, though alchemist and astrologer were both laborious men – men whose patience imbued them with something of the spirit which governs modern scientific research. The ground of the contrast is in the purpose which actuated the two schools of experience. The crucible in which metals are transmuted, on the assumption of alchemy, is still a crucible and the converted metal is still a metal; so also, the astrologer may trace the occult and imponderable influences of the stars, but the stars are material bodies. The practical work of the mystic concerned, on the contrary, the soul's union with God, for, to state it briefly, this, and this only, is the end of mysticism. It is no study of psychic forces, nor, except incidentally, is it the story of the soul and her development, such as would be involved in the doctrine of reincarnation. It is essentially a religious experiment and is the one ultimate and real experiment designed by true religion. It is for this reason that in citing examples of mystics, I have chosen two men who were eminent for sanctity in the annals of the Christian Church, for we are concerned only with the West; while the third, though technically out of sympathy, essentially belonged to the Church. I must not, therefore, shrink from saying that the alternative name of the mystic is that of the saint when he has attained the end of his experiment. There are also other terms by which we may describe the occultist, but they refer to the science which he followed.

The life of the mystic was then in a peculiar sense the life of sanctity. It was not, of course, his exclusive vocation; if we are to accept the occult sciences at their own valuation, more than one of them exacted, and that not merely by implication, something more than the God-fearing, clean-living spirit, which is so desirable even in the ordinary business man. He who was in search of transmutation was counseled, in the first instance, to convert himself, and the device on the wall of his laboratory was Labora but also Ora. The astrologer, who calculated the influences of the stars on man, was taught that, in the last resource, there was a law of grace by which the stars were ruled. Even the conventional magician, he who called and controlled spirits, knew that the first condition of success in his curious art was to be superior to the weakness of the inconstant creatures whose dwelling is amidst the flux of the elements.

I have said that, in most cases, the occult student was, after his manner, a specialist – he was devoted to his particular branch. Deep down in the heart of the alchemist there may have been frequently the belief that certain times and seasons were more favorable than others for his work, and that the concealed materials which he thought of symbolically as the Sun and Moon, as Mercury, Venus or Mars, were not wholly independent of star and planet in the sky; and hence no doubt he knew enough of elementary astrology to avoid afflicted aspects and malign influences. But, outside this, the alchemist was not an astrologer, and to be wise in the lore of the stars was an ambition that was sufficient for one life, without meddling in the experiments of alchemy. On the other hand, the mystic, in common with all the members of his community, having only one object in view, and one method of pursuing it – by the inward way of contemplation – had nothing to differentiate and could not therefore specialize.

Again, occult science justifies itself as the transmission of a secret knowledge from the past, and the books which represent the several branches of this knowledge bear upon them the outward marks that they are among the modes of this transmission, without which it is certain that there would be no secret sciences. The occult student was, therefore, an initiate in the conventional sense of the term – he was taught, even in astrology. There were schools of Kabbalism, schools of alchemy, schools of magic, in which the mystery of certain knowledge was imparted from adept to neophyte, from master to pupil. It is over this question of corporate union that we have at once an analogy and a distinction between the mystic and the occultist. The former, as we find him in the West, may in a sense be called an initiate because he was trained in the rule of the Church; but the historical traces of secret association for mystic objects during the Christian centuries are very slight, whereas the traces of occult association are exceedingly strong. The mysteries of pre-Christian times were no doubt schools of mystic experience. Plato and Plotinus were assuredly mystics who were initiated in these schools. Unfortunately, the nature of this experience has come down to us, for the most part, in a fragmentary and veiled manner. But, outside exoteric writings, it has in my belief come down, and it is possible to reconstruct it, at least intellectually and speculatively, for it is embedded in the symbolic modes of advancement practiced by certain secret societies which now exist among us. A transmission of mystic knowledge has therefore taken place from the past, but the evidence is of an exceedingly complex nature and cannot be explained here. Nor is it necessary to our purpose, for western mysticism is almost exclusively the gift of the Church to the West, and the experiment of Christian mysticism, without any veils or evasions, is written at large in the literature of the Church. It may call to be re-expressed for our present requirements in less restricted language, but there is not really any need to go further. "The Ascent of Mount Carmel," "The Adornment of the Spiritual Marriage," and "The Castle of the Inward Man," contain the root-matter of the whole process. I have also found it well and exhaustively described in obscure little French books, which might appear at first sight to be simply devotional manuals for the use of schools and seminaries. I have found it in books equally obscure, which a few decades ago would have been termed Protestant. There is the same independent unanimity of experience and purpose through all which the alchemists have claimed for their own literature, and I have no personal doubt that the true mystics of all times and countries constitute an unincorporated fellowship communicating continually together in the higher consciousness. They do not differ essentially in the East or the West.

In its elementary presentation, the life of the mystic consists primarily in the detachment of the will from its normal condition of immersion in material things and in its redirection towards the goodwill, which abides at the center. This center, according to the mystics, is everywhere and is hence, in a certain sense, to be found in all; but it is sought most readily, by contemplation, as at the center of the man himself, and this is the quest and finding of the soul. If there is not an open door

– an entrance to the closed palace – within us, we are never likely to find it without us. The rest of the experiences are those of the life of sanctity leading to such a ground of divine union as is possible to humanity in this life.

In the distinction – analogical, as already said – which I have here sought to establish, there lies the true way to study the lives of the mystics and of those who graduated in the schools of occult science. The object of that study, and of all commentary arising out of such lives, is to lead those, and there are thousands, who are so constituted as to desire the light of mysticism, to an intellectual realization of that light. The life of the mystic belongs to the divine degree, and it would be difficult to say that it is attainable in the life of the world; but some of its joys and consolations – as indeed its trials and searchings – are not outside our daily ways. Apart from all the heroisms, and in the outer courts only of the greater ecstasies, there are many who would set their face towards Jerusalem if their feet were put upon the way – and would thus turn again home.

THE LEGEND OF THE HOLY GRAIL AND ITS CONNECTION WITH TEMPLARS AND FREEMASONS

PART I

SKETCH OF THE CONNECTION

If deeper pitfalls are laid by anything more than by the facts of coincidence, it is perhaps by the intimations and suggestions of writings which bear the stamp of allegory or concealed allusion on their surface; as in the cases of coincidence, so in these it is necessary for the historical critic to be very much upon his guard, and not to accept correspondences, however plausible, unless they are controlled and strengthened by more substantial evidence.

But the fact of the correspondences remains; they are important within their own sphere; and it is often through indirect lights of this kind that research has been led into new tracks from which unexpected and indubitable results have ultimately followed. It is the purpose of the present paper to indicate certain analogies which are at least curious and to stimulate further investigation along the lines which they appear to indicate, without attempting at the moment to press any definite conclusion.

Some slight general acquaintance with the Legend of the Holy Grail may for the moment be presupposed in the reader, though the legend itself will be made quite clear as we proceed. It is proposed for the first time in the history of the subject to institute a connection between the knightly quest of the Grail, as undertaken by the chivalry of King Arthur's Court, and the allegorical quest which is undertaken in Freemasonry, as the candidate progresses from grade to grade. The connecting link between the two things, to all appearance so widely divergent, must be sought outside of each, and it is found in the Ancient Order of the Knights Templar who, according to a well-known, though by no means universally accepted view, are the ancestors of the modern Freemason, and, as it will be sought to show, were possibly the originators or conservers of the Grail legend. If such a view should prove to be well-founded, two things will follow of necessity: (1) modern archaeology will have to revise its notions on the subject of the Grail in medieval and romantic literature; and (2) the history of Masonry will require to be rewritten. This statement summarizes in a few words an enormous complexity of issues to which no justice can be done in what must at best be only a preliminary sketch. As much archeological or masonic knowledge must not be assumed in the reader, it may be premised further that he will acquire without difficulty as he proceeds the little that is essential for a proper understanding of the subject. It is not necessary that he should be either a literary scholar familiar with the byways of the mediaeval romances, and with their criticism, or, on the other hand, that he should he himself a member of the masonic fraternity. Attendance will be asked in the first place to the following points, which will simplify the later considerations.

There are at the present time two schools of masonic criticism with regard to the origin of the fraternity. For the one it is the natural descendant of the old building guilds or trade unions of the past, which from a remote period were in the habit of admitting into their ranks influential persons who were neither architects nor builders. At a certain epoch of time, which it is difficult to indicate, except within rather broad limits, but with England as its locality, some of these lay members would appear to have found themselves practically in possession of certain lodges, and they converted the old mystery or mummery of masonry into an allegorical or speculative system applied to the morals of its professors, which new system so spread that it absorbed or ousted the original trading element and laid the ground-work of that vast confederation which at this day covers the whole earth. This, somewhat roughly indicated, is the accepted view, the view taken by the major part of the educated opinion within the ranks of the fraternity, because it tends to minimize the element of mystery and wonder which is inseparable from subjects of the kind by exhibiting things which are unknown or dubious in the aspect of things familiar. By the other school it is believed that at the suppression of the Templars by King Philippe le Bel and Pope Clement in 1307, that knightly order did not in reality, or at least utterly perish, but assumed the disguise of freemasonry, taking refuge in certain lodges of the building guilds, and importing into these the secret speculative and religious doctrine which it had learned in the east, and on account of which the Pope and King combined in the attempt to destroy it. This view finds expression more particularly in France and Germany, but it has had its exponents in England; it has rested so far on insufficient foundations from the standpoint of historical evidence, but it represents a tradition which it is difficult to ignore with justice and entirely, and it is possible that it may yet receive unexpected substantiation. It will be obvious that one important step in this direction will be made by establishing an analogy between masonic symbolism and that of the Grail legend, the Templar connections of which have been put forward successfully by scholars, both in England and Germany, whose decision, if not final, is at least entitled to the very highest respect. The connections, moreover, as will be seen, appear on the face of the legend in some of its most important forms.

With a view to the simplification of an inquiry which touches upon several fields of research which are all of them highly specialized, the first consideration will be given to the Legend of the Holy Grail and its sources in medieval literature; the traces of Templarism therein will be dealt with in the next place, together with a short account of what has been surmised concerning the secret doctrine of the Templars and the alleged survival of the Order; the connection of both with the chief legend of Masonry will be shown in the last place, and a tentative inference will be attempted.

PART II

SOME ASPECTS OF THE GRAIL LEGEND

There are a few legends which may be said to stand forth among the innumerable traditions of humanity, wearing upon them the external signs or characters of some secret or mystery within them which seems to belong rather to eternity than to time. They are, in no sense, connected with one another, and yet, by a suggestion which is deeper than any suggestion of the senses, they would seem as if each of them were appealing to each, one bearing testimony to another and all recalling all. They might be the broken fragments of a primitive revelation which, except in these memorials, has passed out of time and mind. There are also other legends, strange, melancholy and long haunting, which seem to have issued from the depths of aboriginal humanity, below all horizons of history, pointing to terrible periods of a past which is of the body only and not of the soul of man, and hinting that, once upon a time, there was a soulless age of our race, when minds were formless as the mammoths of geological epochs. To the latter class belongs some of what remains to us of the folklore of the cave-dwellers, the traditions of the pre-Ayran races of Europe. To the former, among many others, belongs the Grail

Legend which, at least in its purest aspects, is to be classed among the legends of the soul.

It might seem at first sight almost a superfluous precaution, even in an elementary paper, to give an answer to the question, What, then, was the Holy Grail? Those who are unacquainted with its literature in the old books of chivalry, by which it first entered into the romance of Europe, will know it by the "Idylls of the King." But it is not so superfluous as it seems, and many answers to the question have been attempted which are altogether different from that which is given by the knight Percival to his fellow monk in the poem of Tennyson.

> *"What Is it? The phantom of a cup that comes and goes?"*

> *"Nay, monk! what phantom?" answer'd Percivale.*
> *"The cup, the cup itself, from which our Lord*
> *Drank at the last sad supper with his own.*
> *This, from the blessed land of Aromat...*
> *Arimathsean Joseph, journeying brought*
> *To Glastonbury...*

> *And thus a while It bode; and if a man*
> *Could touch or see It, he was heal'd at once*
> *By faith of all his Ills; But then the times*
> *Grew to such evil that the Holy Cup*
> *Was caught away to Heaven and disappear'd."*

That is the answer with which in one or another of is forms, poetic or chivalrous, everyone is expected to be acquainted, or must be classed as too unlettered for consideration, even in a slight sketch of the present kind. But, as hinted already, it is so little the only answer, and it so little full or exhaustive, that no person acquainted with the literature would accept it otherwise than as one of its aspects, and even the enchanting gift of the laureate's poetic faculty leaves- and that of necessity- something to be desired in the summary of the knight's reply to the direct question of the monk Ambrosius. There is an allusiveness, a pregnancy, a suggestion about the legend in its best forms which escapes in such an answer; it is found in the old romances, especially in the romantic chronicle of Sir Percival and the "Morte d'Arthur." It is found later on in Tennyson's own poem, when Percival's sister, the nun of "utter whiteness," describes her vision :—

> *"I heard a sound*
> *As of a silver horn from o'er the hills. . . .*
>
> *the slender sound*
> *As from a distance beyond distance grew*
> *Coming upon me. .*
>
> *and then*
> *Stream'd thro' my cell a cold and silver beam*
> *And down the long beam stole the Holy Grail.*
> *Rose-red with beatings in it."*
>
> *And again:—*
> *"I saw the spiritual city and all her spires*
> *And gateways in a glory like one ear . . . .*
> *Strike from the sea and from the star there shot*
> *A rose-red sparkle to the city, and there*
> *Dwelt, and I knew it was the Holy Grail."*

So also in the chivalric books the legend is treated with an aloofness, and yet with a directness of circumstance and a manifoldness of detail awakening a sense of reality amidst enchantment which is scarcely heightened when the makers of the old chronicles testify to the truth of their story. The explanation is, according to one version of the Quest, that it was written by Christ himself after the Resurrection, and that there is no clerk, "however hardy," who will dare to suggest that any other scripture is referable to the same hand. Sir Thomas Malory, the latest and best of the compilers of the Arthurian legend, suppresses this ascription, and in the colophon of his eighteenth book is contented with adding that it is "a story chronicled for one of the truest and holiest that is in this world."

But there is ample evidence in Sir Thomas Malory's own book, the "Morte d'Arthur," that the Grail L end was derived into his great chronicle from various sources, and that several elements entered into it which are quite excluded by the description of Sir Percival in the "Idylls," or by the colophon of his own twelfth book, which reads: "*And here followeth the noble tale of the Sancgreal that called is the hooly vessel, and the sygnefycacyon of blessid blood of our Lord Jhesu Cryste, blessid mote it be, the whiche was brought into this land by Joseph of Armathye, therefore on all synful souls Blessid Lord have Thou mercy."*

It is not necessary, or indeed possible, to particularize all these elements, but, as an equipoise to the religious or sacramental side of the legend, it has been pointed out that the French romance, from which the English version is chiefly derived, would appear to have borrowed from old Irish stories of the pagan period something concerning a mysterious magical vessel full of miraculous food. This is illustrated by the "Morte d'Arthur" in the memorable episode of the high festival held by King Arthur at Pentecost. "In the midst of the supper there entered into the hall the Holy Grail covered with white Samite, but there was none might see it or who bore it, and then was all the hall fulfilled with good odors and every knight had such meats and drinks as he best loved in this world." That is a state of the legend which has little connection with the mystic vessel carried out of Palestine by the centurion of the evangelists, but the simple-minded chroniclers of the past did not observe the anachronism when they married the Christian fable to any parallel history which came in their way.

PART III

EPOCHS OF THE LEGEND

A minute enquiry into the materials and their sources of a moving and stately legend are opposed to the purposes and interests of the general reader, for whom the Grail has two epochs only in literature, that of Sir Thomas Malory and that of "The Idylls of the King," and as Tennyson was indebted to Malory, so it is through his gracious poems that most persons have been sent back to the old book of chivalry from which he reproduced his motives and sometimes derived his words. But without entering into the domain of archaeology, the lettered student, and, indeed, the literate reader, will know well enough that there are branches of the legend outside these two great names, and that some of them are close enough to his hand. He will know that the Cornish poet, Robert Stephen Hawker's "Quest of the San Grail" has, as Madame de Stael once said of Saint Martin, "some sublime gleams." He will know that the old French romance of Percival le Gallois recently translated into English of an archaic kind by Dr. Sebastian Evans, is a gorgeous romance, full of richly painted pictures and endless pageants. He will know finally that there is a German cycle of the Grail traditions, and that Titurel, Parsifal and Lohengrin, to whom a strange and wonderful life beyond all common teachings of nature, and beyond all common conventions of art has been given by Wagner, are also legendary heroes of the Holy Grail. There are, therefore, broadly speaking, three points of view as regards this subject, which are—

(1) The Romantic ; and the reversion of literary sentiment at the present day towards romanticism will make it unnecessary to say that this is now a very strong point. It is exemplified by the numerous editions of the "Morte d'Arthur," produced not only for students, but also in the interests of children, and in which a large space is invariably given to the Grail Legend. Lang's "Book of Romance" and Mary McCleod's "Book of King Arthur and His Noble Knights," are instances which will occur to most people; but there are many others.

(2) The Poetic, to which, having regard to what has been said already, it is only necessary to add that it has done something to exalt and spiritualize the legend without removing the romantic element. In the case of Tennyson it has certainly added the elevated emotion which belongs essentially to the spirit of romance, and has saved English literature during the latter half of the 19th century. But taking the work at its highest, it may well be that the Grail Legend has still to receive its treatment more fully by some poet who is to come. The literary form of this particular Idyll of the King, a tale within a tale twice told, leaves something to be desired.

(3) The Archeological, and this has naturally many branches, each of which has the character of a learned inquiry calling for special knowledge, and, in many instances, only of limited interest outside the field of scholarship. The archaeology of the legend would include, of course, its sources, which remain debatable, and certain problems of authorship in connection with the early romances, as, for example, whether Master Blihis did write the first Percival in the latter half of the 13th century. The Grail in the musical epics of Wagner has been the subject of special devotion in the writings of Miss Jessie L. Watson. Outside these admitted branches of research there is a fourth point of view which has emerged more recently, and for want of a better term may, perhaps, be called Spiritual. It cares little for the archaeology of the subject, little for the romantic aspects and as little perhaps, explicitly, for

the poetic side. It would know nothing of Hawker's "Quest," and would regard the Grail simply as one of the sacramental legends of the soul; yet it is not confined, nor is it indeed found, to any important extent, among those who hold extreme Eucharistic views. In other words, it is not specially a high Anglican or a Latin interest; it is found rather among those who regard religious doctrine, institution and ritual, as things typical or analogical, and the Grail as an early recognition of the fact that such things are really symbols and not for literal acceptance. This view cares, perhaps, only in an ordinary degree for the evidences of history, nor can history be said to endorse it. It is a consideration of certain devout minds. Connected with this, although really independent, there is a still more recent disposition to regard the whole legend as hinting at the perpetuation of a secret teaching within the Christian church which is not exactly what is understood commonly by Christianity. There is much to be said for this view, though in the form that we at present possess it, it may be admitted that it still awaits demonstration. There is perhaps a certain sense in which all these views can be accepted, and in which all are capable in the last resource of being harmonized together. No one can read the romances without seeing that the legend has its spiritual side, but it has also, and not less evidently, that side which connects it with folklore. In the hands of the compiler of the "Morte d'Arthur" it is treated openly as an allegory, and the knighthood of King Arthur's Court passes explicitly during the quest into a region of similitude, where every adventure and episode has a supernatural signification which is explained sometimes in rather a tiresome manner. On the other hand, in the romance of Sir Percival, there are assuredly traces of a doctrine or system which is not quite in affinity with the Christianity of its period, and there is also a suggestion of veiled hostility to the church of that period.

PART IV

SOURCES OF THE LEGEND

The sources of the romance-legend are of two kinds, existing and traditional, the second class being represented only by the tradition of a Latin MS., which is referred to by most narrators of the legend, with the exception of Sir Thomas Malory, though it is possible that they have borrowed the reference from one another. On the authority, by no means unquestionable, of a certain chronicle of Helinandus, this book was entitled "Liber Gradalis" and was the work of a British hermit, whose name does not transpire. Moreover, it had not been seen by the historian who mentions it. At the present day it is regarded as mythical by scholars, but, after making every allowance, there does not, perhaps, seem full ground for doubting the fact of its existence. It is pointed out that there are no romance works in the Latin language, but this is not a valid objection, because it does not follow that the Latin original was in the form which we naturally attribute to the word romance. This word originally involved a work written in the romance language, and everything points, as regards the Latin manuscript, to the fact that it was rather in the nature of an apocryphal gospel book, as indeed its imputed authorship would imply, and as such it is not impossible that it may still exist among the uninvestigated treasures of old monastic libraries in the remote corners of Brittany.

The extant sources may be summarized as follows:—

(1) The mediaeval poem of the Grail, begun by Chrestien de Troyes who died between 1181 and 1190, and of whose work there are several continuations which may have been written at any time between the close of the twelfth and the middle of the thirteenth century.

(2) The romance poem of Joseph of Arimathea, very nearly perfect, a single leaf only being wanting in one of the most complete copies. The author was Robert de Borron, who wrote it towards the end of the twelfth century, and died in 1212.

(3) The prose version of this poem, which supplies the defect therein; although in respect of the language it corresponds, like the poem, to the original meaning of the term romance, it is not of the kind which we understand by the word—that is to say—both versions purport to be true histories and are in fact a species of apocryphal narrative, somewhat approaching the canonical Acts of the Apostles, giving the genealogy of Joseph and all his descendants with a pseudo history of his life, travels and imprisonments before and after the Ascension of Christ.

(4) A sequel to the poem of Borron by a later hand, known as the Didot Percival, of which there is only a single manuscript in existence.

(5) The quest of the San Grail, corresponding in all respects to what the ordinary literate reader would understand by the romance of chivalry. It is the most famous of the whole cycle.

(6) The romance of Sir Percival le Gallois, which of recent years

has come into the hands of many thousands of English readers in the translation of Dr. Sebastian Evans. This is an elaborate, highly pictorial narrative of the best romantic kind, and it contains the presumptive evidence out of which the present hypothesis has arisen.

(7) Sir Thomas Malory's "Birth, Life and Acts of King Arthur," more commonly known under the name of "Morte d'Arthur." It was originally printed by Caxton and the modern editions are numerous. The Quest of the Grail (see *ante*, No. 5) occupies several books of this great compilation, to the production of which a singular genius was brought by the compiler, and it is and will remain one of the great epoch-making books of English literature. Sir Edward Strachey, one of its modern editors, has well pointed out that the narrative is almost epical in its form, and has so digested the confused materials on which Malory wrought, that something of sustained purpose appears throughout, and it has, so to speak, a beginning, middle and end.

(8) A distinct cycle of the Grail Legend is filled by the German romances, as already noted. Their place is a little difficult to settle on satisfactory grounds. Some French scholars have endeavored to show that the source of the Arthurian legends is to be sought in Germany, but it is a hypothesis advanced b those who seek to minimize their merit in favor of the superior claims of the Charlemagne cycle, and this does not bear consideration. The German cycle may be classified as follows:-

A. The Romance of Titurel.

B. That of Parsifal.

C. That of Lohengrin.

They are all interconnected, and the order given above is in a sense almost chronological. Titurel was the first knight called to the guarding of the Grail, and is supposed to have built a temple in which it was placed during the period that it abode on Earth. Parsifal is of course the German version of Percival, and Lohengrin is the latest and closing legend, corresponding to that of Galahad in the "Morte d'Arthur," in which, however, the chronological succession is entirely lost.

(9) For the sake of completeness two other romances may be mentioned: that of Peredur, the son of Earl Evrawe, a Welsh legend of the thirteenth century or earlier, and the English metrical romance of Sir Percyvelle; but they do not call for consideration in the present connection.

It should be added that the above list is not chronologically arranged.

PART V

THE SECRET OF THE GRAIL

Whatever the elements which entered into the composition of the Grail conception, all the chief versions of the legend unite in connecting it with the mystery and power of certain secret words. These words, in the earlier romances, are entrusted by Christ Himself to the custody of Joseph of Arimathea. Those who can acquire and retain them, can exercise at will a strange power and mastery over all about them and will possess great credit in the sight of God. They never need fear being deprived of their rights, sufferings from evil judgment, or conquest in battle, so long as their cause is just. It is impossible, however, to communicate these words in writing; they are too precious and holy, and, moreover, they are the secret of the Grail itself, in which a strange power of speech also resides. Joseph himself was only permitted to reveal them to a single person, a mysterious rich fisherman who figures continually in the stories, sometimes following the craft which his name suggests, sometimes as the lord of a stately castle, in several instances as a king. He, in his turn, and by virtue of some mysterious power or license vested in him, does appear to have committed them to writing, together with other secrets, but they are to be concealed forever from the world.

In the prologue or preamble of the Grand San Grail legend, the hermit who receives the revelations and the custody of the mysterious book of the legend, testifies that the greatest secret of the world has been confided to him, and that the communication took place amidst inexpressible experiences in that third heaven to which St. Paul was translated. The description of his ecstasy is written in fervent language. On the other hand, in the Didot Percival, the putative sequel to the poems of Robert de Borron, the secret words appear as those which Christ spoke to Joseph on the Cross. After they have been imparted to one of the heroes of the story, he is translated by angels. It is needless to add that the maker of this chronicle is forbidden to transcribe them.

In another class of the romances the unutterable words reappear in a simplified or substituted form, and we have in this manner the legends of a suppressed word, of the sorrow and the misery which is wrought by that suppression, and of the joy and the deliverance which follow the utterance of the word, whereby great enchantments are determined, great wrongs redressed, and the wounds and sufferings endured through many years are healed and annulled. This mystery of the word which is withheld, or in reservation, would offer some curious points to criticism if the subject could be pursued here. It takes the form of a simple question which should have been asked and was not, and as such it is, so to speak, the reverse side or antithesis of the old classical legend of the sphinx. The sphinx asked questions and devoured those who did not reply, or whose answers blundered. Percival in the romances kept silence, when he should have urged his inquiries, sometimes through carelessness, sometimes through false modesty, sometimes because he had been cautioned against idle questioning, but in all cases indifferently, by the working of some apparently blind destiny, the omission carries with it the long series of its disastrous consequences.

The higher sense of the mysterious word or words is of course removed to heaven when the Grail is itself removed, the departure of which is described in many ways, of which the following from the "Morte d'Arthur" may serve as an example. *"And when he had said these words Galahad went to Percival and kissed him and commended him to God, and so he went to Sir Bors, and kissed him, and commended him to God, and said, Fair lord, salute me to my lord Sir Lancelot, my father, and as soon as you see him, bid him remember of this unstable world. And therewith he kneeled down before the table, and made his prayers, and then suddenly his soul departed to Jesu Christ and a great multitude of angels bore his soul up to heaven, that the two fellows might well behold it. Also the two fellows saw come from heaven an hand, but they saw not the body. And then it came right to the vessel, and took it and the spear, and so bare it up to heaven. Since then was there never man so hardy to say that he had seen the Sangraal."* But the lesser word, the word which can be withheld or spoken, has performed in the meantime a certain office of amelioration, so that it is not by a mere vain observance that it has been in a sense substituted by the later romances for that which could neither be spelt nor written.

Of such is the Grail Legend, and those who are acquainted with it in the most choice of its early forms will agree not only that many portions of it are singularly winning, but that it is indeed

"a part Of the hunger and thirst of the heart."

It is also a very melancholy legend; it is the passing of a great procession and a great sacrament which is destined never to return; it is a portion of the loss of humanity; and it is no matter for surprise that in these late days which are so full of this thirst and this hunger, several persons have attempted to read into it a more profound significance than could have been consciously intended by its makers.

PART VI

THE TEMPLAR CONNECTION

The slight investigation here attempted has proceeded so far solely on the basis of the documents, though it must be admitted that, as regards the last section there has not been any special attention paid to the subject by English scholars. The Templar connections of the Grail Legend lie also on the face of the documents, but these are recognized by scholarship. Some are trivial in themselves, but are noticeable by their continual recurrence throughout the romances, as, for example, the characteristic Templar symbolism of the white alb and the scarlet cross, varied by the scarlet cross on the white banner, or on the white sails of fairy ships, and so forth. Other connections are rooted more deeply and of great significance. There are indications of a confraternity, partly military and partly religious, connecting by the legend of a lineage with a kind of secret history of Christendom, written under the guise of knight errantry. This feature is more especially noticeable in the German versions. The later adaptations of the Lohengrin Legend are literally and verbally Templar, but the German Parsifal, written by Wolfram von Eschenbach, prior to 1215, is the romance of a brotherhood of the Holy Grail, strong, mighty and powerful, while that of Titurel is the legend of the building of a Temple. And this leads to a still more important point, also fully acknowledged by scholars, namely, that current through all the stories we have the hint of the existence of what has been termed a Grail Church, that is to say, of a secret doctrine which, by the hypothesis, is higher than the open doctrine which at the time was taught in Christendom. The inmost heart of this doctrine is no doubt typically represented by the Grail itself, and in accordance with this view, it will be sufficient to point out the amazing statement that the Eucharist was first entrusted to Joseph of Arimathea, that he was the first priest who ever celebrated the Mass and was the first bishop of the Church, consecrated by Christ himself and the angels. The book of the Grail also claims Christ as its author and thus stands in a position of inexpressible superiority to the gospels. Behind this blasphemous ascription, which in itself could not have been literally intended, there could be only the implied existence of some concealed instruction of religion, which claimed for itself a more sacred sanction than that of orthodox Christianity. Equally designed to enforce this claim, and signifying equally something which did not appear on the surface, is the pretense that among the treasures of the Grail Church were the crown and sword of David and the wood of the Tree of Life. The precise intention of these allegories may perhaps never be unraveled, but their general design is apparent, and this corresponds broadly to the chief accusations brought against the Knights Templar at the time of their suppression. The two centuries of their existence are also the two centuries during which the Grail legends were originated and for the most part developed. Most of the accusations raised against the brethren were not so much unfounded as baser constructed, and after every allowance has been made, there is reasonable ground for inferring that they acquired strange knowledge in the East, on the basis of which they raised claims to a priestly and religious preeminence, and these claims found in the romances of the west, which seem to have been inspired by them and to have grown up to some extent under their auspices, an indirect and veiled expression.

The specific considerations which tend towards the substantiation of this view are of course highly technical, and they involve issues which have been long and hotly debated. There is, firstly, so much light as can be obtained from the name of the order and from the improbability of the pretense that it was so called because its first house was situated near the site of King Solomon's Temple. It is advanced that the Knights were brethren of the Temple in a less accidental sense, and were secretly pledged to the erection, symbolically speaking, of another house of God which was neither precisely of Israel nor of Christendom. In this connection there is a legend of Solomon within the Grail legend which calls for the elucidation of scholarship; but there is, above all, the fact that the Grail heroes were Temple-builders. Secondly, there is the use among the Templars of secret words which did not carry their significance on their surface, and were therefore, in a sense, substituted words, by which the true and more secret words were suppressed and concealed from the lower ranks of the brethren. In the third place, amongst alleged Templar remains, there are examples of fonts or vases which have been regarded as Grail vessels, and in this connection it may be noted, because of the alleged sympathies between the Templars and some of the survivals of the

194

Gnostic sects, that, according to Epiphanius, the Marcosian heretics made use of similar vases in their celebration of the Eucharist. They were filled with white wine, which was supposed to undergo transformations of color and other magical changes which recall the marvelous permutations of the Grail cup in the old books of chivalry.

But the most important consideration of the whole is one which so far has passed entirely unnoticed, and this is, that about the period when the Grail romances may be supposed to have originated, the Latin Church denied the Chalice to the laity, and Communion was limited to one kind. Is it too much to suppose, that when the most sacred rite and highest sacrament of the Christian religion was thus tampered with, and, in appearance, violated, there must have arisen a very strong feeling of hostility? Is it too much to suppose, when about the same period we find a cycle of legend springing into existence, the central point of which was the very Cup Of Mystery which was thus withheld from the faithful, that between the two there is some connection corresponding to cause and effect? And at the back of this hostility, and at the back of these legends, is there any class of society at the period more possible, and even probable, than those Knights Templar who were themselves a priestly order, to whom as such the Communion in both kinds was doubtless continued, and to whom the Eucharistic rite seems in some form always to have been a special object of veneration?

As, on the one hand, it is by no means pretended that this account does common justice to an exceedingly complex subject, so on the other, it cannot be affirmed that the fullest analogies would lead up to a demonstration in the existing state of knowledge. But after every allowance has been made for the greed and duplicity of the French King, who coveted the Templar possessions, and for the criminal weakness of the servile Pontiff who acted as his tool, there is much to be said for the view, that the Church and perhaps the State were guided by no mistaken instinct when they regarded the Templar pretensions as inimical to their own safety, and so also, amidst much exaggeration and much invention, their enemies of latter days, the Romish historians, who have connected the order with the Gnostics, the Manicheans, the Albigenses and kindred heresies which overran several parts of Europe when the Templars were at the height of their power, may not have been so profoundly mistaken as has been sometimes supposed.

PART VII

THE CONNECTION WITH MASONRY

The theory that Masonry of the speculative kind was developed somehow from the Building Guilds, explains very little of itself, and to speak of its comparative simplicity, which is that which has recommended it chiefly, is not really to press one of its advantages. Those who adopt it will have in the end to admit, as already indicated, that the operative craft was assumed by persons who were not operative Masons, and this is all that is asked for by the Templar or any other hypothesis. At present, and after the persistent investigations of many generations less or more equipped for the purpose, it must he confessed that speculative Freemasonry is still in the position of Melchizedek, without father or mother; but so far as presumptive evidence is concerned, the Templar explanation is not in reality more difficult than any Of its competitors, if it can be shown that the knightly order survived the destruction which was attempted by the Pope and the King. And as to this no two opinions are really possible, and those who maintain the negative are doing but little better than playing with the words. For, in the first place, the Order in Portugal was never suppressed at all, but was transformed into the Order of Christ. In the second place there was no suppression in Germany in the sense that we attach to the term, and there the Knights Templar became the Teutonic Knights, though there is a break in the succession. In the third place, there are several other countries where the proscription was partial and halfhearted only, and, lastly, in Scotland there is valid ground for believing that the quarrels of the Scottish king with his English neighbor were at that period far too strenuous to admit of his interfering with an Order of Knighthood from which he had better reason to look for material assistance. The suppression, no doubt, in France, and in some other countries, took the form of practical destruction, but even there the apologists of the Latin Church, who also figure among those who maintain the complete overthrow of the Fraternity, are the first to deny that anything like the majority of the Knights Templar suffered more than the ordinary canonical punishments of the period. Now it is precisely in Scotland that the consistent tradition of modern Templarism points to the continuation of the old Order, and later on to its identification with the Operative Masonry of that country. Here, again, the evidences are practically impossible to summarize, as they would involve a minute examination not only of many historical documents, real or alleged, but also of the Templar Rituals of Masonry, and of the literature which has grown out of the claim. The following statements have been advanced on historical ground. In 1309, the Grand Preceptor of Scotland was Walter de Clifton, who subsequently became Grand Master, and five years later the Templars joined the standard of the Bruce, and being instrumental in placing him on the throne, their former grants were confirmed by him. The Templars are mentioned in two charters, one of which is dated 1340, and the other about a century later. They are now in possession of the Chapter General of Scotland. In the reign of James IV, there was a union of the Templars and Hospitallers, the evidence for which is a charter dated October 19th, 1488, confirming grants of lands to the Knights of the Temple and St. john. After the Act of 1560 prohibiting allegiance to Rome, Sir William Sandilands, Preceptor of Torphichen, and successor to Sir William Lindsay as Master of the Temple, gave territories of both Orders to the State, which were then made over to him, with the lordship of Torphichen, in return for a certain payment. The Knights thereupon drew off in a body with the Grand Prior, David Seton. We must turn, however, from special points to an indication of the wider lines of the argument, which, to put it as shortly as possible, takes in the first place the Masonic legend of Hiram, which is that of the Third Degree, and refers it, with the majority of Masonic historians, to its prototype in the Compagnonage or Building Guilds of France; it connects the Compagnonage itself through Templarism with the religious sects of the South of Europe, who drew like the Templars from the East; it seeks to show that modern Masonry deriving, as it is allowed, from the one is also referable to the other. We are concerned, however, with an analogy which is more important for our purpose, and having shown that, according to the best scholarship of the present period, the Grail legends exhibit Templar marks, and possess Templar connections, it remains to indicate that the Masonic legend is but another version of what has been termed here the Secret of the Grail.

The great and chief legend of Masonry, which is that of the Third Degree, the head and crown of the symbolic edifice, gives account of the circumstances under which a great and sacred knowledge summarized in a word of mysterious power was lost through a deed of treason, since which time, as in the Grail Legend, a substituted word only is conferred upon the candidate, to be kept in his heart until the restoration of the true word. The latter, also like the Grail Legend, is one of Divine power and is actually the building word of the first Master Mason, who died rather than communicate it, much after the same manner as we find it stated in the romance legends. In a supplementary degree, called the Royal Arch, the Lost Word is ostensibly recovered, but as a fact the word imparted is only another substitute. There are also other grades belonging to various classes and sources, all passing under the name of High Grades, being superadded to the original Craft degrees, and in many of these the true word is supposed to be found and joy restored to the seekers, even as in the Grail Legends the punishments and sufferings were removed; but they are all of the same character, that is to say, they are merely makeshifts and evasions. The true initiates of masonry, of whom there are comparatively speaking very few, know well the reason, which is that given by the hermit in the preamble of the Grand San Grail, namely, that the last secrets are incommunicable; but they know also that they exist. In any case this loss and this alleged restoration are the whole concern of Masonic symbolism; they are that to which the profane person cannot penetrate, at least by the hypothesis. There is, therefore, from the Masonic standpoint, a lost knowledge which Masonry assuredly memorizes, and which the Worshipful Master, in the charge to the candidate who has been raised to the Third Degree, confesses to be lost, even as the Holy Grail was removed from earth, and for the same reason, that is to say, on account of the unworthiness of the world. The building word of the Master Architect was removed when he was slain, and though the Temple was finished by a species of substitution, it was not after the original plan. Thus the Masonic legend, like that of the Grail histories, has throughout a note of sadness and of want. The echoes of the old legend of Eden, so often referred to by the makers of the romances, the memory of that loss which is the world's loss, reverberate through the mysteries of the Building Craft, uplifted into the sphere of symbols, dimly and unaccountably.

Such are the outlines of the analogy which it has been sought to establish. It is not pretended that it approaches demonstration, but merely that it offers an interesting light on obscure fields of research, and that something has been accomplished towards showing that the mystery of secret teaching hinted at almost everywhere in the Grail legends, the mystery which has for centuries shrouded the inner teaching imparted by the Templar initiation, and the mystery which involves the origin of the great legend of Masonry are not in reality three mysteries, but rather a single mystery exhibited through various vehicles. The further elucidation of the problem must be left to specialists of the several branches of research, which, if even for a moment only, it has so unexpectedly brought together.

198

THE VEIL OF ALCHEMY

I should perhaps begin by saying that the Veil with which I am concerned is not only one of the most deeply inwoven of those which have been held to cover the mysteries of secret knowledge but that it is also triple in its character. In other terms, the records of the literature present Alchemy under three analogical aspects. One of them embodies the Hermetic doctrine concerning the macrocosm and its development. It is therefore a department of transcendental philosophy and does not as such pass into experience with the adept, except in so far as the physical work of Alchemy in the transmutation of metals is, by the hypothesis, an exact pattern and reproduction of the unfoldment from within which took place in the work of creation. The so-called Hermes Trismegistus, saluted as father of sages, affirms in *The Emerald Table* that the art is true, without any shadow of falsehood, is true indeed above all things, and that after the self-same manner the world was made. The fundamental correspondence is developed curiously by numerous writers and might be extended still further than the adepts seem to have carried it. It rests literally on the text of Genesis, which opens, however, by affirming the creation or making of heaven and earth—thus presupposing an antecedence when these were not—and it is obvious therefore at the beginning that the strict correspondence is stultified, because the First Matter— which constitutes the initial mystery in Alchemy—is not of the adept's making. The knowledge concerning it is either the gift of God by a sudden illumination, as the reward of toil and the zeal of a right spirit, or it is transmitted by one who knows.

Among the cryptic doctrines concerning it, there is the affirmation of its identity with the primordial matter out of which the world was formed. The authority in chief is the text already quoted, which says that all things whatsoever have come forth from One by the mediation of one, according to the mode of adaptation. If I may somewhat interpret the analogy, it follows therefore that on the threshold of adeptship God created in the elect alchemist that knowledge of the First Matter which is necessary to the work of the wise, and the alchemist perceived at once that it was an earth which was without form and void, immersed also as if in the primeval waters. Having few concerns as an exponent of the physical side, I do not attempt to indicate at what stage he assumed on his own part a species of demiurgic work, so that his experimental spirit moved like that of God over the face of the waters and his operations became as a formulation of light in the darkness. Nor does the process which took place in his vessel itself concern us. It is enough that the analog followed the path indicated till the cosmos was produced in that vessel as it was produced at the term of creation in the greater world—a perfect work of Nature and of Art. It is thus summarized in part by the rare Latin tract entitled *Cato Chemicus*: (a) In creation there was firstly the confused chaos, without distinction of anything, and a similar confusion in the philosophical work hinders the discernment of the matter; (b) But as there were earth and water in the greater world, so there are dry and humid in the chaos of adepts; (c) There is also a night of great darkness in the vessel, the appearance of which is, however, a cause of joy, as a sign of progress in the work; (d) After such darkness there came light in creation, which answers to the White State of the Stone supervening after the Black State; (e) But the sun was in fine created, to which corresponds the Red State of the Stone, and this is the desire of our eyes.

I have described here two analogical veils of the Hermetic subject. The third is that of the microcosm, understood as the human being, and to discern the nature of this veil we must approach another form of the symbolism, forgetting our analogy between the work on metals and the work in creation. It is now the question of a medicine which can be administered to metals and to man. This medicine is the same at the root but not in the mode of production, though the loose terminology of the literature seems often to identify them too closely. The philosophical analogy is found, under a certain distinction, in the traditional doctrine of the Fall. This is not to say that the inferior metals, which it is the design of Alchemy to transmute, were once gold and have degenerated from that state of perfection. The intent of Nature was always to produce gold, but owing to imperfection in the media through which Nature works it has often failed in the design. The operation of the Fall of man corresponds roughly to the imperfection of media in the metallic kingdom. Again the relation is fantastic, but it serves a certain purpose. There is a way of saving the metals and raising them to a perfect state, and this kind of medicine signifies the successive operations in the performance of the

Great Work. There is the Medicine of the First Order, which is the separation and purification of the elements; it is followed by that of the Second Order, which is a process of fermentation and conjunction; there is lastly the Medicine of the Third Order, which is a method of multiplication. The first is a work of Nature, the second of Art and the third of Art and Nature in the marriage thereof. There is a tract entitled *Libellus de Alchymia* which may be consulted for the process of the work; it is attributed to Albertus Magnus, the great master of the greater St. Thomas Aquinas, and is actually included in the collected edition of his works which was published in the seventeenth century. Its authenticity is, of course, doubted and is indeed dubious enough. To his pupil, the angel of the schools, there is also ascribed a *Thesaurus Alchymie,* which is certainly spurious, but it is interesting as a summary memorial respecting the transmutation of metals and maintains that the work of their redemption is accomplished in a single vessel, by one mode and with one substance.

According to Hermetic doctrine, the body of man also can be saved from disease and raised to a state of perfection which corresponds to that of gold in the metallic kingdom. The Medicine in this form is called Elixir *par excellence,* Potable Gold, and Medicine of the Superior Order. It prolongs life to the furthest limits, but the true adepts do not say that it confers immortality. This is rather the intervention of romanticism extending the horizon of the texts for its own objects. It is also the claim attributed to adventurers like Cagliostro and to mysterious personalities after the manner of Comte de Saint-Germain. It is inconceivable and yet true that there are persons at the present day who take these claims seriously. Now, it is out of this hypothesis concerning the Medicine of Men that the mystical side of Alchemy more especially arises. The new life of the body, the youth renewal, the suggestion of immortality in the physical part are phases of a dream on the external side and a reflection of that which takes place within as a result of those processes with which transcendental religion is concerned. This consanguinity is recognized indifferently by the physical alchemists and by those who seem to have been concerned only with the spiritual work. The preparation of the philosophical Magistery is in analogy with the work of regeneration, and the state of divine beatitude in the arch-natural part of man, with the vision and the union therein, is symbolized by the perfect Stone. This also in the metallic region corresponds to the office of the Holy Eucharist, which imparts a Divine tincture to the spirit of man as the tingeing Stone of Alchemy multiplies the gold of the sages and communicates its glorious state to all prepared substances. Hence it is said that the operation of the Stone is "a certain metaphysical work, not a work of words but real, not doctrinal but experimental." And this is the truth concerning it on the mystical side—a work of experience in the spirit of man for the attainment—at the end of our separation as individual beings—of a

Divine Union with the one and eternal nature.

Some of the most curious intimations concerning mystical Alchemy are in *The Amphitheatre of Eternal Wisdom,* by Henry Khunrath, a poor and obscure student who died in 1601, aged about forty-five years, leaving his work unfinished, so far as the description of the plates is concerned, and these unfortunately are the most important part of the work. As an exponent of the Hermetic doctrine of analogy, he believed in the physical Stone but was concerned with the mystic side. He delineates the process as follows:—(a) Purification of the personal part, that we may come to see God, (b) The closing of the avenues of sense, stillness of soul, sanctification, illumination, tincture by the Divine Fire, (c) Hereof is the path of attainment for the Stone of the Philosophers, (d) which Stone is the living Spirit of the Elohim and (e) the outbreaking of Jehovah, the Divine Power, the Word of God in Nature, (f) That Word is made flesh, so to speak, in the virginal womb of the greater world and (g) is manifested as Jesus, in the virginal womb of Mary, but also (h) in the soul of man as a light super-added to that of Nature; hereby the knowledge of God and His Christ is communicated.

I have spoken very briefly here of a great and important literature. I may add that it is a matter for satisfaction that Alchemy on the external or material side has been taken over of recent days by a practical chemist, Mr. H. S. Redgrove, who has given us a sane and enlightened review of the subject in his work entitled *Alchemy, Ancient and Modern.* He is alive to the main issues, including the mystical aspect, and it is by collaboration of this kind that the desired canon of criticism in respect of the literature will be established ultimately. I do not know much of the outlook otherwise, save in respect of France, where there is an Alchemical Society, the efforts of which were once mentioned courteously by Berthelot. To judge, however, by the work of its Secretary-General, F. Jollivet de Castelot, there is no especial encouragement. He establishes a ridiculous program, some heads of which may be given for the entertainment of my readers. It is entitled *Comment on devient Alchimiste,* and the postulant in the path of Hermeticism is invited to take notice— on the assumption that he is also a Frenchman—that the true adept, as the son of Hermes, is always a royalist, while the *Fleur-de-lys,* which is the *apanage* of Mgr. le duc d'Orléans, expresses (a) the doctrine of analogy and (b) the relation between macrocosm and microcosm. Qualified after this manner in the political sense, he may begin the study of the Tarot, which throws great light on chemical combinations. He must cultivate a certain status of the moral

202

kind, but it is conveniently relaxed in respect of the sixth commandment and does not insist on marriage. He should cultivate the psychic faculties and practice magic, for he must be a magus before an alchemist. He should also play the violin, but I am not sure that this counsel is peremptory. A study of the texts is not unnaturally enjoined, but those which are most recommended are the work of contemporary writers belonging to the same school. They do not know the First Matter or the process of the Art—these Martinists and Rosicrucians of Paris—but they testify one of another, they cleave one to another, and they have a stock of admiration in common which belongs to the heroic degree.

SOME DEEPER ASPECTS OF
MASONIC SYMBOLISM

PART I

The subject which I am about to approach is one having certain obvious difficulties, because it is outside the usual horizon of Masonic literature, and requires, therefore, to be put with considerable care, as well as with reasonable prudence. Moreover, it is not easy to do it full justice within the limits of a single lecture. I must ask my Brethren to make allowance beforehand for the fact that I am speaking in good faith, and where the evidence for what I shall affirm does not appear in its fullness, and sometimes scarcely at all, they must believe that I can produce it at need, should the opportunity occur. As a matter of fact, some part of it has appeared in my published writings.

I will introduce the question in hand by a citation which is familiar to us all, as it so happens that it forms a good point of departure:--"But as we are not all operative Masons, but rather Free and Accepted or speculative, we apply these tools to our morals." With certain variations, these words occur in each of the Craft Degrees, and their analogies are to be found in a few subsidiary Degrees which may be said to arise out of the Craft-- as, for example, the Honorable Degree of Mark Master Mason. That which is applied more specially to the working implements of Masonry belongs to our entire building symbolism, whether it is concerned with the erection by the Candidate in his own personality of an edifice or "superstructure perfect in its parts and honorable to the builder," or, in the Mark Degree, with a house not made with hands, eternal in the heavens, or again with Solomon's Temple spiritualized in the Legend of the Master Degree.

A SYSTEM OF MORALITY

It comes about in this manner that Masonry is described elsewhere as "a peculiar system of morality, unveiled in allegory and illustrated by symbols." I want to tell you, among other things which call for consideration, something about the nature of the building, as this is presented to my mind, and about the way in which allegory, symbols and drama all hang together and make for one meaning. It is my design also to show that Craft Masonry incorporates three less or more distinct elements which have been curiously interlinked under the device of symbolical architecture. That interlinking is to some extent artificial, and yet it arises logically, so far as the relation of ideas is concerned.

There is, firstly, the Candidate's own work, wherein he is taught how he should build himself. The method of instruction is practical within its own measures, but as it is so familiar and open, it is not, properly speaking, the subject-matter of a Secret Order. There is, secondly, a building myth, and the manner in which it is put forward involves the Candidate taking part in a dramatic scene, wherein he represents the master-builder of Masonry. There is, thirdly, a Masonic quest, connected with the notion of a Secret Word communicated as an essential part of the Master Degree in building. This is perhaps the most important and strangest of the three elements; but the quest after the Word is not finished in the Third Degree.

THE FIRST DEGREE

Let us look for a moment at the Degree of Entered Apprentice, and how things stand with the Candidate when he first comes within the precincts of the Lodge. He comes as one who is "worthy and well recommended," as if he contained within himself certain elements or materials which are adaptable to a specific purpose. He is described by his conductor as a person who is "properly prepared." The fitness implied by the recommendation has reference to something which is within him, but not of necessity obvious or visible on his surface personality. It is not that he is merely a deserving member of society at large. He is this, of course, by the fact that he is admitted; but he is very much more, because Masonry has an object in view respecting his personality--something that can be accomplished in him as a result of his fellowship in the Brotherhood, and by himself. As a matter of truth, it is by both. The "prepared" state is, however, only external, and all of us know in what precisely it consists.

Now the manner of his preparation for entrance to the Lodge typifies a state which is peculiar to his ward position as a person who has not been initiated. There are other particulars into which I need not enter, but it should be remarked that in respect of his preparation he learns only the meaning of the state of darkness, namely, that he has not yet received the light communicated in Masonry. The significance of those hindrances, which place him at a disadvantage, impede his movements, and render him in fact helpless, is much deeper than this. They constitute together an image coming out from some old condition by being unclothed there from - partially at least - and thereafter of entering into a condition that is new and different, in which another kind of light is communicated, and another vesture is to be assumed, and, ultimately, another life entered.

THE MEANING OF INITIATION

In the first Degree the Candidate's eyes are opened into the representation of a new world, for you must know, of course, that the Lodge itself is a symbol of the world, extending to the four corners, having the height heaven above and the great depth beneath. The Candidate may think naturally that light has been taken away from him for the purpose of his initiation, has been thereafter restored automatically, when he has gone through a part of the ceremony, and that hence he is only returned to his previous position. Not so. In reality, the light is restored to him in another place; he has put aside old things, has come into things that are new; and he will never pass out of the Lodge as quite the same man that he entered. There is a very true sense in which the particulars of his initiation are in analogy with the process of birth into the physical world. The imputed darkness of his previous existence, amidst the life of the uninitiated world, and the yoke which is placed about him is unquestionably in correspondence with the umbilical cord. You will remember the point at which he is released there from - in our English ritual, I mean. I do not wish to press this view, because it belongs of right, in the main, to another region of symbolism, and the procedure in the later Degrees confuses an issue which might be called clear otherwise in the Degree of Entered Apprentice. It is preferable to say that a new light--being that of Masonry--illuminates the world of the Lodge in the midst of which the Candidate is placed; he is penetrated by a fresh experience; and he sees things as they have never been presented to him before. When he retires subsequently for a period, this is like his restoration to light; in the literal sense he resumes that which he set aside, as he is restored to the old light; but in the symbolism it is another environment, a new body of motive, experience, and sphere of duty attached thereto. He assumes a new vocation in the world.

The question of certain things of a metallic kind, the absence of which plays an important part, is a little difficult from any point of view, though several explanations have been given. The better way toward their understanding is to put aside what is conventional and arbitrary-- as, for example, the poverty of spirit and the denuded state of those who have not yet been enriched by the secret knowledge of the Royal and Holy Art. It goes deeper than this and represents the ordinary status of the world, when separated from any higher motive--the world-spirit, the extrinsic titles of recognition, the material standards. The Candidate is now to learn that there is another standard of values, and when he comes again into possession of the old tokens, he is to realize that their most important use is in the cause of others. You know under what striking circumstances this point is brought home to him.

ENTERED, PASSED, RAISED

The Candidate is, however, subjected to like personal experience in each of the Craft Degrees, and it calls to be understood thus. In the Entered Apprentice Degree it is because of a new life which he is to lead henceforth. In the Fellowcraft, it is as if the mind were to be renewed, for the prosecution of research into the hidden mysteries of nature, science, and art. But in the sublime Degree of Master Mason it is in order that he may enter fully into the mystery of death and of that which follows thereafter, being the great mystery of the Raising. The three technical and official words corresponding to the successive experiences are Entered, Passed, and Raised, their Craft-equivalents being Apprentice, Craftsman and Master--or he who has undertaken to acquire the symbolical and spiritualized art of building the house of another life; he who has passed therein to a certain point of proficiency, and in fine, he who has attained the whole mystery. If I may use for a moment the imagery of Francis Bacon, Lord Verulam, he has learned how to effectuate in his own personality "a new birth in time," to wear a new body of desire, intention and purpose; he has fitted to that body a new mind, and other objects of research. In fine, he has been taught how to lay it aside, and yet again he has been taught how to take it up after a different manner, in the midst of a very strange symbolism.

IMPERFECT SYMBOLISM

Now, it may be observed that in delineating these intimations of our symbolism, I seem already to have departed from the mystery of building with which I opened the conference; but I have been actually considering various sidelights thereon. It may be understood, further, that I am not claiming to deal with a symbolism that is perfect in all its parts, however honorable it may be otherwise to the builder. In the course of such researches as I have been enabled to make into the Instituted Mysteries of different ages and countries, I have never met with one which was in entire harmony with itself. We must be content with what we have, just as it is necessary to tolerate the peculiar conventions of language under which the Craft Degrees have passed into expression, artificial and sometimes commonplace as they are. Will you observe once again at this stage how it is only in the first Degree that the Candidate is instructed to build upon his own part a superstructure which is somehow himself? This symbolism is lost completely in the ceremony of the Fellowcraft Degree, which, roughly speaking, is something of a Degree of Life; the symbols being more especially those of conduct and purpose, while in the Third Degree, they speak of direct relations between man and his Creator, giving intimation of judgment to come.

THE THIRD DEGREE

I have said, and you know, that the Master Degree is one of death and resurrection of a certain kind, and among its remarkable characteristics there is a return to building symbolism, but this time in the form of a legend. It is no longer an erection of the Candidate's own house- -house of the body, house of the mind, and house of the moral law. We are taken to the Temple of Solomon and are told how the Master-Builder suffered martyrdom rather than betray the mysteries which had been placed in his keeping. Manifestly the lesson which is drawn in the Degree is a veil of something much deeper, and about which there is no real intimation. It is assuredly an instruction for the Candidates that they must keep the secrets of the Masonic Order secretly, but such a covenant has reference only to the official and external side. The bare recitation of the legend would have been sufficient to enforce this; but observe that the Candidate assumes the part of the Master-Builder and suffers within or in him--as a testimony of personal faith and honor in respect to his engagements. But thereafter he rises, and it is this which gives a peculiar characteristic to the descriptive title of the Degree. It is one of raising and of reunion with companions--almost as if he had been released from earthly life and had entered into the true Land of the Living. The keynote is therefore not one of dying but one of resurrection; and yet it is not said in the legend that the Master rose. The point seems to me one of considerable importance, and yet I know not of a single place in our literature wherein it has received consideration. I will leave it, however, for the moment, but with the intention of returning to it.

PART II

There are two ways in which the Master Degree may be thought to lapse from perfection in respect of its symbolism, and I have not taken out a license to represent it as of absolute order in these or in any respects. This has been practically intimated already. Perhaps it is by the necessity of things that it has recourse always to the lesser meaning, for it is this which is more readily understood. On the other hand, much must be credited to its subtlety, here and there, in the best sense of the term. There is something to be said for an allegory which he who runs may read, at least up to a certain point. But those who made the legend and the ritual could not have been unaware of that which the deeper side shows forth; they have left us also the Opening and Closing as of the great of all greatness--so it seems to me, my Brethren --in things of ceremony and ritual. Both are devoid of explanation, and it is for us to understand them as we can.

For myself it is obvious that something distinct from the express motives of Masonry has come to us in this idea of Raising. The Instituted Mysteries of all ages and countries were concerned in the figuration, by means of ritual and symbolism, of New Birth, a new life, a mystic death and resurrection, as so many successive experiences through which the Candidate passed on the way of his inward progress from earthly to spiritual life, or from darkness to light. The Ritual or Book of the Dead is a case in point. It has been for a long period regarded by scholarship as intimating the after-death experiences or adventures of the soul in the halls of judgment, and so forth; but there are traces already of the genesis of a new view, chiefly in the writing of Mr. W. Flinders Petrie, according to which some parts at least of this great text are really a rite of initiation and advancement, through which Candidates pass in this life.

THE BOOK OF THE DEAD

If I am putting this rather strongly as regards one important authority, it is at least true to say that he appears to discern the mystical side of the old Egyptian texts, while there are others, less illustrious than he, who have gone much further in this direction. It is very difficult for one like myself, although unversed in Egyptology, to study such a work as "Osiris and the Egyptian Resurrection," by E. Wallis Budge, without feeling very strongly that there is much to be said for this view, or without hoping that it will be carried further by those who are properly warranted.

So far as it is possible to speak of the Cabiric Mysteries, there was in those an episode of symbolical death, because Kasmillos, a technical name ascribed to the Candidate, was represented as slain by the gods. Some of the rites which prevailed within and around Greece in ancient times are concerned with the idea of a regeneration or new birth. The Mysteries of Bacchus depicted the death of this god and his restoration to light as Rhea. Osiris died and rose, and so also did Adonis. He was first lamented as dead and then his revivification was celebrated with great joy. There is no need, however, to multiply the recurrence of these events in the old Mysteries nor to restrict ourselves within their limits, for all religions have testified to the necessity of regeneration and have administered its imputed processes. That which is most important-- from my point of view--is the testimony belonging to Christian times and the secret tradition therein.

THE CHRISTIAN MYSTERIES

Of course, to speak of this it is necessary to trend on subjects which at the present are excluded, and very properly so, from discussion in a Craft Lodge, when they are presented from a religious and doctrinal angle. I shall not treat them from that standpoint, but rather as a sequence of symbolism in the form of dramatic mystery, alluding slightly, and from a philosophical point of view only, to the fact that in certain schools they are regarded as delineating momentous experiences in the history and life of man's soul. That new birth which conferred upon the Eleusinian mystae the title of Regenerated Children of the Moon-- so that each one of them was henceforth symbolically a Son of the Queen of Heaven-- born as a man originally and reborn in a divine manner--has its correspondence on a much higher plane of symbolism with the Divine Birth in Bethlehem, according to which a child was "born" and a son "given," who, in hypothesis at least, was the Son of God, but Son also of Mary--one of whose titles, according to Latin theology, is Queen of Heaven.

The hidden life in Egypt and Nazareth corresponds to the life of seclusion led by the mystae during their period of probation between the Lesser and Greater Mysteries. The three years of ministry are in analogy with the Temple-functions of the mystagogues. But lastly, in Egypt and elsewhere, there was the mystic experience of the Pastos, in which the initiate died symbolically, as Jesus died upon the Cross. The Christian "Symbolum" says:--Descendit ad inferos: that is, "He descended into hell"; and in the entranced condition of the Pastos, the soul of the Postulant was held or was caused to wander in certain spiritual realms. But in fine, it is said of Christ:--Tertia die resurrexit; "the third day he rose again from the dead." So also the Adept of the Greater Mysteries rose from the Pastos in the imputed glory of an inward illumination.

THE MYSTICAL FACT

There was a period not so long ago when these analogies were recognized and applied to place a fabulous construction upon the central doctrines of Christian religion, just as there was a period when the solar mythology was adapted in the same direction. We have no call to consider these aberrations of a partially digested learning; but they had their excuses in their period. The point on which I would insist is that in the symbolism of the old initiations, and in the pageant of the Christian mythos, there is held to be the accurate delineation of a mystical experience, the heads and sections of which correspond to the notions of mystic birth, life, death and resurrection. It is a particular formula which is illustrated frequently in the mystic literature of the western world. Long before symbolical Masonry had emerged above the horizon, several cryptic texts of alchemy, in my understanding, were bearing witness to this symbolism and to something real in experience which lay behind it. In more formal Christian mysticism, it was not until the 16th century and later that it entered into the fullest expression.

Now, that which is formulated as mystic birth is comparable to a dawn of spiritual consciousness. It is the turning of the whole life-motive in the divine direction, so that, at a given time-- which is actually the point of turning--the personality stands symbolically between the East and the North, between the greatest zone of darkness and that zone which is the source of light, looking towards the light-source and realizing that the whole nature has to be renewed therein. Mystic life is a quest of divine knowledge in a world that is within. It is the life led in this light, progressing and developing therein, as if a Brother should read the Mysteries of Nature and Science with new eyes cast upon the record, which record is everywhere, but more especially in his own mind and heart. It is the complete surrender to the working of the divine, so that an hour comes when proprium meum et tuum dies in the mystical sense, because it is hidden in God. In this state, by the testimony of many literatures, there supervenes an experience which is described in a thousand ways yet remains ineffable. It has been enshrined in the imperishable books of Plato and Plotinus. It glimmers forth at every turn and corner of the remote roads and pathways of Eastern philosophies. It is in little books of unknown authorship, treasured in monasteries and most of which have not entered into knowledge, except within recent times.

THE PLACE OF DARKNESS

The experience is in a place of darkness, where, in other symbolism, the sun is said to shine at midnight. There is afterwards that further state, in which the soul of man returns into the normal physical estate, bringing the knowledge of another world, the quest ended for the time being at least. This is compared to resurrection, because in the aftermath of his experience the man is, as it were, a new being. I have found in most mythological legends that the period between divine death and resurrection was triadic and is spoken of roughly as three days, though there is an exception is the case of Osiris, whose dismemberment necessitated a long quest before the most important of his organs was left finally lost. The three days are usually foreshortened at both ends; the first is an evening, the second a complete day, while the third ends at sunrise. It is an allusion to the temporal brevity ascribed in all literatures to the culminating mystical experience. It is remarkable, in this connection, that during the mystic death of the Candidate in the Third Degree, the time of his interned condition is marked by three episodes, which are so many attempts to raise him, the last only being successful.

OPERATIVE MASONRY

Two things follow unquestionably from these considerations, so far as they have proceeded. The interest in Operative Masonry and its records, though historically it is of course important, has proceeded from the beginning on a misconception as to the aims and symbolism of

Speculative Masonry. It was and it remains natural, and it has not been without its results, but it is a confusion of the chief issues. It should be recognized henceforward that the sole connection between the two Arts and Crafts rests on the fact that the one has undertaken to uplift the other from the material plane to that of morals on the surface and of spirituality in the real intention. Many things led up thereto, and a few of them were at work unconsciously within the limits of Operative Masonry. At a period when there was a tendency to symbolize everything roughly, so that it might receive a tincture of religion--I speak of the Middle Ages--the duty of Apprentice to Master, and of Master to pupil, had analogies with relations subsisting between man and God, and they were not lost sight of in those old Operative documents. Here was a rudiment capable of indefinite extension. The placing of the Lodges and of the Craft at large under notable patronage, and the subsequent custom of admitting persons of influence, offered another and quite distinct opportunity. These facts notwithstanding, my position is that the traces of symbolism which may in a sense be inherent in Operative Masonry did not produce, by a natural development, the Speculative Art and Craft, though they helped undoubtedly to make a possible and partially prepared field for the great adventure and experiment.

THE OLD CHARGES

The second point is that we must take the highest intention of symbolism in the Third Degree to some extent apart from the setting. You will know that the literary history of our ritual is rather non-existent than obscure, or if this is putting the case a little too strongly, it remains that researches have so far left the matter in a dubious position. The reason is not for our seeking, for the kind of enquiry that is involved is one of exceeding difficulty. If I say that it is my personal aspiration to undertake it one of these days, I speak of what is perhaps a distant hope. That which is needed is a complete codification of all the old copies, in what language so ever, which are scattered through the Lodges and libraries of the whole Masonic world, together with an approximate determination of their dates by expert evidence. In my opinion, the codices now in use have their roots in the 18th century, out were edited and re-edited at an even later date.

I have now brought before you in somewhat disjointed manner-- as I cannot help feeling-- several independent considerations, each of which, taken separately, institutes certain points of correspondence between Masonry and other systems of symbolism, but they do not at present enter into harmony. I will collect them as follows:--

(1) Masonry has for its object, under one aspect, the building of the Candidate as a house or temple of life. Degrees outside the Craft aspire to this building as a living stone in a spiritual temple, meet for God's service.

(2) Masonry presents also a symbolical sequence, but in a somewhat crude manner, of Birth, Life, Death and Resurrection, which other systems indicate as a mystery of experience.

(3) Masonry, in fine, represents the whole body of its Adepti as in search of something that has been lost, and it tells us how and with whom that loss came about.

These are separate and independent lines of symbolism, though, as indicated already, they are interlinked by the fact of their incorporation in Craft Masonry, considered as a unified system. But the truth is that between the spiritual building of the First Degree and the Legend of Solomon's Temple there is so little essential correspondence that the one was never intended to lead up to the other. The symbolism of the Entered Apprentice Degree is of the simplest and most obvious kind; it is also personal and individualistic. That of the Master Degree is complex and remote in its significance; it is, moreover, an universal mythos. I have met with some searchers of the mysteries who seem prepared to call it cosmic, but I must not carry you so far as this speculation would lead us, and I do not hold a brief for its defense. I am satisfied in my own mind that the Third Degree has been grafted on the others and does not belong to them. There has been no real attempt to weld them, but they have been drawn into some kind of working sequence by the Exhortation which the Worshipful Master recites prior to the dramatic scene in the last Master Degree. To these must be added some remarks to the Candidate immediately after the Raising. The Legend is reduced therein to the uttermost extent possible in respect of its meaning, though it is possible that this has been done of set purpose.

LIVING STONES

It will be seen that the three aspects enumerated above fall under two heads in their final analysis, the first representing a series of practical counsels, thinly allegorized upon in terms of symbolical architecture. The Candidate is instructed to work towards his own perfection under the light of Masonry. There is no mystery, no concealment whatever, and it calls for no research in respect of its source. Its analogies and replicas are everywhere, more especially in religious systems. It is a reflection of the Pauline doctrine that man is or may become a temple of the Holy Spirit. But it should be observed in this connection that there is a rather important-though confusing mixture of images in the address of the Worshipful Master to the Candidate, after the latter has been invested and brought to the East. It is pointed out to him that he represents the cornerstone of a building--as it might be, the whole Masonic edifice but he is immediately counseled to raise a superstructure from the foundation of that corner-stone--thus reversing the image. That of the corner-stone is like an externalization in dramatic form of an old Rosicrucian maxim belonging to the year 1629: - "Be ye transmuted from dead stones into living, philosophical stones."

From my point of view, it is the more important side of the symbolism; it is as if the great Masonic edifice were to be raised on each Candidate; and if every Neophyte shaped his future course both in and out of Masonry, as though this were the case actually, I feel that the Royal Art would be other than it now is and that our individual lives would differ.

PART III

Recurring to the Legend of the Third Degree, the pivot upon which it revolves is the existence of a building secret, represented as a Master-Word, which the Builder died to preserve. Owing to his untimely death, the Word was lost, and it has always been recognized in Masonry that the Temple, unfinished at the moment of the untoward event, remained with its operations suspended and was completed later on by those who obviously did not possess the Word or key. The tradition has descended to us and, as I have said, we are still on the quest.

Now what does all this mean? We have no concern at the present day, except in archaeology and history, with King Solomon's Temple.

What is meant by this Temple and what is the Lost Word? These things have a meaning, or our system is stultified. Well, here are burning questions, and the only direction in which we can look for an answer is that which is their source. As to this, we must remember that the Legend of the Master Degree is a Legend of Israel, under the aegis of the Old Covenant, and though it has no warrants in the Holy Writ, which constitutes the Old Testament, it is not antecedently improbable that something to our purpose may be found elsewhere in Jewish literature.

THE KABBALAH

I do not of course mean that we shall meet with the Legend itself; it would be interesting if we did but not per se helpful, apart from explanation. I believe in my heart that I have found what is much more important, and this is the root-matter of that which is shadowed forth in the Legend, as regards the meaning of the Temple and the search for the Lost Word. There are certain great texts which are known to scholars under the generic name of Kabbalah, a Hebrew word meaning reception, or doctrinal teaching passed on from one to another by verbal communication. According to its own hypothesis, it entered into written records during the Christian era, but hostile criticism has been disposed to represent it as invented at the period when it was written. The question does not signify for our purpose, as the closing of the 13th century is the latest date that the most drastic view-- now generally abandoned-- has proposed for the most important text.

We find therein after what manner, according to mystic Israel, Solomon's Temple was spiritualized; we find deep meanings attached to the two pillars J. and B.; we find how the word was lost and under what circumstances the chosen people were to look for its recovery. It is an expectation for Jewish theosophy, as it is for the Craft Mason. It was lost owing to an untoward event, and although the time and circumstances of its recovery have been calculated in certain texts of the Kabbalah, there has been something wrong with the methods. The keepers of the tradition died with their faces toward Jerusalem, looking for that time; but for Judaism at large the question has passed from the field of view, much as the quest is continued by us in virtue of a ceremonial formula but cannot be said to mean anything for those who undertake and pursue it. It was lost owing to the unworthiness of Israel, and the destruction of the First Temple was one consequence thereof. By the waters of Babylon, in their exile, the Jews are said to have remembered Zion, but the word did not come back into their hearts; and when Divine Providence inspired Cyrus to bring about the building of the Second Temple and the return of Israel into their own land, they went back empty of all recollection in this respect.

THE DIVINE NAME

I am putting things in a summary fashion that are scattered up and down the vast text with which I am dealing--that is to say, Sepher Ha Zohar, The Book of Splendor. The word to which reference is made is the Divine Name out of the consonants of which, He, Vau, He, Yod, we have formed Jehovah, or more accurately Yahve. When Israel fell into a state which is termed impenitence it is said in the Zoharic Symbolism that the Vau and the He final were separated. The name was dismembered, and this is the first sense of loss which is registered concerning it. The second is that it has no proper vowel points, those of the Name Elohim being substituted, or alternatively the Name Adonai. It is said, for example: "My Name is written YHVH and read Adonai." The epoch of restoration and completion is called, almost indifferently, that of resurrection, the world to come, and the advent of the Messiah. In such day the present imperfect separation between the letters will be put an end to, once and forever. If it be asked: What is the connection between the loss and dismemberment which befell the Divine Name Jehovah and the Lost Word in Masonry, I cannot answer too plainly; but every Royal Arch Mason knows that which is communicated to him in that Supreme Degree, and in the light of the present explanation he will see that the "great" and "incomprehensible" thing so imparted comes to him from the Secret Tradition of Israel.

It is also to this Kabbalistic source, rather than to the variant accounts in the first book of Kings and in Chronicles, that we must have recourse for the important Masonic Symbolism concerning the Pillars J. and B. There is very little in Holy Scripture which would justify a choice of these objects as particular representatives of our art of building spiritualized. But in later Kabbalism, in the texts called "The Garden of Pomegranates" and in "The Gates of Light," there is a very full and complicated explanation of the strength which is attributed to B., the left-hand Pillar, and of that which is established in and by the right-hand Pillar, called J.

THE TEMPLE

As regards the Temple itself, I have explained at length elsewhere after what manner it is spiritualized in various Kabbalistic and semi-Kabbalistic texts, so that it appears ever as "the proportion of the height, the proportion of the depth, and the lateral proportions" of the created universe, and again as a part of the transcendental mystery of law which is at the root of the secret tradition in Israel. This is outside our subject, not indeed by its nature but owing to limitations of opportunity. I will say only that it offers another aspect of a fatal loss in Israel and the world-- which is commented on in the tradition. That which the Temple symbolized above all things was, however, a House of Doctrine, and as on the one hand the Zohar shows us how a loss and substitution were perpetuated through centuries, owing to the idolatry of Israel at the foot of Mount Horeb in the wilderness of Sinai, and illustrated by the breaking of the Tables of Stone on which the Law was inscribed; so does Speculative Masonry intimate that the Holy House, which was planned and begun after one manner, was completed after another and a word of death was substituted for a word of life.

THE BUILDER

I shall not need to tell you that beneath such veils of allegory and amidst such illustrations of symbolism, the Master-Builder signifies a principle and not a person, historical or otherwise. He signifies indeed more than a single principle, for in the world of mystic intimations through which we are now moving, the question, "Who is the Master?" would be answered by many voices. But generically, he is the imputed life of the Secret-Doctrine which lay beyond the letter of the Written Law, which "the stiff-necked and disobedient" of the patriarchal, sacerdotal and prophetical dispensations contrived to destroy. According to the Secret Tradition of Israel, the whole creation was established for the manifestation of this life, which became manifested actually in its dual aspect when the spiritual Eve was drawn from the side of the spiritual Adam and placed over against him, in the condition of face o face. The intent of creation was made void in the event which is called the Fall of Man, though the particular expression is unknown in Scripture. By the hypothesis, the "fatal consequences" which followed would have reached their time on Mount Sinai, but the Israelites, when left to themselves in the wilderness, "sat down to eat and rose up to play." That which is concealed in the evasion of the last words corresponds the state of Eve in Paradise, when she had become affected by the serpent.

To sum up as regards the sources, the Lost Word in Masonry is derived from a Kabbalistic thesis of imperfection in the Divine Name Jehovah, by which the true pronunciation--that is to say, the true meaning-- is lost. It was the life of the House of Doctrine, represented by the Temple planned of old in Israel. The Master-Builder is the Spirit, Secret or Life of the Doctrine; and it is the quest of this that every Mason takes upon himself in the ceremony of the Third Degree, so that the House, which in the words of another Masonic Degree, is now, for want of territory, built only in the heart, "a superstructure perfect in its parts and honorable to the builder."

CRAFT MASONRY

But if these are the sources of Craft Masonry, taken at its culmination in the Sublime Degree, what manner of people were those who grafted so strange a speculation and symbolism on the Operative procedure of a building-Guild? The answer is that all about that period which represents what is called the transition, or during the 16th and 17th centuries, the Latin writing scholars were animated with zeal for the exposition of the tradition in Israel, with the result that many memorable and even great books were produced on the subject. Among those scholars were many great names, and they provided the materials ready to the hands of the symbolists. What purpose had the latter in view? The answer is that in Germany, Italy, France and England, the Zeal for Kabbalistic literature among the Latin-writing scholars had not merely a scholastic basis. They believed that the texts of the Secret Tradition showed plainly, out of the mouth of Israel itself, that the Messiah had come. This is the first fact. The second I have mentioned already, namely, that although the central event of the Third Degree is the Candidate's Raising, it is not said in the Legend that the Master-Builder rose, thus suggesting that something remains to come after, which might at once complete the legend and conclude the quest. The third fact is that in a rather early and important High Degree of the philosophical kind, now almost unknown, the Master-Builder of the Third Degree rises as Christ, and so completes the dismembered Divine Name, by insertion of the Hebrew letter Shin, this producing Yeheshua - the restoration of the Lost Word in the Christian Degrees of Masonry.

Of course, I am putting this point only as a question of fact in the development of symbolism. Meanwhile, I trust that, amidst many imperfections, I have done something to indicate a new ground for our consideration, and to show that the speaking mystery of the Opening and Closing of the Third Degree and the Legend of the Master-Builder come from what may seem to us very far away, but yet not so distant that it is impossible to trace them to their source.

Printed in Great Britain
by Amazon

17375828R00128